Writing Baseball

THE SOUTHERN ILLINOIS UNIVERSITY PRESS SERIES

Other Books in the Writing Baseball Series

THE NEW YORK GIANTS

Series Editor's Note

In 1943, G. P. Putnam's Sons began a series of major league team histories with the publication of Frank Graham's history of the New York Yankees. From 1943 to 1954, Putnam published histories for fifteen of the sixteen major league teams. The Philadelphia Athletics ball club was the only one not included in the series, though Putnam did publish a biography of Connie Mack in 1945.

Thirteen of the fifteen team histories in the Putnam series were contributed by sportswriters who were eventually honored by the Hall of Fame with the J. G. Taylor Spink Award "for meritorious contributions to baseball writing." Three Spink recipients actually wrote eleven of the team histories for the series. The famed New York columnist Frank Graham, after launching the series with the Yankees history, added team histories for the Brooklyn Dodgers and the New York Giants. Chicago sports editor and journalist Warren Brown, once dubbed the Mencken of the sports page, wrote both the Chicago Cubs and the White Sox team histories. Legendary Fred Lieb, who, at the time of his death in 1980 at the age of ninety-two, held the lowest numbered membership card in the Baseball Writers Association, contributed six team histories to the Putnam series. He also wrote the Connie Mack biography for Putnam.

For our reprints of the Putnam series, we add a foreword for each team history by one of today's most renowned baseball writers. The bibliography committee of the Society for American Baseball Research has also provided an index for each team history. Other than these additions and a few minor alterations, we have preserved the original state of the books, including any possible historical inaccuracies.

The Putnam team histories have been described as the "Cadillacs" of the team history genre. With their colorful prose and their delightful narratives of baseball history as the game moved into its postwar golden age, the Putnam books have also become among the most prized collectibles for baseball historians.

Richard Peterson

THE NEW YORK
GIANTS

*An Informal History
of a Great Baseball Club*

Frank Graham

With a New Foreword by Ray Robinson

Southern Illinois University Press
Carbondale and Edwardsville

Library of Congress Cataloging-in-Publication Data

Graham, Frank, 1893–
    The New York Giants : an informal history of a great baseball
club / Frank Graham ; with a new foreword by Ray Robinson.
        p. cm. — (Writing baseball)
    Includes index.
        1. New York Giants (Baseball team)—History. I. Title. II. Series.

GV875.N42 G7 2002
796.357'64'097471—dc21
ISBN 0-8093-2415-6 (alk. paper)   2001020709

Reprinted from the original 1952 edition published by G. P. Putnam's Sons.

Contents

Illustrations

Foreword

I have had a troubled past as a baseball partisan. For some reason impossible to fathom, I rooted, as a nine-year-old, not for any team but for individual players. I liked Lou Gehrig and Herb Pennock, both Yankees, and didn't care much for Babe Ruth, which may have indicated a form of perversity. Then, for a while, I dropped the players and started to root for the Philadelphia Athletics, even though, as a kid living in Manhattan, I hadn't the slightest notion where Philadelphia was.

But starting around 1932, when the New York Giants were still under the guidance of that old tyrant, John McGraw, I turned to his team. This growing infatuation came about by way of an elderly ex-bootlegger who lived in an apartment next to mine on the upper west side of Manhattan. My father was a lawyer who believed only in college wrestling, for he was pure of heart and didn't care about going to ball games, since the Black Sox shenanigans were still in his mind. It was left to the bootlegger to invite me to that old bathtub, the Polo Grounds (a newspaper photographer had called it the Polish Grounds), where he had two wonderful box seats. That introduction sealed my rabid interest in the Giants. It was somehow fitting that a bootlegger converted me into a Giants fan, for their clientele in those days consisted mainly of cab drivers, unemployed actors, bookmakers, hooky players, beer-soaked Tammany wardheelers, and, of course, bootleggers.

When a young journeyman infielder out of Holy Cross, Blondy Ryan, joined the Giants in midseason 1933 and sent a telegram to the manager, Memphis Bill Terry, saying, "I'm on my way, they can't beat us," I was in seventh heaven. Inspiration like this may not have matched Knute Rockne's Gipper exhortation, but Blondy's words still struck a chord with me. For better or for worse, the Giants of the Meeker Marvel (Carl Hubbell), the Gause Ghost (Joe Moore), Rowdy Richard (Dick Bartell), Prince Hal (Hal Schumacher), and Master Melvin (Mel Ott) became my cherished team.

It hasn't always been an easy relationship. But periodic visits to the Polo Grounds made me almost senselessly happy, although I must admit that I feel the same way about other ball parks these days, including that cavernous cathedral in the Bronx, Yankee Stadium.

By some quirky throw of the dice, I actually watched the Giants *lose* two no-hitters. One, right after World War II, was by a wild-throwing Dodger, Rex Barney, on a rainy night. The other was by Brooklyn's Carl Erskine at Ebbets Field. How many fans have watched their favorite team lose two no-hit games!

In July 1940, I watched Harry "The Horse" Danning's home run in the ninth inning beat Cincinnati's Bucky Walters, after Bucky held a 4-to-1 lead going into the inning. My pals and I had already headed for the exit when Danning unloaded, and suddenly we became hysterical with joy. It was one of those epiphanic moments one doesn't easily forget. But it was the aftermath of that game that sticks in my mind to this day. The second-string catcher of the Reds, Willard Hershberger, blamed himself for Danning's home run pitch. He told his manager, Bill McKechnie, that it was his fault. Several days later, Hershberger's body was found in a hotel bathroom. He had cut his throat with a razor blade.

Yes, sometimes it's the sad things that jolt the memory. But there are funny things, too, that also cause us to remember. In October 1951, I wasn't on hand when Bobby Thomson, that bright-eyed, decent fellow, hit you-know-what to win the National League pennant over the Dodgers. However, only the day before, I had been at the Polo Grounds to witness the Dodgers' slaughter

xii

of my Giants to tie the playoff at one all. Thereby hangs a tale both comic and memorable.

It was a bright, sunny day at the Polo Grounds, and some thirty-eight thousand were there, most of them begging the Giants to wrap it up. I was sitting behind first base with my wife, Phyllis, who was pregnant at the time, and Fred, my bushy-browed father-in-law, who had rooted for the Giants in the days of the indomitable Matty and High Pockets Kelly and Fred Merkle. Fred became outwardly testy when he realized that Giants manager Leo Durocher had put the game in the hands of right-hander Sheldon "Available" Jones, for whom my father-in-law had scant respect. He kept protesting out loud about Jones. He was right, of course, for within minutes the Dodgers assaulted Jones, putting the game out of reach. Along about the sixth inning, Fred bolted from his seat and angrily stormed out of the ball park. When he was gone, a man who had been sitting behind us tapped me on the shoulder.

"Would you tell me who that fellow was?" he asked, not impolitely. Obviously he had never seen such choleric behavior at a ball game.

"He's my father-in-law," I confessed. "But he's a kind man when he's not at the ball park."

"You're lucky he's not your mother-in-law," my inquiring neighbor concluded.

Of that tough, opportunistic Giants team of 1951, I got to know the team's slugger, Monte Irvin, well enough to proclaim him as my friend—and he still is. By any standards, Monte was a thoughtful gentleman and a perfect guardian for the effervescent newcomer, Willie Mays.

It wasn't long after the Thomson home run heard 'round the world that I met, for the first time, Frank Graham. Shyly, I asked him for some information about the Giants, and he supplied the answers quickly. I had been reading Graham's warm "conversation pieces" for some years, first in the *New York Sun,* then in the *Journal-American,* but I had no idea how kind and modest he was.

The columnist Red Smith, Graham's good friend, once referred to him as "a digger for truth, a reporter of facts . . . with an incredibly accurate ear and an implausibly retentive memory." To Smith, Graham was the finest sports columnist of his time and also the man entitled to receive official credit for reporting Durocher's infamous words, "Nice guys finish last."

Graham was still writing his insightful essays in 1957 when the Giants, now managed by Bill Rigney, made their last hurrah at the Polo Grounds before they went west. On a late September afternoon, my friend Arnold Hano, who had written a gem of a book, *A Day in the Bleachers,* about the first game of the 1954 World Series between the Giants and the Cleveland Indians, asked me if I'd like to join him for the last time in the cheap seats. About eleven thousand depressed and betrayed Giants fans showed up to watch Mays, Johnny Antonelli, Dusty Rhodes, and other holdovers from the 1954 Championship team lose a dismal 9-to-1 game to Pittsburgh. When the demoralizing event was over, souvenir collectors stormed the field, like so many crazed ants. They tore up the pitching rubbers, carted off chunks of grass, walked away with the bases, ripped off advertising signs, and uprooted the green-painted seats. Many of the old-timers seemed to have stayed away from the scene that day, for it was a farewell that they did not choose to participate in—it hurt too much.

Hano swore to me as we took the subway home that he'd never again give his heart to another baseball team. But within a year, the two of us were listening to the San Francisco Giants late at night, via Les Keiter's game reconstructions on the radio.

After all, there was still Mays to cheer for, and Willie McCovey and Orlando Cepeda. The Giants habit was very hard to break.

Ray Robinson
April 2001

THE NEW YORK GIANTS

1

"We Are the People!"

⊖ THIS was New York in the elegant eighties and these were the Giants, fashioned in elegance, playing on the Polo Grounds, then at 110 Street and Fifth Avenue. It was the New York of the brownstone house and the gaslit streets, of the top hat and the hansom cab, of oysters and champagne and perfecto cigars, of Ada Rehan and Oscar Wilde and the young John L. Sullivan. It also was the New York of the Tenderloin and the Bowery, of the slums and the sweat shops, of goats grazing among shanties perched on the rocky terrain of Harlem.

The Giants, however, were the darlings of the brownstone set and drew the carriage trade. They were owned by John B. Day, a wealthy manufacturer, whose factory was on the lower East Side but who lived in a brownstone house, wore a top hat and a frock coat, carried a cane, and rode in his own coach. They were managed by James Mutrie, who lived in a sedate hotel in the Twenties, wore a top hat and frock coat, carried a cane, and rode in hansom cabs. Their players were cut to their pattern, so that, gazing on their likenesses in fading photographs, you might be tempted to think they had been chosen as much for their looks as for their ability as ball players.

This was not the first New York team in the National League. When the league was organized at a meeting held on February 2, 1876, in the Grand Central Hotel on lower Broadway, William H. Cammeyer, president of the Mutual Club, purchased a franchise, and so it appears in the records that New York was a charter member. But Cammeyer's club was a New York club in name only. It played on the Union Grounds in Brooklyn, then a city in itself, and still was referred to by its followers as "The Mutuals." Before the season was over, it was expelled from the league for the reason that Cammeyer and his players refused to go on the road.

It was not until 1883 that the club destined to become known as the Giants entered the league. Day, who had been an amateur player of considerable skill, was not without experience in professional baseball. He was the proprietor of the Metropolitan club, or "Mets," which he had assembled in 1881. He had operated it as an independent club for a year and then had placed it in the American Association, a cut-rate circuit that had dim aspirations, never to be fully achieved, of some day rivaling the National League. Mutrie, who managed the Mets, had been a shortstop of meager reputation in New England, best remembered around New Bedford.

Day's opportunity to place a team in the big league came when the Troy club, a member since 1879, had a disastrous season in 1882 and disintegrated at its conclusion. Day picked up the discarded franchise and transferred it to New York. As a playing site, he leased the Polo Grounds, logically so called because on that field polo was introduced in this country by James Gordon Bennett, publisher of the *New York Herald*. It was large enough for two baseball fields, so Day had two laid out, placing his National League team on one and the Mets on the other. A ten-foot-high canvas fence was placed between them, but it nevertheless was possible, on days when both teams played, for customers in the top row of the bleachers on either field to see two games concurrently for one price of admission. Mutrie operated in a dual capacity, managing both clubs, although, like Day, he centered most of his attention on the National Leaguers.

The New Yorks, as they were called, were built around the worth-while players Day had salvaged from the wreck of the Troy club. Among them were William (Buck) Ewing, still regarded by surviving patrons of the time as the greatest player baseball ever has known; Roger Connor, a towering, wide-shouldered first baseman; Mickey Welch, a small but tough-fibered and redoubtable pitcher; Ed Caskins, who had played shortstop in Troy but could play anywhere in the infield save at first base; and Pat Gillespie, a tall, hearty, and hard-hitting outfielder. John Montgomery Ward, a pitcher who also could play in both the infield and the outfield, and who, like Ewing, still has a magic name with the graybeards, was bought from Providence. James (the original Tip) O'Neill, a first-rate pitcher, was discovered on the local sandlots. Frank Hankinson, an infielder, was moved up from the Mets, as was John Clapp, a catcher. John (Dasher) Troy, an infielder, was bought from Detroit. Joe Humphries, a catcher, was signed out of the independent ranks. Since Gillespie was the only full-time outfielder on the squad, Mutrie picked up two others. One was Mike Dorgan, a veteran "leaguer," who was at a loose end. The other, purchased from Baltimore, was Grayson (Grace) Pearce.

A newspaper account of the first game, played on May 1, 1883, is reproduced in full, save for the box score that accompanied it:

About 12,000 people witnessed the opening game of the league season between the gilt edged New York and Boston clubs. Many prominent people were interested spectators, among them General Grant. The New Yorks put in Welch and Ewing as their battery, while the Bostons presented Whitney and Hines. Whitney's pitching was hard hit and his support behind the bat was poor. John Troy played a miserable game at short, having no less than five errors in nine chances and the Bostons are indebted to him for most of their runs.

The score, incidentally, was 7 to 5. Ewing led the batting order, followed by Connor, first base; Ward, center field; Gillespie, left field; Dorgan, right field; Welch, pitcher; Caskins, second base; Troy, shortstop; and Hankinson, third base.

Welch, in later years still a lively little man who explained that he never had had time to grow old, frequently was in attendance at the Polo Grounds. One day he told John Kieran, then sports columnist on the *New York Times,* "Mutrie was what you would call today the business manager of the club. The real manager and leader on the field was Buck Ewing. In fact, Mutrie often sat up in the grandstand."

"And did he continue as manager of the Mets, too?" Kieran asked.

"Oh, yes."

6

"What did he do about them when he went on the road with you?"

"I don't know," Mickey said, grinning. "I guess he just left word."

As was the custom in that time and for many years afterward, not only in New York but elsewhere, most of the players lived close to the ball park and, like the precinct policemen, were well known by the neighbors. Ewing, the Babe Ruth of his day, must have felt, as the Babe did in his time, that he must maintain a position suitable to his eminence on the field, for he had a suite of rooms in a private home on 110 Street off Madison Avenue. Many of the others lived in the Harlem House, a hotel at 115 Street and Third Avenue. Ward, socially and intellectually the superior of the others—he was to become a successful lawyer and achieve prominence as an amateur golfer—but as popular with his teammates as he was with the public, lived further downtown and found companionship in the bluebook set.

Ewing, although he never led the league in batting, was a very good hitter, fast on the bases, the possessor of an arm that terrorized opposing base runners, and had that flair for the dramatic that marks most great players. Once, in the tenth inning of a scoreless game, he singled, stole second and third, and then announced to the crowd that he would steal home—and did. Some enterprising soul bobbed up a few days later with a gaudy lithograph titled "Ewing's Famous Slide," and sold thousands of copies of it, mostly, it seemed, to saloon keepers, who displayed it proudly back of their bars.

Despite their brave beginning and the furor they had caused, the New Yorks could not hold to the pace and as

7

the summer dragged, so did the athletes. They finished in sixth place, and Mutrie knew some changes would have to be made. That winter he sold Tip O'Neill to St. Louis and bought Alexander McKinnon, a first baseman from Philadelphia. Troy and Pearce were demoted to the Mets and Danny Richardson, a small but sprightly youngster who was to become a favorite with the fans, was picked up for use as a utility player, since he was equally skilled as an infielder and outfielder. One Bagley, not otherwise identified in available records, was added to the pitching staff.

When the season of 1884 got under way, McKinnon was on first base, Hankinson remained at third, and Caskins was at shortstop. Ward, who had been a very good pitcher with Providence—he had hurled a no-hit game against Buffalo in 1880—was convinced he had lost his effectiveness, since he had won only twelve games while losing fourteen the year before, and was eager to make a permanent place for himself in the infield. Between pitching assignments in 1883, he had played second base, third base, shortstop, and the outfield and now, with Mutrie's approval, he picked second base for his spot. Connor, displaced at first base, filled in frequently for Ward, Hankinson, or one of the outfielders, Richardson, Dorgan, and Gillespie. Ewing was the catcher and Welch, who had been in eighty-eight games in 1883, winning twenty-seven and losing twenty-one, again bore the burden with scant help from Bagley and Ward, the latter taking an occasional fling in the box but managing to win only three games. "Smiling Mickey," as they were calling him by now, won thirty-eight games that year, but fifth place was the end of the road for the young men. However, the attendance, which had fallen off toward the end of the 1883 campaign, picked up again. Here, the fans seemed to feel, was a team that was going places.

They were right. It was in 1885 that it started to roll. Tim Keefe, a pitcher who had come with the Troy franchise but had been shunted off to the Mets, where he won forty-one games in 1883, and thirty-five in 1884, was brought up in 1885 and paired with Welch. Ward moved to shortstop, a position in which he was to reap new fame. Jim O'Rourke who, with Buffalo the year before, had led the league in batting with an average of .350, was bought and posted in the outfield. These, with Ewing, were the key players as the club roared up through the league, chased Chicago to the wire, and missed the pennant by a margin of only two games. Welch having another of his astonishing years, won forty-seven games, seventeen of them in a row between July 18 and September 4, and Keefe won thirty-two. Connor, back on first base and smashing the ball at a .371 clip, was the league's leading hitter.

It was in that year that Mutrie, in the heat of a thrilling game, leaped to his feet yelling, "My big fellows! My giants!"

They'd had no nickname before but they had one now. Forever after they would be called the Giants.

Now another cry, springing from Mutrie's lips, echoed though the gaslit streets, "We are the People!"

The Giants had become a power in the league, challenging the domination of the Chicago White Stockings, managed by Adrian C. (Cap) Anson. Many favored them to win the pennant in 1886, but they finished third as Chicago won again and, in 1887, slipped to fourth. They were not to be held back long, however. Mutrie, although he sometimes sat in the grandstand at a ball game, was the one responsible for changing the make-up of the team and by 1888 he had rebuilt it around Welch, Keefe, Ewing, Ward, Gillespie, Richardson, Dorgan, and Connor.

Ewing, most versatile player of his time and one of the most versatile of any time, not only still was the first string catcher but played the infield and outfield as well and, on occasion, pitched. "Cannonball" Ed Crane, bought from Washington, had been added to the pitching staff, along with Ledell Titcomb, from Washington. From Buffalo, Mutrie had got Gilbert Hatfield, an infielder, and Pat Murphy, a catcher. George (Piano Legs) Gore, purchased from Chicago, and "Silent Mike" Tiernan, a rookie from Trenton, New Jersey, joined the outfielders. Arthur Whitney was obtained from Pittsburgh.

They really were "The People" now. Keefe, at the very top of his form, won thirty-five games and, between June 23 and August 10, set a record that would stand for twenty-four years—and then only be tied—by winning nineteen consecutive games. Welch won twenty-six games, and Titcomb fourteen. Behind this pitching, the Giants hit hard, fielded brilliantly, and won the pennant for the first time. As the town rocked with excitement, they then dashed off a victory in the world series (primitive vintage) by beating the St. Louis club of the American Association.

Although only six series' games had to be won, and the Giants racked up that many in eight starts, it was decided to play out the string of ten games. As a reward for their contributions to the victory, Mutrie sent Keefe, Ewing, and Ward home after the eighth game, Keefe having won four games, Ewing having demonstrated that he still was the greatest of catchers, and Ward having played so well, at least one critic wrote that if he had been at shortstop on the other side the Browns conceivably might have won. Their departure so weakened the Giants that the Browns took the last two games, but it didn't matter, and nobody cared.

In 1889, the Giants won the pennant again and, in the world series, defeated the Brooklyn club of the Association. The pennant race was the closest in the league up to that time. The Giants won it by taking seventeen of their last twenty games, beating out Boston by a half game and eleven percentage points—.659 to .648. Hank O'Day, later to become famous as a National League umpire but then a pitcher, was bought from Washington in July. Since he had won only two games for the Capitals, little interest in the deal was expressed at the time but, as it developed, it meant the pennant for the Giants. O'Day won seven games as the Giants nosed out Boston by only eleven points in the closest race in the thirteen-year history of the league. Hank also won two games in the world series, but the pitching hero of the inter-league clash was Cannonball Crane, who hurled the Brooklyns back four times. Ward, who hit .417, again was lauded as the Giants, having lost three of the first four games, swept the next five.

Day and Mutrie had reached the pinnacle of their success and popularity. The descent would be swift and would end in bleak dispair.

2

The Decline of Day

⊝ LOOKING back, it almost seems that an augury of
the defeat of these two men, who built a solid, famous,
and profitable club in the space of seven years, could have
been seen in the first major setback they suffered. This
was the result of a decision by the Board of Aldermen in
1889, in accord with plans for the development of Harlem,
to cut a street through the Polo Grounds. So short was the
notice of eviction served on Day and Mutrie that, with
the season little more than half over, they had no time to
prepare another field in Manhattan and were compelled to
play the remainder of their home games at St. George on
Staten Island. It was inconvenient and it was costly, since
many Polo Grounds regulars shied from the ferryboat ride,
but since the Giants were winning the pennant again,
owner and manager struggled through an awkward situation uncomplaining.

It was during the winter of 1889-90 that their fate
was sealed and, although they may not have been aware
of it at the time, a certainty of it was pressed upon them
shortly. It was brought about by a revolt of the National
Brotherhood of Base Ball players and the formation of
an eight-club Players League that waged a brief but bitter

war against the National. Financial losses on both sides were heavy, but since the Players made their fiercest assault on New York, Day was the chief casualty and, as he tottered, Mutrie fell.

The Brotherhood was organized by John Montgomery Ward in 1885. It was not a union in the beginning and was not intended to be so, but when the time came for it to be used as such, there it was, a ready-made and effective—if double-edged—sword. In 1887, when the members declared themselves opposed to the reserve clause in their contracts, Ward while agreeing with them in principle advised them it must be retained since no equitable substitute had been found for it. But two years later as their president and spokesman, he not only led them in their breakaway but was instrumental in lining up financial backers for their own league in New York, Boston, Philadelphia, Brooklyn, Buffalo, Chicago, Cleveland, and Pittsburgh. The war was on, and while all the National League clubs were hard hit by the departure of players, the Giants were hit hardest of all.

The cause of the rupture was the classification rule adopted by the club owners in 1888 as a dodge to avoid impending trouble over a salary limit of $2,800 they had set in 1887. The new rule was, actually, a graded salary limit. The owners would be the sole judges of the player's worth and, in effect, would group them in salary brackets. What the players wanted was the right to bargain individually. When it was denied, they voted to act collectively. The break would have been made a year before if Ward had been at home, but as he was on a world tour with teams organized by A.G. Spalding, the decision was deferred until the others could consult with him. Since his return was delayed until March of 1889, action was post-poned until the end of the season. When it came, it was sharp and violent.

Day and Mutrie reeled under a blow from which neither ever recovered. Ward, their shortstop, leader of the revolt, became the manager of the Brooklyn club of the Players League. Ewing, their greatest player and as much of a hero to them as he was to the fans, was appointed manager of the New York club. With Ewing went Connor, Richardson, Whitney, Hatfield, Keefe, Crane, and O'Day. The only Giants who stuck by their owner and manager were Welch, Tiernan, and Murphy.

Day had ended the season of 1889 with the pennant and the world championship, but without a ball park he could call his own. Now, with the season of 1890 coming on, he had three ball players and still no ball park. All that he had built was crumbling from under him.

Help was at hand but it would give him but a short stay. John T. Brush, who owned the Indianapolis club in the National League, turned in his franchise—he was to move to Cincinnati within the year—and put some of his players up for sale. Day bought them. One was Amos Rusie, one of the greatest and fastest pitchers that ever lived. Fast as Walter Johnson or "Lefty" Grove or Bob Feller, the old-timers say. With him in the deal were Harry Boyle, also a pitcher; Dick Buckley and Jack Sommers, catchers; and Jack Glasscock, Jerry Denny and Charlie Bassett, infielders. Other players were picked up here and there to pad out the team.

New York was moving uptown and Day moved with it, leasing Manhattan Field, at 155 Street and Eighth Avenue. To his consternation, the Players League club, which had taken most of his best players and plotted a schedule of conflicting dates, built a plant on the ground immediately adjacent to him and called it Brotherhood Park.

The buying of players and the leasing of a new field took most of the money Day had in the ball club and all he felt he safely could drain from his factory. He was able to continue only because he borrowed money from Arthur Soden, one of the owners of the Boston club, and sold stock in the Giants to Edward B. Talcott, a New York lawyer and financier.

With a ragtag team behind him, Rusie won twenty-nine games in 1890, but was charged with thirty-two defeats, and Welch won twenty while losing fifteen. Old Giant fans were divided in their allegiance, as the players had been. Most of them followed the old Giants to Brotherhood Field. Few were there to see the Giants as they finished sixth, and Day's debts mounted.

The season over, those who had visioned fortunes as they rushed to the financial support of the Players League, ruefully counted their losses, for while attendance had been good in New York it had been meager elsewhere and operational costs had been high. The members of the Brotherhood, too, were disillusioned, for they had fared no better in their own league than they had in the National and, in many cases, had fared much worse. So they, the backers and the players, sued for peace and found their adversaries eager to deal with them, for they had been badly hurt as well. A third injured party was the American Association which, in spite of monetary help from the National League to keep it in the field as an ally against the Brotherhood, had suffered fatal wounds.

And so, when the final settlement was made, the rebellious players returned to their clubs and the Association was merged with the National League. Day and Mutrie struggled on, abandoning Manhattan Field, taking over the Brotherhood Park and calling it the Polo Grounds. Ewing was back, but Ward remained in Brooklyn to manage the National League club. Rusie won thirty-three games in 1891, and lost twenty. But Welch, the almost indestructible Smiling Mickey, was almost through. He won only six games and lost ten. The Giants finished third —but Mutrie's number was up.

Day, still hard pressed for money, sold more stock to Talcott and Talcott, in consenting to buy it, drove a bargain so hard that it completely broke Day's spirit. As a consideration in the transaction, Mutrie must be released as Manager. Gaunt... tired... graying... Mutrie withdrew. They no longer were his "big fellows," his "Giants." "We" no longer were "the People." With complete understanding of the situation in which Day struggled, Mutrie remained steadfast in his friendship for his erstwhile employer and associate. Steadfast unto death.

At Talcott's dictation, Pat Powers, who had managed the Rochester club in the American Association in 1890, was hired as Mutrie's successor. In 1892, Ewing still was catching or playing in the infield. Rusie again headed the pitching staff, winning thirty-two games and losing thirty, but it was Welch's last year and, starting only two games, he failed to win either. Bassett and Denny were among the infielders; O'Rourke, Gore, and Tiernan were in the outfield, but there had been numerous additions to the squad. One was Jack Doyle, a catcher. Another, an infielder by the name of Willie Keeler. Willie was to become famous as an outfielder and as explanation for his greatness as a hitter he was to say, "I hit 'em where they ain't." But then a kid out of Brooklyn and playing his first season in the big league, he was a third baseman, and little used at that.

It was another bad season. The Giants finished eighth in the twelve club league. The club lost money and Day, his business gravely imperiled by the withdrawal of his capital from it, and himself on the verge of bankruptcy, sold his remaining shares of stock to Talcott. Six years later he was to appear on the Giant scene again. But then he was a fleeting and futile figure. Now, aged before his years and poor in pocket, his top hat the symbol of a withered glory, he returned to his factory.

Talcott, in full control of the Giants, fired his man Powers, bought Ward from Brooklyn, installed him as playing manager, appointed a friend, C. C. Van Cott, as president.

Ward's popularity was unimpaired by his Brotherhood activities and his two-year absence in Brooklyn, and hope for a revival of the Giants' fortunes were bright as the season of 1893 was launched. John made a number of changes in the team but only three were important. He bought Mark Baldwin, a winning pitcher save for the year before, from Pittsburgh. He brought Connor back from Philadelphia, where Powers had sent him, and he traded Buck Ewing to Cleveland for George Davis, an infielder.

Ward undoubtedly was the only manager who could have traded Ewing and got away with it. Even so, there were some who said that he sent Buck to Cleveland merely to rid himself of a potential rival, pointing out that while the departed hero was thirty-four years old, he had caught or played first base in ninety-seven games in 1892 and hit .319. Those who supported Ward said he must have known Buck was slipping and wanted to unload him, for the good of the team, before he slipped all the way. (The argument was revived in the fall, for Buck, as a regular outfielder in Cleveland, played in 114 games, more than ever before, and hit .371, thus helping his team to finish ahead of the Giants!)

At any rate, with Rusie winning thirty-three games and losing twenty, the Giants were in the fifth slot when the final bell rang, but since they had won four more games than they had lost and had an average of .515, both Talcott and Ward were encouraged.

Ward strengthened the Giants for the 1894 season by buying Jouett Meekin and Charlie (Duke) Farrell, a first-rate battery from Washington, and George Van Haltren, a hard-hitting outfielder, from Pittsburgh. Meekin kept pace with Rusie, winning thirty-five games and losing but eleven, as Amos, having his best season, won thirty-seven and lost thirteen. Farrell, if not a great player, as Ewing was, was the best catcher in the league that year, and Van Haltren hit .333. The Giants couldn't quite win the pennant but they did finish second.

There seemed every reason to believe that within another year or so Ward, as able a manager as he was a ball player and steadily building the Giants, would have them at the top of the league. Then, on January 17, 1895, Talcott, whose interest in baseball was confined to the financial returns it yielded, sold the controlling block of stock in the Giants to Andrew Freedman.

For eight years Freedman ruled the Giants and almost completely wrecked them. Had he not been restrained, he would have wrecked the league as well.

3

A Time of Tumult

⊖ CONSIDERING the time in which he lived and the frame within which he operated, Andrew Freedman was a very important man in New York. He had a lot of money. His political connections were the best, since he was closely allied with Tammany Hall and, in 1895, there was no other political force in the city. Coarse, vain, arrogant, and abusive, he insulted, threatened, or assaulted any who opposed him and many who, however inadvertently, merely got in his way.

Managers . . . ball players . . . umpires . . . fans . . . newspapermen . . . police officers . . . even some of his colleagues felt the impact of his violence. Among his principal targets were the newspapermen. He broke one, forcing him to beg for his job after Freedman, a friend of his paper's managing editor, had threatened to bar him from the Polo Grounds and have him fired. The others, to their credit, stood up to him and fought back. Charlie Dryden of the *American,* one of the celebrated writers of the era, drew his wrath deliberately by simply quoting him verbatim.

"You tell Dryden," Freedman roared at another newspaperman, "that he is standing on the brink of an abscess and if he ain't careful, I'll push him in!"

When that was reported to Charlie, he printed it and, forthwith, was barred from the park. Thereafter he got the details of the games from his fellow craftsmen and embellished his stories with imaginary interviews with Freedman that caused his readers to howl with joy and Freedman to fume.

Meanwhile, the first thing Freedman had done on taking control of the Giants was to dismiss John Montgomery Ward. Ward was too decent for him and he knew it and, in effect, he drove John out of baseball. It was, apparently, one of the few good things he ever did in his life. Another was the founding of a home for the aged which, happily, still flourishes on the Grand Concourse in the Bronx. But this, the firing of Ward, was not planned that way. It worked out that way, however. Ward, having put baseball behind him, soon became one of the foremost lawyers in the town.

In Ward's stead, Freedman appointed George Davis, the third baseman, as manager of the Giants. This, too, was a mistake on his part. Davis, who looked very like Ward, except that there was a bit more curl to his blond mustache, was a decent man, as Ward was. By June 5, he'd had it, and resigned in disgust. But Freedman refused to release him as a player and, perforce, he remained in that capacity.

Freedman's next choice was Jack Doyle who, having joined the Giants three years before as a catcher, had switched to first base. Doyle, unlike Ward and Davis, was rough, tough, and ruthless on the field. "Dirty Doyle," the other players called him, and Freedman must have thought he was the one that should have been the manager in the first place. But Freedman underestimated him, or overestimated him, as you will. By August 2, Doyle had taken all he could from the boss and gave the baton back to him. He couldn't quit the club, however. The boss had him bound 'round with a player's contract, too, even as he had Davis.

Next came Harvey Watkins. It may be that some time, somewhere, Watkins was a ball player, a manager, or in some other way connected with baseball. If so, there is no record of such activity on his part. It is known that he was an actor and that he was an enthusiastic Giant fan, as so many actors much more famous than he were in the happy time when the Giants were new and John B. Day was in his prime. Whatever prompted his appointment remains a mystery but it is a fact that from August 2, 1895, to the end of the season, he was manager of the Giants. Does it surprise you that the Giants finished ninth in a field of twelve?

Watkins was gone by the spring of 1896 and in his place was Arthur Irwin, an old hand in baseball as player and manager, who had piloted the Philadelphia club the year before. Under him, the Giants finished seventh, and he was dismissed. His successor was "Scrappy" Bill Joyce, a veteran player who had been acquired from Washington the previous season. Joyce not only brought the club home in third place in 1897 but, much to every one's amazement, also endured for the entire season and, unlike Irwin, was engaged for another. He quit in June of 1898, after the team had lost six home games in a row, and Cap Anson, who had retired at the close of the 1897 season after a long and brilliant career as player and manager in Chicago, somehow was induced by Freedman to take another whirl, this one with the Giants. He lasted a few weeks and went into retirement again, this time to stay. Joyce took another crack at the job and, when the team wound up in seventh place, he went to his home in St. Louis, opened a saloon, and never came back.

The grotesque parade of managers took a pathetic turn at the outset of the 1899 race. The new manager was John B. Day, aging, still dogged by ill fortune, his factory gone, willing, in his straits, to go to work for Freedman. His stay in the raffish atmosphere of the Polo Grounds was mercifully brief. He gave up on July 5, with the team in the ninth spot. After him came one Fred Hoey. Of him there is known only that he managed the Giants for the balance of the season and that they were tenth when he departed, to be seen no more.

In 1900, Buck Ewing made his reappearance. He had gone from Cleveland to Cincinnati as playing manager in 1895, had quit the playing ranks in 1898, and for the past two seasons had managed the Reds from the bench. Now Freedman was asking him to put the Giants on their feet again. That was the year the National League was reduced to eight clubs, and when Buck found himself locked in eighth place on July 13 he chucked it and followed Anson, Joyce, and the others—including Watkins and Hoey—into the shadows. It must be said that a definite air of finality pervaded the dugout at the Polo Grounds. When a manager was through with Freedman, he really was through.

The sorry task of conducting the Giants through the remainder of the campaign fell to George Davis, who had hung around all this time as a player. He couldn't get them out of last place either.

Along about the time that Ewing quit, a young pitcher arrived at the Polo Grounds, lingered for a while almost unnoticed, then drifted back to Norfolk, whence he had

come. But he was to return. His name was Christy Mathewson.

The frequent managerial changes, the constant shuffling
and reshuffling of players, the steady loss of prestige by
the Giants, and the alarming dwindling of the attendance
at the Polo Grounds, all went on against a background of
repeated outbursts by Freedman. One precipitated the
"Ducky Holmes" riot in 1898.

Holmes, an outfielder who had been with the Giants the
year before but now was with Baltimore, verbally was
assailed by a spectator at the Polo Grounds when he struck
out in the fourth inning of a game. When he replied in
kind, Umpire Tom Lynch (later to become president of
the league) ordered him to go to the bench, which he did.
But when the Baltimore team had been retired, Freedman,
who had been out of the city for three weeks or so and was
in his box for the first time since his return, strode on the
field and angrily demanded that Lynch remove Holmes
from the game. Lynch refused and Freedman declared the
Giants would not continue as long as Holmes was on the
field and summoned policemen to place the player under
arrest. Recognizing the hopelessness of the situation, Lynch
declared the game forfeit to Baltimore.

This brought the crowd of 3,000 out of the stands to mill
around, not the umpire, but Freedman, calling him a cheat,
demanding their money back, and telling him he was killing baseball in New York. He tried to bluster his way
through the aroused fans but when it seemed he was
about to be mauled, he announced he would refund their
money and as he walked toward the clubhouse, they
trooped at his heels, hissing, and booing.

Charlie Dryden, who long since had been banished from

23

the grounds, was waiting on a bench in City Hall Park to get the daily report from his friend, Joe Vila of the *Sun*. He sat facing a huge bulletin board on a newspaper office across Broadway from the park on which had been chalked: RIOT AT THE POLO GROUNDS!

When Vila arrived, but before he had a chance to say anything, Dryden, gesturing toward the board, said, "I see Andy's back."

He and Vila were perhaps the only ones to get a chuckle out of the incident, and the general indignation was reflected not only on the sports pages but in the editorial columns of the newspapers. There were many who felt very deeply that Freedman and a few others in baseball—who of their own volition or because they had been cowed by him were on his side—constituted a menace to the future of the sport comparable to the drinking and gambling evils that had been wiped out some years before. Prominent among them was A. G. Spalding who had had a distinguished career as a player, manager, and president of the Chicago club, and was a forceful figure in the founding of the National League, and who now was engaged in the manufacture of sporting goods.

Writing of this critical period in the history of the Giants, and of baseball as a whole, in his book, *Base Ball,* brought out by his own American Sports Publishing Company in 1911, he said in part:

> I do not know how better to characterize the monstrous evil which at this time threatened the life of baseball than to denominate it "Freedmanism"; for Andrew Freedman, owner of the New York franchise, absolutely held sway over one-half the League interests

Jim Mutrie's pennant-winning Giant team of 1888. (l. to r.) Bottom row: Welch, Ewing, and Tiernan. Middle row: Whitney, Ward, Foster, Manager Jim Mutrie, Connor, O'Rourke, Murphy, and Brown. Top row: Titcomb, Keefe, Slattery, Richardson, Crane, George, Hatfield, and Gore.

John B. Day

Andrew Freedman

John T. Brush

The first three owners of the New York National League team.

and was the incarnation of selfishness supreme. Surrounding himself by a coterie of men willing to follow such a leader; dictating policies that were suicidal to the League of which these men were an important integral part, it is no wonder that this destructive element in those years worked havoc to our national pastime ...

Freedman's personal course had become so obnoxious to most of those connected with the game that nobody outside his own following could endure his eccentricities of speech or action. He would apply to other members of the League, in ordinary conversation, terms so coarse and offensive as to be unprintable. Taking umbrage at some personal newspaper criticism, he would openly declare his intention of ruining the game. My brother, Mr. J. Walter Spalding, who was a Director of the New York Club, was compelled to resign in order to retain his self-respect.

All that had happened before, however, was as nothing compared to Freedman's attempt, in August of 1901, with the aid of three of his sycophants, to convert the National League into a syndicate. This was launched at a secret meeting at his home in Red Bank, New Jersey, which was attended by representatives of the Boston, Cincinnati, and St. Louis clubs, the other clubs being unaware of the plot. So well did the conspirators cloak their movements and purposes that it was not until December 11, the opening day of the winter meeting in New York, that the story was broken in the newspapers.

"This scheme," the *Sun* said, "contemplates the organization of the National League Base Ball Trust, to be divided into preferred and common stock to draw a dividend of 7 per cent, all of which is to belong to the National League, as a body; the common stock to be used in payment for the present eight League Clubs, as follows . . ."

(New York was to receive 30 per cent; Cincinnati, St. Louis, and Boston, 12 per cent each; Philadelphia and Chicago, 10 per cent; Pittsburgh, 8 and Brooklyn, 6.)

"The management of the company," the article continued, "is to be placed for a term of years in the hands of not more than five men, to be selected by the stockholders and designated as a Board of Regents. From this board of managers a President and a Treasurer are to be chosen, although the Secretary need not necessarily be a member of the board. The salary of the President must not exceed $25,000, a year and the Treasurer not over $12,500. As the eight clubs will lose their identity by being merged into and becoming a part of the National League Trust, the different clubs will be under the direction of the managers, who will each receive a salary of $5,000 a year."

Spalding now ceased to be a mere concerned bystander and, at the pleadings of the Philadelphia, Pittsburgh, Chicago, and Brooklyn clubs, plunged into the fracas that began as the meeting got under way. Before it was over, Spalding, a reluctant candidate who promised only that, if elected, he would resign as soon as Freedman got out of baseball, was chosen president, succeeding Nicholas E. Young, who in his seventeenth year in office, and weary of the conflict all about him, was more than willing to retire. It was not however, a legal election, since Freedman and his three supporters refused to attend and the Spalding faction, in a great bluff, tried to claim a majority had been present merely because Fred Knowles, secretary of the

26

Giants, was observed at one time peering nervously into the room where the meeting was held.

Freedman properly challenged the election by asking the courts to enjoin Spalding from serving, which they properly did. But months of artful dodging by Spalding followed and it was not until the spring of 1902, as the season was about to open, that the battle ended. Freedman, realizing that in his bold attempt to refashion baseball to fit his own curious pattern he had succeeded only in splitting the league wide open and that further measures on his part were bound to fail, sent word to Spalding at his home in Point Loma, California, that he would sell the Giants as soon as he could do so with some grace. It appears he did not want to admit publicly that he had taken a licking. On receipt of this information, Spalding withdrew, Young was re-elected, harmony was re-established throughout the league, and there were no more alarms, for Freedman's quondam pals had turned their backs on him and hit the sawdust trail.

While all this had been going on, a complacent Freedman presided at the Polo Grounds in the season of 1901. He made peace with the newspapers. He didn't abuse the ball players, his own or his opponents'. If he ever was tempted to leap from his box and assault an umpire, he restrained himself. He reappointed George Davis as manager and stuck to him all year, although the club, hopeless from the beginning, was seventh at the wire.

Few of the players he had that year will be remembered, even by baseball historians. Davis still was active at shortstop. There were four catchers: Jack Warner, Frank Bowerman, Alex (Broadway) Smith and Joe Wall. John Ganzel, puchased from Chicago and in his first season in

New York, was at first base. Sammy Strang, whose square name was Samuel Strang Nicklin but who was always to be known as Sammy Strang, had come from Chicago with Ganzel, and was the second baseman. He was to jump to the American League the following year but he would be back, eventually. The old standby, George Van Haltren was one of the outfielders. One of the pitchers was the mute, Luther (Dummy) Taylor. He, like Strang, was to leap to the American League in 1902. Like Strang, he was to return. Also on the pitching staff were Ed Doheny, Bill Phyle, Chauncey Fisher, Roger Denzer, and the boy, Christy Mathewson.

Remember, Matty, as he soon was to be called all across the country and wherever the game of baseball was played, had been up from Norfolk the year before but had been sent back before the season was over. Then the Cincinnati club had drafted him for $100 and promptly traded him to New York for Amos Rusie, who had not pitched a game for the Giants since 1898 and was so close to the end of his string that he reached it with the Reds in 1901, when he took part in only three games and had a record of no victories and one defeat.

Does it strike you as strange that Brush, having got Mathewson for $100, should hand him over to the Giants for a worn-out pitcher with nine great years and two years of idleness behind him and nothing ahead of him? Or does it strike you, on second thought, that Brush simply was arranging a rendezvous between himself and the young Mathewson at the Polo Grounds? In Freedman's fight to gain complete control of the National League and turn it into a syndicate, he had the support of three clubs, Boston, St. Louis, and Cincinnati—and Brush owned the Cincinnati club. Freedman had given his word to Spalding—and for once he would keep his word—that he would get out of baseball as soon as he could do so gracefully. Had it already been arranged between him and Brush that when he moved out, Brush, forsaking Cincinnati, would move into New York? There were certain persons who suspected as much when they saw Mathewson shunted from Norfolk to New York by way of Cincinnati, but since they could prove nothing, they merely yawped for a while and then were silent. At all events, there was Mathewson with the Giants.

Christopher Mathewson was born in Factoryville, Pennsylvania, on August 12, 1880. He attended Keystone Academy and, at the age of seventeen, entered Bucknell University at Lewisburg, where he was better known as a football player than as a pitcher, being exceptionally talented as a field goal kicker. As a collegian he played summer baseball in the nearby town of Honesdale and, in 1899, pitched for the Taunton, Massachusetts, club of the New England League. In 1900, he was with Norfolk, in the Virginia League. There his record, with time out for his brief fling in New York—where he appeared in five games, winning none and losing three—was twenty-one games won, and only two lost.

He was not yet twenty-one years old when he reported to the Giants for the second time in the spring of 1901. He was blond, blue-eyed, weighed 190 pounds and was six feet, one and one half inches tall. He was a Greek god in flannels and he had the effortless motion and the speed, curve ball and control that baseball scouts dream of in a pitcher, yet never see, unless they are touched by great good fortune.

He was called "Big Six" and there are legends about that. One is that he got the name from Sam Crane, baseball writer with the *New York Evening Journal.* Once a ball player himself, Crane had served briefly with the Giants in the time of the trouble, or Brotherhood war. Sam was said to have recalled that in the days when volunteer firemen had put out New York fires, there was an engine known as Big Six . . . and . . . and what? Sam, born in Springfield, Massachusetts, never knew New York when the vamps were hauling their hand-drawn hand-pumped engines through the streets and, even if he only had read of them, what connection could there have been in his mind between an antique fire engine and this handsome young pitcher?

More plausible, although this, too, is but a legend, is that one of the other Giants, looking at Mathewson warming up one day and not having seen him before, said, "There's a nice looking kid. How big do you think he is?"

And when another hazarded a guess that the boy was six feet, the first said, "He's the biggest 'six' you ever saw."

However Matty got the name, there it was. Through all his days, as a Giant, in story and in headline, he would be Big Six.

Matty won twenty games and lost seventeen in 1901, which was better than fair to middling for a boy who wasn't twenty-one until August and was pitching for a seventh-place club. Even more impressive was his earned run average of 1.99 per nine-inning game and the fact that, on July 15, he pitched a no-hit, no-run game against St. Louis.

Within the next few years he was to be extolled by the baseball writers not only as the almost perfect pitcher but as the practically perfect man. He was held up to the youth of the nation as one who did not smoke, did not drink, would not play ball on Sunday (a desecration of the Sabbath permitted only at that time in Cincinnati, St. Louis, and Chicago in the National League), eschewed all card games, and found pleasure only in a whopping game of chess or checkers. The Greek god in flannels had become a knight in shining armor.

Fortunately, the knight was intensely human under the armor the baseball writers had placed upon him. He smoked cigars, cigarettes, and a pipe. He was no drinker in the broad sense of the term, but he knew the difference between Scotch and rye. He was a master at chess and checkers but he also was an expert bridge player, and when he sat down at a poker table, he knew when, and when not, to draw to an inside straight. But the illuminated picture of him was precise in one respect. He would not play ball on Sunday.

The eventful season of 1902 at the Polo Grounds began very much as most others had during the Freedman regime, for he whom Charlie Dryden always referred to as "Andy," quiescent in 1901, was having his final fling.

Over the winter he had fired George Davis and sold him to Chicago, replacing him as playing manager with George Smith, a second baseman bought from Pittsburgh. Meanwhile, somewhere along the line, he had added to his entourage one Horace Fogel, who had managed the Indianapolis club as far back as 1887, filled various executive positions of a minor nature in baseball in the years between, and ultimately was to become president of the Philadelphia club. Now, although his status was undefined, he wandered in and out of the clubhouse, sat on the bench when he chose, was free with his advice to one and all, and caused the players to wonder who was managing the team, Smith or Fogel?

Possibly it didn't make any difference, since it was a very bad team, although surely the confusion generated by the omnipresent Fogel didn't help. Dummy Taylor having jumped to the Cleveland club of the American League, Matty was the only pitcher of quality remaining on the staff, and behind him, when he pitched, there was rabble on the field. Naturally, the club quickly found its level in last place.

This was the drabbest, bleakest time in the history of the Giants, with only an occasional brawl by Freedman to enliven the dismal scene. The only fans who paid to see them play were there to mock them and many, although they hated him, had the low instincts of the owner. They howled at him to remove Smith as manager, then howled again when he announced Smith would remain only as a player and that Fogel was the manager.

A high note of comedy was struck when Fogel decided that since Matty couldn't win regularly he wasn't much of a pitcher and might be used to better effect in another position. He tried him at first base, at shortstop, in the outfield, and then in despair returned him to the box.

How long this sort of thing could have gone on and what the end would have been defies speculation. But late in June, Freedman learned that John McGraw, youthful manager of the Baltimore club of the American League and already one of the most exciting figures in the game, was at loggerheads with Byron Bancroft Johnson, president of the league and with the directors of his club as well, and was eager to move.

He sent the Giants' secretary, Knowles, to Baltimore to

see McGraw and invite him to New York for a conference. On McGraw's acceptance of the invitation, Freedman offered him both the management of the club and the concessions at the Polo Grounds. McGraw was willing to take the first but rejected the second for two reasons. One was that he was a baseball man and knew nothing of the catering business, the other that his friend, Harry M. Stevens, had had the concessions since 1894, and he was of no mind to usurp them. At that point, negotiations broke down and McGraw returned to Baltimore.

A few days later, however, he was back. Freedman wanted him as manager and was willing to drop the matter of the concessions. Only one detail remained to be cleared up in Baltimore before McGraw would be free to pull out in a manner that he felt would make him appear as something more than a mere deserter. He was prepared to bring that about. The club owed him $7,000 of his own money that he had advanced the year before. He had attempted several times to get it back but without success. Now he would demand it on pain of quitting if it were denied him. It was a perfect plan. He knew the directors didn't have $7,000.

That having been attended to, he notified the Baltimore newspapers of his withdrawal, threw in a blast at Ban Johnson and the directors and, to the accompaniment of an answering blast from Johnson, hopped back to New York and signed with Freedman.

The other National League club owners were delighted. Johnson, they knew, was preparing to invade New York, having the backing for such a move and needing only a field on which to play. Freedman, by reason of his Tammany connections, had been able to keep him from getting his hands on the desired real estate up to that time but it was inevitable that, sooner or later, he would get in. Then, however, he would find the going even rougher than he had thought before. Then McGraw would be there to combat him.

4

The Arrival of John McGraw

⊝ McGRAW, son of an Irish immigrant, was born in
Truxton, New York, on April 7, 1873, so that he was twenty-
nine years old when he arrived in New York, where he was
to lead the Giants to greatness and remain for the rest of
his life.

He was five feet, seven inches tall, dark-haired, dark-
eyed, and slightly built. Restless, aggressive, and quick
tempered, he would fight anybody—and frequently did.
His actual experience as a manager had been scant but
already he had demonstrated that he was the type, and
wherever he managed, his players would reflect his per-
sonality. They, too, would fight—the enemy players, the
umpires, the crowds and the cops, if necessary. Coming
from behind in a ball game, they wouldn't sacrifice to get
on even terms with their opponents, hoping to go on from
there. They would hit away, driving for the lead from
away back, scorning a tie, wanting only to win. That was
to be their hallmark through the years ahead.

As a youth, McGraw had worked briefly as a candy
butcher on the Elmira, Cortland, and Northern Railroad,
but a career as a railroad man, such as his father had visioned for him, had no attractions for him, nor had any

other career save one in baseball. Beginning as a pitcher but soon switching to the infield, he played with teams in Truxton, East Homer, and other small towns nearby, and at seventeen quit selling candy on the steam cars and joined the Olean club of the New York and Pennsylvania League. Elated at first that he was with a genuine professional team in an organized league, he soon grew dissatisfied because he was not allowed to play regularly and, as he had no contract, he moved on—to Hornellsville, to Canisteo, and before the season of 1890 had expired to Wellsville.

That winter, as a member of a barnstorming team managed by Al Lawson, his friend who also managed the Wellsville club, he toured the South and spent a month in Havana where, as he grew older, he was to spend many winters. Back in this country in the early spring of 1891, the wandering players completed their tour in Gainesville, Florida, and as they started north he parted company with them.

He remained in Gainesville where the Cleveland club, then in the National League, trained and caught on with another troupe of itinerant athletes who called themselves the All-Americas. In a practice game with Cleveland one afternoon, he made three doubles and a single off Leon Viau, then one of the best pitchers in baseball. When minor league owners, especially in the Middle West, read of this, he received wires from many of them offering him a job, and he accepted the best, which was from the Cedar Rapids club of the Illinois-Iowa League. That summer he moved up to the Baltimore club of the American Association and when the Association folded in the winter of 1891-1892 and the club was absorbed by the National League he became, within two years of his beginning as a professional in Olean, a big leaguer.

It was in Baltimore that McGraw not only attained fame as a ball player but received the training that ultimately was the background of his success as a manager.

The Orioles, at their peak, were more than a great club managed by Ned Hanlon, one of the greatest of managers. They had a flaming team spirit and, encouraged by Hanlon to exercise their initiative, devised new plays such as the hit-and-run and so improved on the old ones that they drove their rivals to distraction. Inspired chiefly by McGraw, they thought up so many tricks they forced lasting changes in the rules of the game. One of these brought about the introduction of the two-umpire system, since it became obvious after a while that no lone umpire could cope with them. So well, incidentally, did Hanlon instruct and encourage his players that four of them—McGraw, Hughie Jennings, Joe Kelley, and Wilbert Robinson—became major league managers.

McGraw was the first of the four to advance. In 1898 the Orioles were slipping fast. So was the attendance and so, H. B. Von der Horst thought, was the town, at least in so far as its interest in baseball was concerned. Since Von der Horst owned the Orioles and felt that changes had to be made, they were. And promptly. It was a fairly loose time in baseball, when the club owners could do pretty much as they pleased, and it pleased Von der Horst, though retaining ownership of the Orioles, to buy a piece of the Brooklyn club and send most of his remaining good players there with Ned Hanlon, too, to manage them.

McGraw, who was included in the package deal, wouldn't go. Neither would Wilbert Robinson. They had several reasons for not wanting to leave Baltimore. Most important was that they were doing a good business as partners in a saloon called the Blue Diamond. When he was convinced the two of them wouldn't budge, Von der Horst compromised. He allowed them to remain, with the proviso that McGraw would manage the remnant of the Orioles when the others went to Brooklyn.

The next few years in the life of John McGraw were pieces out of a picture of baseball that never can be reproduced, for this was a time of trouble and strife unthinkable in the solidly molded sport now contained within the iron frame of a business.

As playing manager of what was left of the Orioles, he did a good job and, although he could not win, he was in such demand on the part of rival club owners that Von der Horst succeeded in stopping the almost frantic bidding for his services only by announcing dramatically, "I would not take $10,000 for his contract!"

Meanwhile, Ban Johnson, who had been a baseball writer in Cincinnati and was now president of the Western League, had seen very clearly the possibility of upsetting the monopoly enjoyed by the National League. He already was expanding his league and the National Leaguers, aware of the direction in which he was about to move, determined to tighten their ranks the better to meet the inevitable onslaught. Thus, in the winter of 1899, they reduced their circuit from twelve clubs to eight by tossing out Washington, Cleveland, Louisville, and Baltimore.

Following this second shake-up in two years, McGraw and Robinson were sold to St. Louis and rebelled again. Finally, they agreed to go, but only as the season was about to open and only on two conditions laid down by

McGraw, who always did the talking for the pair: McGraw would not manage the club as Frank de Haas Robison, who owned it, wanted him to do. Neither he nor Robbie would have a reserve clause in their contracts, and both would be free agents at the end of the season. Thus they went to St. Louis for the 1900 campaign on their own terms.

Now, in the fall, McGraw was back in Baltimore, waiting bids for his services and in a position to accept the best. It came from Johnson who, lining up an Eastern battle front, had seized on the open spot in Baltimore. Who, he reasoned, would be better suited to lead the club, in what he now called the American League, than the young McGraw, Baltimore's favorite ball player? McGraw agreed he was just the man for the job, and so, in 1901, he was a playing manager in the "outlaw" league and certain that in this league lay his future.

It was, for him, a pleasant day dream . . . and faded as dreams will. Before the season was half over, he and Ban were in angry disagreement over what Ban called rowdyism on the field. They managed to patch up their quarrel during the winter but when spring came through again they were at each other once more. Besides, there was the matter of the $7,000 loan to the club, which in the end McGraw found a handy tool in prying himself loose from Baltimore but which actually had been a source of irritation to him before. This, then, was his situation when Freedman beckoned.

McGraw's first move on taking charge at the Polo Grounds was to slash the squad, dispatching nine players and Fogel along with them. Jack Hendricks, who was to manage the Cincinnati Reds years later and was a Giant outfielder at the time of McGraw's arrival, once said, "There is a story that McGraw fired me the first day. That is a big lie. It was the second day. I hid in the clubhouse the first day."

There were nine down—ten, including Fogel—and more to go as rapidly as possible. McGraw's original intention was to send Smith on his way with the first batch because he had heard Smith agreed with Fogel that Matty wasn't so hot as a pitcher. But on second thought he decided to keep him for the balance of the season. Now he set about gathering first-rate players to take the place of the vanished incompetents.

In two trips to Baltimore—and two raids on the outlaw club he had just left—he came off with "Iron Man" Joe McGinnity and Jack Cronin, pitchers; Roger Bresnahan, recognized even then as the best catcher in baseball and, as Buck Ewing had been, capable of playing any position and fast enough to be the lead-off man; Dan McGann, the first baseman; and Steve Brodie, the outfielder. He had several other raids planned but they could wait.

The Giants were defeated, 5 to 3, by the Phillies in McGraw's first game. It was played on July 19 and there were 10,000 in the stands. The fans didn't seem to mind the outcome. They were used to seeing the Giants lose. Besides, they had faith in McGraw and believed he soon would develop a winning team. Even losing, this one looked better than the one he had shaken up and all but thrown away. He played shortstop himself, with McGann on first base, Smith on second, and Billy Lauder, later to be the baseball coach at Yale for many years, on third. Brodie, Jimmy Jones, and Louis Washburn were in the outfield. Bresnahan was the catcher and McGinnity the pitcher.

McGraw made one other raid, this one by remote control. He knew just how good a pitcher Dummy Taylor was and wanted him back. After all, hadn't Dummy won eighteen games the year before with the worst team the Giants ever had put on a field, not even barring the mob that John B. Day had scraped together when his heroes had fled to the Brotherhood league? He had written several letters to Taylor but had no response. Now he sent an emissary.

Frank Bowerman had been Taylor's battery mate with the Giants and Taylor had taught him the deaf-and-dumb finger-language.

"Go see him in Cleveland," McGraw said to Bowerman. "Bawl the hell out of him . . . and give him what he wants. Don't come back without him."

A couple of days later Bowerman was back, Taylor with him. He told McGraw, through Bowerman, he was very happy to be back and, now that McGraw was there, he would not leave the Giants ever again as long as he could get the ball up to the plate. He didn't either. His next jump was to a school for the deaf in Kansas, where he was trained as an instructor for three or four winters and where he became a member of the faculty after the season of 1908.

McGraw now had the nucleus of a real staff—Mathewson, McGinnity, and Taylor. They were to figure largely in Giant triumphs in the very near future. In 1902, or what was left of it after Matty had been rehabilitated as a pitcher by McGraw, and McGinnity and Taylor had been snatched from the American League, Matty won thirteen games, McGinnity nine, and Taylor eight. What if among them they were charged with thirty-nine defeats? Better times, better teams, lay just ahead. Come the times, come the teams, the three would be ready for them—and there would be other pitchers, some good, a few great, to go with them.

This, quite possibly, was the only ball club ever to finish in last place that had so bright an outlook.

5

The New Owner of the Giants

⊖ IN the winter of 1902-03, that which must have been arranged a year and a half before came to pass. Freedman sold the Giants to Brush. This seems to have made every one happy, especially the Giant fans.

John Tomlinson Brush was tall, gaunt, hard-faced, and a curious combination of the businessman and the sportsman. He had made a lot of money in men's clothing and need never have gone into baseball yet he bought the Indianapolis club, gave it back to the league and sold his players to Day, bought the Cincinnati club, now sold it and bought the Giants. That he was not exactly a starry-eyed fan was indicated by his willingness to go along with Freedman in the proposed syndication of the National League. No fan would have wanted that. And no far-seeing businessman normally would have wanted it either, since, had the plan come off, the league would have been ruined and all the money invested in it lost. He may have been bewitched by Freedman's bluff assurance that they could not fail.

From that ill-conceived venture, Brush must have learned a lesson. In New York he was the perfect club owner. He gave McGraw all the money he wanted with which to buy ball players and never asked a question. He poured thousands of dollars into the repair and maintenance of the weather-beaten tumble-down wooden stands that Freedman had left behind him and, when the grandstand burned to the ground in 1911, he reared the steel and concrete horseshoe that, for all that it has been extended and built upon, still is the core of one of the most celebrated sports arenas in the world.

He hated Ban Johnson, regarded the American League with contempt, and on entering New York was determined to keep Ban and the upstart circuit out of it. He would have supported McGraw to any length in further forays in quest of American League players but, suddenly, his hands were tied. That same winter the National League, weary of fighting the American and spattered with red ink that was as blood to some of the club owners, worked out a settlement with Johnson. One of the terms demanded by Ban and granted over the bitter protests rasped by Brush in the meeting, was permission for the American League to put a club in New York. An angry signatory to the peace pact, Brush remained an implacable enemy of Johnson's, whom he first had known when Ban was a baseball writer in Cincinnati, and did all he could to hinder him and belittle his league.

It must have made his fingers itch when he looked on the American League players he and McGraw would like to have snared, yet who were beyond his grasp now that peace had come to baseball again. But they were bound, he and McGraw, and had to round up reinforcements without breaking the rules set upon them. McGraw knew where to look. He bought George Browne, who was to become one of the best right fielders the Giants ever have had, from Philadelphia, and by a stroke of extreme good fortune signed Billy Gilbert, a second baseman, who had been released outright by the Baltimore club of the American League. Other players, bought or obtained in barter or on waivers, were to loom large in the Giant successes that lay just ahead, but none would serve better than Browne and Gilbert.

In the spring of 1903 the Giants trained at Savannah, Georgia. Through the years McGraw always brought home well conditioned, well drilled teams. This one was the mold in which those that came after were cast. It hustled, it won ball games, and it was a crowd pleaser, smashing attendance records all over the league, once drawing 32,000 against the champion Pirates at the Polo Grounds. It was the most exciting season the Giants had known since Mutrie's team won its first pennant fifteen years before.

That was the year in which McGinnity, who won thirty-one games all told, expanded his reputation as an iron man —a reputation first gained in Baltimore two years before when he twice pitched two games in one day, winning one double-header and breaking even in the other. In 1903, he did it three times, all in the month of August—on the first, the eighth and the thirty-first, winning all six games.

For the first time Matty was a thirty-game winner, and Taylor tossed thirteen games into the drive that landed the Giants in second place. A young pitcher named Leon Ames, called "Red," who was out of Warren, Ohio, and joined the Giants straight from the Ilion, New York, town team, arrived too late and was too green to accomplish much that year, but in time he was to be one of the mainstays of the club. Another newcomer was Sam (Sandow)

45

Mertes, a barrel-chested, piano-legged outfielder and a six-year veteran on the big time with the Phillies and the Cubs.

Before the season was out, McGraw bought Arthur Devlin, a twenty-five year old third baseman from Newark, and Harry (Moose) McCormick, a twenty-four year outfielder and extraordinary pinch-hitter from Philadelphia. Devlin would become the greatest third baseman ever to wear a Giant uniform. McCormick was no sensation as an outfielder but he could walk up cold from the bench and maul the enemy pitchers.

That winter McGraw made a deal that he always believed was the most important he ever conjured. He traded Jack Cronin, a pitcher, and Charlie Babb, an infielder, to Brooklyn for Bill Dahlen, shortstop. Dahlen was thirty-three years old and had broken into the league with Chicago in 1891 when McGraw himself was a busher in Cedar Rapids. From Chicago he had gone to Brooklyn in 1898. To almost every one else, he was strictly a run-of-the-mill shortstop, good enough to hold a major league job but one a manager could take or leave alone. To McGraw, who had played against him many a time, he was just what the Giants needed.

"With Dahlen," he told Brush, "we can win the pennant."

"If you think that much of him," Brush said, "get him, no matter what he costs."

McGraw got him virtually for nothing. Cronin couldn't win for even the improved Giants of 1903. Babb had been used at shortstop only because no one else was available.

The team now was set for 1904. McGann was on first base, Gilbert on second, Dahlen at shortstop, and Devlin on third. Browne, Mertes, and McCormick were in the outfield. Bresnahan was back of the bat, with Bowerman and Jack Warner to spell him when needed. The pitching staff was headed by Matty and McGinnity and included Ames and another youngster, this one a twenty-three year old left-hander called George (Hooks) Wiltse, who also could hit and play first base.

The Pirates, three-time pennant winners were, of course, the team to beat. After them, the Reds and the Cubs. As the season rolled along, the Giant infield clicked and the pitching was great, but there was need of another slugging outfielder to pair with Mertes, since neither Browne nor McCormick was a window-breaker. McGraw found him in Cincinnati. His name was Michael Joseph Donlin and they called him "Turkey Mike."

Donlin was but twenty-six years old at the time but he had been around: with St. Louis in 1899, the year he came out of Erie, Pennsylvania, and again in 1900; with McGraw on the American League club in 1901; then back to the National League in 1902. He had been around in other spots, too. In one of them, some one had knifed him in the face, leaving a scar that extended from his left cheek bone to his jaw. But that hadn't stopped Mike from going around. Years later, long after he had called it a career in baseball and was working on another in the movies, and night baseball had begun to flourish in the minors, he said, "Jesus! Think of taking a ball player's nights away from him!"

No one ever took many away from him when he was young and roaming the baseball trails. He could hit ...329...340...351...He was hitting .356 in Cincinnati in 1904, when Garry Herrmann, the president of the club, simply got tired of upbraiding him and fining him for his nocturnal prowlings, and asked for waivers on him, planning to send him to the St. Louis Browns. He got them from six clubs, but McGraw, who liked Mike—and his hitting and fielding—and was willing to take a chance on him, claimed him.

That was it. The Giants, with Donlin in the line-up, romped home, winning 106 games to set a record for both leagues as the Reds, Cubs, and Pirates, in that order, finished up the stretch. McGinnity and Matty, comprising the hardest one-two pitching punch in the league, were dynamite, McGinnity winning thirty-five games and Matty thirty-three.

McGraw had gone from the bottom of the league in 1902 to the top in 1904, and the only stop on the way had been in second place. Brush ordered more lumber and enlarged the stands.

Peace having come to baseball in 1903, there had been a world series that fall between the Pirates and the Boston Red Sox, but in 1904 there was no series. That was Brush's decision, brought about by his intense hatred for Johnson and his adamant refusal, no matter the terms of the peace treaty, to recognize the American League as the equal of the National. The fans wanted a series; the newspapers clamored for one. The players, wanting the money they would get from a series, petitioned for one. McGraw, though he had no love for either Johnson or the rival league, sought to persuade Brush to change his mind. They wasted their time, all of them.

That was the last time participation in a series was left to the discretion of a pennant-winning club owner. The National Commission, created in 1903 and consisting of the presidents of the two leagues, and Garry Herrmann as chairman, had no ruling to cover Brush's balk, not having anticipated such an attitude on the part of any owner. But at their meeting that winter they fashioned one. Beginning with 1905, the world series has been, automatically, the climax of the season.

6

"Hey, Barney!"—And Another Pennant

⊖ THE year 1905 was one of tumult and triumph for the Giants, a year in which McGraw's first great feud within the league had its beginning. Reasonably tractable though his first two seasons in New York, he reverted sharply to type as he led his champions into this campaign and was again the turbulent, often downright offensive, character he had been as a member of the Orioles and for the short time he spent in the American League. Now there was none to curb him. When the mild Harry C. Pulliam, president of the league, tried it, McGraw tongue-lashed him pitilessly. Barney Dreyfuss, who owned the Pirates, challenged him and received a frightful verbal beating. Brush urged him on, although, in truth, he needed no urging. The baseball writers applauded him in print and denounced all who dared oppose him. The blood cries from grandstand and bleachers at the Polo Grounds when he descended upon a quailing umpire or visiting player were remindful of the bull ring.

His Giants, with few exceptions—Matty, Browne, one or two others—took their cue from him and were as ruthless on the field. Idolized at home, they were hated on the road and they reveled in it. The presence of policemen, posted about their dugout in the hostile towns, was to them a symbol of their prowess—and the cops were there almost everywhere they went, especially in Pittsburgh, Chicago, and Cincinnati. Reporters traveling with the team frequently referred to themselves in print as war correspondents. There was at least some slight justification for the appelation. Scarcely a day went by that their stories of the ball game weren't interwoven with blow-by-blow descriptions of squabbles and fist fights.

McGraw was capable, of course, of hurtling into a violent rage in a split second, where he had been all sunshine and sweetness before. But many of his seemingly sudden charges on the field were carefully plotted and perfectly timed. This was particularly true where the Pirates were concerned.

The year before, as the Giants had rushed to the pennant, the Pirates, favored in the spring to repeat their victories of the three preceding years, had buckled and lagged as the campaign neared its end. However, McGraw still looked upon them as the Giants' most dangerous rivals. His own team was but little changed, save for the return of Sammy Strang, this time as a full-blown outfielder, by way of Brooklyn. On the Pittsburgh side were the likes of Fred Clarke, the manager and left fielder; Hans Wagner, Tommy Leach, Otto Knabe, Ginger Beaumont, George Gibson, the catcher who was second only to Bresnahan; and a fine pitching staff built around Sam Leever, Deacon Phillippe, Lefty Leifield, and Pat Flaherty.

His plan was to ride them hard, soften them up, get them off balance and, having thus reduced their effectiveness, to slay them. As a result, every time the teams met in New York or Pittsburgh their meeting was marked by violence. Clarke was McGraw's pet target, but when he really was heated up he scattered his fire. The only Pittsburgh player on whom he could make no impression whatever was Wagner. Throwing insults at the Dutchman was like pitching pebbles at Gibraltar.

This animosity between the two clubs, deliberately planted and fostered by McGraw, reached an eerie peak in the "Hey, Barney!" incident and its aftermath which, absurd as it sounds—and as it was—threw the entire league into a turmoil and all but crowded the pennant races in both leagues off the sports pages. The New York writers fulminated against Barney or lampooned his heavy German accent as they repeated his charges against McGraw, and the writers in Pittsburgh and the other cities tore McGraw to pieces.

Barney Dreyfuss, a spry but dignified little man of middle age, owned the Pirates. He charged, in a letter to Pulliam, made public by the league president, that on the nineteenth of May, as he sat with friends from Pittsburgh in a box at the Polo Grounds, McGraw addressed insulting remarks to him from the field, and on the following day as he was standing near the main entrance to the grounds, again in the company of friends, McGraw had yelled "Hey, Barney!" at him.

When he ignored this "too familiar greeting," he continued, McGraw defied him to make a bet with him on the game, accused him of controlling umpires and of welshing on his bookmaker.

In reply McGraw flayed Pulliam, who had been Dreyfuss' secretary in Pittsburgh and before that in Louisville, for having pilloried him without giving him an opportunity to defend himself against Barney's allegations

52

and called upon the president to give him that opportunity forthwith. Pulliam, possibly fearing he might be adjudged biased in the matter in view of his past employment by Dreyfuss referred it to a meeting of the league's board of directors, which he called for June 1, in Boston. McGraw countered by getting Pulliam on the telephone and calling him names that curled his ears. For that Pulliam suspended him for fifteen days and fined him $150.

McGraw and Dreyfuss appeared before the directors in Boston and gave their versions of the story and, after scant time for deliberation, the directors found McGraw not guilty and censured Dreyfuss for, in their judgment, making an ass of himself!

McGraw promptly demanded of Pulliam a statement as to what he intended to do about the fine and suspension, and when the president said the Giant manager would have to pay the one and serve the other Brush's lawyers got an injunction restraining him. So ended the affair. By that time McGraw was impossible.

Meanwhile, the Giants were moving on toward their goal of another pennant and, having finished off the Pirates in the last week of September, reached it by beating the Cardinals in St. Louis on October 1.

The Athletics having won the pennant in the American League, the fans across the nation looked forward eagerly to a clash of Matty and Rube Waddell, the A's eccentric, but great left-hander. An injury to Rube's left shoulder, suffered on September 1 in a friendly scuffle between him and Andy Coakley—with the Rube trying to grab and tear up Andy's straw hat, since the seasonal bell for skimmers had tolled that day—had kept the great man out of action through the final month of the campaign. Yet hopes were high that he would recover in time for the series. He didn't, and such hopes were shattered and the A's plainly were handicapped going into the series without him.

There is no telling, of course, what might have happened if the Rube had been able to pitch. What actually happened was this: The Giants won, four games to one, and a pitching standard for the series was set that in all likelihood never will be met, since in no contest did the losing team score a run. Matty, opposing Eddie Plank, in his own right a great southpaw, yet not quite the equal of Waddell, shut out the A's in the opening game. In the second game, Chief Bender of the Chippewa tribe, hooking up with McGinnity, shut out the Giants. Matty, drawing Coakley as his opponent in the third game, shut out the A's. McGinnity and Plank, each in his second time around, hooked up in the fourth game and the Iron Man shut out the A's. In the final game Matty, making his third start and this time opposed by Bender, pitched his third shutout.

Twenty-two years later when the Yankees, under Miller Huggins, tore the American League apart and beat the Pirates in four games in the world series, a reporter asked Wilbert Robinson how they compared with the fabulous Baltimore Orioles of the nineties and Robbie said, bluntly, "They would have kicked the hell out of us."

For this he was assailed by all the living Orioles, including McGraw, who said, "I've known for a long time he was daffy but the old ——— must have blown his top for sure."

It is too bad the one who was talking to him didn't ask him to rate the Orioles of 1894-96 and the Giants of 1905. He had said before, and would say again, that the 1905

Giants were the best team he ever managed and when some one challenged him with the 1922 team that won the pennant in a stirring western drive and beat the Yankees four straight in the series, he insisted that the 1905 team was the greatest. Had the passing years colored his judgment of the heroes who had won his first world championship? Perhaps.

7

The Afternoon of September 23, 1908

⊖ IT may sound odd that the season of 1906, in which the Giants finished second, was by McGraw's own appraisal one of his worst. But it was. It was a season he never forgot.

When the team moved north from its training camp at Memphis in the spring, he did not doubt that it would repeat its smashing victory of the year before, nor was he hesitant about expressing his confidence. He not only told every one who asked him that he thought his athletes would win in a breeze but, to make sure the public would recognize them for what they were, the legend "World's Champions" replaced "New York" on their shirt fronts.

He was, of course, totally unaware that he was riding for a fall. Even when Matty came down with diphtheria shortly after the opening he was upset only for the sake of the pitcher, for already there was a bond of friendship between them that would be broken only by Matty's death about twenty years later. Young Ames had achieved real major league stature the year before by winning twenty-two games; Wiltse was improving regularly, and there was always McGinnity. Let Matty take it easy. The

Roger Bresnahan

"Iron Man" McGinnity

Rube Marquand

The Giants of 1904, who won a record-breaking 106 games to bring John J. McGraw his first pennant. (l. to r.) Standing: Roger T. Bresnahan, George R. Wiltse, "Dummy" Taylor, George R. Browne, Arthur Devlin, Jack Dunn, and Harry E. "Moose" McCormick. Seated: "Sandow" Mertes, Joe "Iron Man" McGinnity, Dan McGann, Jack Warner, John J. McGraw, Leon K. Ames, Frank Bowerman, Billy Gilbert, and "Doc" Marshall. Not shown in this picture are Mathewson, Dahlen, and Donlin.

Giants would be in front when he was ready to pitch again.

Actually they were in front, and Matty, making a remarkable recovery from a malady that in those years was very often fatal, won thirty-one games, and the always reliable McGinnity won twenty-seven. But Ames, in an unexpected form reversal, won only twelve. Then, in one series with Cincinnati, Donlin suffered a broken leg and McGann a broken arm, and Bresnahan was knocked out by a blow on the head from a pitched ball. Injuries . . . ailments . . . batting slumps . . . a sudden slow-down by Billy Gilbert at second base . . . all of these, none of which could have been foreseen in the spring, took the Giants off the pace as the Cubs came with a rush.

Here, it developed, was just the team to wrap up the Giants, great as they had been the year before and great as they now were supposed to be. For four years Frank Selee, little remembered now but one of the most able managers of all times, had been rebuilding the Cubs. For three years they had been a threat to the Giants and Pirates. A change in the administration of the club, which saw the volatile Charles Webb Murphy elected to the presidency in the winter of 1905-06, resulted in the release of Selee and the appointment of Frank Le Roy Chance as manager. Rough as the deal may have been on Selee, it apparently was just what the Cubs needed. Chance, who had been a catcher and was now a first baseman, and one of the best, was a savage driver, yet one who inspired a fierce loyalty in his men.

McGraw, suddenly realizing his peril, sought to bolster his team against the onslaught of Chance, Tinker, Evers, Slagle, Schulte, and Sheckard, of Lundgren and Reulbach

57

and "Three Fingered" Brown, and their catcher, Johnny Kling. Seeking added power and with it the experience needed in a spot like this, he bought two veteran outfielders, Spike Shannon from St. Louis and Cy Seymour from Cincinnati.

Shannon, red-faced, bull-necked and one of the first, if not the first, outfielders ever to wear sun glasses, was posted in left field, while Seymour took Donlin's place in center. For Seymour, his arrival in New York was a home coming, as he had been a pitcher with the Giants for a part of the Freedman era. His return also meant a reunion with McGraw who, in 1901, had induced him to quit the Giants and take up with the American League club in Baltimore.

But Shannon and Seymour couldn't stop the Cubs, nor could any of the other Giants or all of them put together, and they won the pennant. The Giants, standing off the Pirates through September, were second. That year the Cubs won 116 games, which still is the major league record and, at the same time, involved McGraw in another of his long standing feuds. Chance, called "Husk" by his players and "The Peerless Leader" by Charlie Dryden—who had left New York and now was writing for the *Chicago Examiner*—was every bit as rough and tough as McGraw on the field and delighted in drawing McGraw's fire and then counterattacking.

"He had us all doing it," Johnny Evers said in later years. "If we didn't ride McGraw and his players, Husk would have fined us and maybe beat the hell out of us."

The loss of the championship, after such a brief whirl in glory, impressed upon McGraw that he must never brag about one of his teams again—and that he must start immediately to make this one over, supplanting his aging heroes with young men fresh from the bushes. Two of his recruits for 1907 were Larry Doyle, a second baseman, and Fred Merkle, a first baseman. Each was destined for fame at the Polo Grounds, and it was Doyle who was to say, "It's great to be young and a Giant."

They were discovered by Dick Kinsella, for many years McGraw's one-man scouting staff. Dick was dark, portly, and suave, and a fastidious dresser in a manner that became fashionable in the nineties and never went out of fashion with him—square-topped derby, square-toed shoes, long sack coat, high stiff collar, and a heavy gold watch chain across his middle. He was the proprietor of a flourishing paint shop in Springfield, Illinois, but he had been in or around baseball all his life. Whenever the spirit—or his friend McGraw—moved him, he left his shop to the care of his assistant and was off on a prowl through the high-grass leagues. McGraw having started a youth movement of his own, the class C and D ball parks would see more of Kinsella than the paint shop for the next couple of years, and many a good young ball player would turn up at the Polo Grounds.

The Giants were fourth that year but McGraw didn't mind too much. This was a team that was being made over as it ran along and at times it had shown flashes of skill and drive that had made him confident of its future.

By 1908, Devlin was the only survivor of the 1905 infield, McGann having gone to Boston, Gilbert back to the minors and thence to St. Louis, and Dahlen to Brooklyn.

The new first baseman was new in a Giant uniform only. He was Fred Tenney, who had been with Boston for fourteen years, the last three as manager. He was thirty-seven years old but still agile and McGraw figured he could hold up, which he did, until Merkle was ready to take over. Doyle was at second base and Al Bridwell, also obtained from Boston, was at shortstop. On the youthful side were Charlie Herzog, an infielder; Josh Devore and Fred Snodgrass, outfielders; and Otis (Doc) Crandall, a pitcher.

That spring, for the first time, the Giants trained at Marlin, a town of some 4,000 in the north central part of Texas, already famous as far away as Dallas because of its natural hot wells. By training there for eleven years, the Giants would make its name known to baseball fans all over the country.

That summer McGraw caused a sensation by paying $11,000 to the Indianapolis club of the American Association for a young left-handed pitcher called Rube Marquard. This was the highest price that ever had been paid for a minor-league player and the Rube promptly was tagged "The $11,000 Beauty." Within a short while, because he could not win, he became "The $11,000 Lemon." But the day was not far off when he would be worth many times over the amount laid out for him.

Everything else that happened to the Giants in 1908, however, was overshadowed by what happened at the Polo Grounds late in the afternoon of September 23, in the ninth inning of a game with the Cubs.

The race had been a three-way scuffle all along among the Giants, the Cubs, and the Pirates. Now, in a vital game, the score was tied at 1-1 and with two out the Giants had Moose McCormick on third base, Merkle on first base, and Bridwell at bat. Bridwell drilled a ball into center field,

McCormick raced home, and the crowd, thinking the game was over, swarmed on the field. But McCormick hadn't scored and the game wasn't over. Merkle, as he had seen older players do in similar circumstances, cut second base and ran for the clubhouse when he saw the Moose nearing the plate, and now Evers was standing on the bag, screaming for the ball, screaming to the umpires, Hank O'Day and Bob Emslie.

Exactly what happened immediately thereafter never has been definitely established. It is incontrovertible that Evers eventually was in possession of a ball when he demanded, first of Emslie, who paid no attention to him, and then of O'Day, who only growled at him, that Merkle be called out in a force play. Evers said the ball was thrown to him by "Circus Solly" Hofman, the Cubs' center fielder. Joe McGinnity swore Hofman's throw was wild and that he, having recovered the ball, threw it into the crowd. No one was more confused than the umpires. Emslie fled to the dressing room and O'Day tried to follow him but was caught in the swirl of players and fans. Did he declare Merkle out? The Cubs said he did; the Giants that he didn't. In the press box, evening newspaper reporters flashed to their offices that the Giants had won, 2 to 1.

It was not until ten o'clock that night that O'Day announced his decision. Merkle was out. The game had ended in a tie.

McGraw was choleric when he heard it.

"If Merkle was out," he yelled, as soon as he became articulate, "O'Day should have cleared the field and gone on with the game! But Merkle wasn't out and we won and they can't take it away from us!"

He was disillusioned on that point the following day

when President Pulliam upheld O'Day and ruled that, if necessary to decide the race, the game must be replayed. McGraw promptly appealed to the league's board of directors to reverse Pulliam's ruling and as promptly was rebuffed.

Little more than a week remained of the season. When it was over, the Giants and the Cubs were tied. In the play-off, set in a riotous scene at the Polo Grounds, the Cubs won, 4 to 2, the clinching blow being a triple by Joe Tinker off Matty.

Around the town the fans blamed Merkle for the loss of the pennant. On the vaudeville stage, a comedian said, "I call my cane 'Merkle' because it has a bone head."

The quip was picked up by the newspapers, by the mob. That was it! "Bonehead Merkle!"

McGraw furiously rushed to the defense of the unhappy youngster, praising him for his skills and his intelligence, absolving him of blame for merely having aped older players, and pointing to a dozen games or more through the season which the Giants should have won but didn't. He said that was how the pennant had been lost. Then, his temperature at the boiling point, he roared, "We were robbed of the pennant and nobody can blame Merkle for that!"

Another unpleasant aftermath of the play-off was a rumor that an attempt had been made to bribe the umpires, Bill Klem and Jim Johnstone, to favor the Giants. It was hinted that some one "connected with the ball club" was guilty. Pulliam announced an investigation would be held, then deferred it until the league meeting in December. At that time, Klem and Johnstone testified that Dr.

William Creamer, the Giants' physician and part-time playboy, was the one. Over Creamer's tearful protestation of his innocence, Pulliam and the club owners took the word of the umpires, and sentenced him to a lifetime of exile from all major and minor league ball parks.

8

The Old Guard Fades Out

⊖ GONE were most of the old heroes as the Giants wheeled into 1909. Now others would follow. McGinnity still had a lot of pitches left in his sturdy arm but he no longer could hold to the major league pace and went to Newark to manage the club and pitch as well—and to rack up a total of fifty-nine victories in two years and start a round of the minors that would end in Dubuque when he was fifty-two. Incidentally, he attributed his longevity as a pitcher to the fact that he never warmed up for more than three or four minutes. He said most pitchers took years off their careers throwing practice pitches.

Donlin, the captain of the team, had been getting $4,000 a year. He had spent the winter in vaudeville with his wife, Mabel Hite, and when his demand that his salary be doubled was rejected, he said he would remain on the stage. Brush thought he was fooling, but he wasn't, and, his employer being obdurate too, the Giants had to get along without him.

Bresnahan was slowing up and McGraw made a trade for him that was greatly to his liking. He went to the Cardinals as manager. In return, the Giants got John (Red) Murray, an outfielder; Arthur (Bugs) Raymond, a pitcher; and George (Admiral) Schlei, a catcher, bought by the Cardinals from the Reds and shunted on to the Polo Grounds.

Raymond, a very good pitcher, was not called Bugs for nothing. He would and did drink anything that came in bottles, and when he was on the loose there was no telling where he would go or what he would do. But McGraw was willing to take a chance on him, as he had on Donlin. Murray, red-thatched and with a jaw like the prow of a battleship, took Donlin's place in right field and quickly became a favorite with the fans. Schlei, a veteran, would do most of the catching.

Among the newcomers in the camp at Marlin that spring were Arthur Fletcher, a shortstop who, playing with Dallas the previous spring, had caught McGraw's attention by outrageously riding him and his players; Arthur (Tillie) Shafer, a young infielder from the Coast; and John Tortes (Chief) Meyers, Mission Indian out of Riverside, California, and a Dartmouth man, who had been bought from St. Paul.

It was a young club and, with Matty at his peak—he won twenty-five games that year while losing only six—McGraw thought it might win, but it didn't, winding up third behind the Pirates and the Cubs. Two years later it crashed to the top but by that time other changes had been made, although Matty was standing off the enemy hitters and he and Meyers were called the best battery in baseball. Meyers took no bows on that, however.

"Anybody can catch Matty," he would say. "You could catch him sitting in a rocking chair."

Matty had amazing control and it was a joy to see him pitch. He worked very easily, operating on the theory that with eight teammates to help him, it would be senseless for him to tear himself apart trying to fog the ball past the hitters. Among his greatest admirers were the umpires. His control made their task a simple one and, when they called a pitch wrong as, of course, they sometimes did, he never gave them so much as a dirty look.

Meanwhile, for laughs, although sometimes the laughter was worn a little thin, there was always Bugs Raymond. McGraw sent most of Bugs's pay to his wife and kept him on a meager allowance, but Bugs managed that all right. He simply bought cheaper liquor or sometimes stayed on the wagon for a few days, thus saving his money for a real twister. McGraw hired a keeper for him, but the keeper quit when Bugs threatened to bash in his head. Once McGraw tried to straighten him out by putting him in a sanitarium for a few days—he thought. The first night the doctor who owned the place called McGraw.

"Get that man out of here!" he yelled. "The rest of my patients are nutty enough and he is making them nuttier!"

But between sprees Bugs was useful. There were days when he was reasonably dried out, and nobody could beat him.

There was nothing really new in 1910. Even Bugs stuck to the old routine. Although the Giants were second for a short time in the spring, they never got to the front. The Cubs, in a spectacular comeback, drove the Pirates from the peak and won the pennant for the fourth time in five years.

9

A Pennant Is "Stolen"

IT was, McGraw felt, like old times in the spring of 1911. That spring he knew he had a winner, as he had known back in 1904. Maybe this team wasn't as good as his first championship array but it was younger and faster: Merkle, Doyle, Fletcher, and Herzog in the infield; Murray, Snodgrass, and Devore in the outfield, with a real speedster named Beals Becker as a spare. Meyers was not precisely a gazelle but he was a thumping hitter. Matty still was the greatest pitcher in the league, and Marquard was gaining constantly in effectiveness. There were also Crandall, Wiltse, and Ames.

McGraw was his old truculent self, fighting with practically everybody—umpires, players, even his own players once in a while. He hated Charlie Herzog but benched Devlin to make room for him at third base. Herzog, for his part, had no use for McGraw but he was a great competitor and played for him as he would have played for the devil himself. McGraw had a fist fight with Dan McGann in Boston and another with Ad Brennan, a pitcher, in Philadelphia. He was getting the worst of it with Brennan when Fletcher stepped between them, pushed him aside, and was outpointing Brennan when the cops broke it up.

"It's a great system they have," Sid Mercer of the *Globe* said. "McGraw starts the fights and Fletcher finishes them. The only time Mac gets licked is when Fletch isn't around."

On the night of April 14, the telephone rang on the desk of Al Steimer, veteran sports editor of the *New York Herald*. Steimer could be gruff and short-tempered when he was busy, and now he was very busy indeed. He picked up the receiver.

"Yes?" he snapped.

The voice on the other end of the wire said, "The Polo Grounds is on fire."

Steimer slammed the receiver back on the phone.

"—— —— clowns!" he said. "Why don't they get something new? 'The Polo Grounds is on fire! A jeweler set fire to it. He wanted to get the diamond!' I shut that —— —— —— —— off before he could tell me the rest of it."

But this time it was no joke. Even as Steimer spoke, there was a red glare in the Harlem sky and the fire engines were racing toward the park. The wooden grandstand that John B. Day had taken over from the Brotherhood in 1891, and on which Brush had built in the years since McGraw had been in New York, collapsed in a horseshoe of flaming debris as the firemen poured tons of water on it.

Again, as when the aldermen cut a street through the original Polo Grounds in 1889, the Giants were homeless, but this time for only a few hours. Before morning, Frank Farrell who, with Bill Devery, the former police chief, owned the Yankees, or Highlanders as they were called then, offered Brush the use of their park at 168 Street and Broadway. Brush accepted the offer, and the following day the Giants moved into their temporary quarters.

Brush, who had been thinking of tearing down the old stand and building a new one of concrete, worked swiftly. The bleachers, wetted down by the firemen as the grandstand was consumed, remained intact. Now, with almost incredible swiftness, a double-decked steel and concrete structure was reared, and long before the season was over the Giants came home again.

It has been said of them that that year they stole the pennant, and so they did, setting a modern record (i.e., dating from 1900) of 347 thefts. They were a ragged crew at the finish—ragged but triumphant for, hitting the dirt day after day and fraying their uniforms, they had hurled back the Cubs, winners of four pennants in the last five years.

The unfortunate Raymond was not around at the finish. At least he was not around the Polo Grounds. During a game with the Pirates on the last home stand, McGraw gave him a new ball and sent him to the bull pen to warm up, as Marquard was in trouble. The Rube righted himself and it was not until the following inning that Raymond was called in. Wagner was at bat with two out and men on first and third. Bugs's first pitch hit the grandstand and now there was a run in and a man on third. Hans hit the next pitch back to Bugs who, instead of tossing the ball to Merkle for an easy out, tried to get the runner at the plate and threw it over Meyers' head.

"I took him out," McGraw said, "and as he reached the bench, I saw he was bleary-eyed. He hadn't stopped at the bull pen when I sent him down to warm up but kept going, right out of the park and across the street to a gin mill, where he traded in the ball for three shots of whisky."

Poor Bugs never appeared in a Giant uniform again. His last appearance in New York, as the world series was coming on, was in a Sunday game with a sandlot semi-pro team.

The Athletics had won in the American League and, as it had been in 1905, McGraw and Connie Mack opposed each other in the series. This was known as the marathon series. It didn't start until October 14. Bad weather set in, and the teams were holed up in Philadelphia for six days in a row. It was not until October 26 that the A's wound it to a finish, four games to two. Until the last game, as Matty, Marquard, and Crandall tilted with Jack Coombs, Eddie Plank, and Chief Bender, the pitching, while not quite up to the 1905 standard, was exceptionally good; but in the finale Ames cracked and the Giants along with him, and a Polo Grounds crowd looked on glumly as the A's won, 13 to 2. In this series Frank Baker, the A's third baseman, hit two home runs, one off Marquard and the other off Matty, and forever after was known as "Home Run Baker."

McGraw's disappointment at losing the series was tempered somewhat by the fact that he lost it to Mack, for whom he had a genuine affection.

"You have one of the greatest teams I've ever seen, Connie," he said when it was all over. "It must be. I have a great team, too, but you beat us."

10

McGraw Loses a Friend

⊖ THE year of 1912 was a crowded one. Marquard won nineteen straight, tying the record set by Tim Keefe in 1888; the Giants won the pennant again, picked up Jim Thorpe along the way—and lost the world series to the Boston Red Sox in a heart-breaking finish. And, in November, Brush died.

Marquard started his streak on the opening day of the season when he beat Brooklyn. He won three games in April, seven in May, eight in June, and one in July, beating every club in the league at least once. His streak was rounded out as it had begun, for on July 3, he took a decision over Brooklyn.

The Rube's march through the first three months of the season naturally made it possible for the Giants to take command early and, in a repetition of their sharp hitting and daring base running in 1911, they won the flag easily, being ten games ahead of the second place Pirates at the wire.

McGraw, a showman as well as a great manager, hired Jim Thorpe when the Indian returned from the Stockholm Olympics and was deprived of the trophies and medals he had won over there, the Amateur Athletic Union having learned that during his summer vacations from Carlisle he had played professional baseball in the Carolinas.

"How do you know he can play ball in the big leagues?" a friend of McGraw's asked.

"I don't know," John said, adding, "All I know is that he is the one all the sports fans in the country want to see. I've got the ball players I need to win—and Thorpe isn't going to hurt us at the gate."

Actually, Thorpe was a better ball player than McGraw might have thought, and a better one than most persons were to recall in later years. Although never a star, he could run and throw—but he had an aversion to curve ball pitchers—and he played eight seasons in the National League, six of them with the Giants. As McGraw had predicted, he didn't hurt the Giants at the gate, especially in 1912.

Few defeats were ever felt as keenly by McGraw as that which the Giants suffered in the world series with the Boston Red Sox. The second game ended in a tie. In the eighth game they were deadlocked at 1-1 at the end of the ninth, with Matty pitching against "Smokey" Joe Wood. The Giants scored once in the tenth and Matty, having another of his great years, had only one more inning to go and the Giants would be champions of the world. But, the way it worked out, Big Six never had a chance.

Clyde Engle, pinch-hitting for Wood, led off and flied to center, but Snodgrass muffed the ball and Engle pulled up at second. Harry Hooper smashed a line drive to right center and Snodgrass caught it on the run, but Steve Yerkes walked. Tris Speaker then raised a pop foul between first base and the plate, but Merkle was slow starting for it and it fell to earth as he and Matty and Meyers tried frantically to catch it. Speaker then singled, scoring Engle, and sending Yerkes to third. When Larry Gardner flied deep to Devore, Yerkes crossed the plate with the run that decided the series.

Thoughtless fans and newspapermen, too, immediately tagged Snodgrass as the goat of the series, and he was flayed for his "$30,000 Muff," the sum representing the approximate difference between the winners' and losers' shares of the receipts. McGraw was quick to rush to the defense of the unhappy center fielder, as he had rushed to give comfort to Merkle four years before. This time, ironically, it was Merkle who had to take the rap.

"Snodgrass didn't lose the game," he said. "It was lost when Merkle didn't catch Speaker's foul. We were all yelling at him from the bench that it was his ball but the crowd made so much noise he couldn't hear us. Besides, he should have caught it without anybody yelling at him."

Brush, who had been in ill health for a number of years, had spent the winters in the warm sunshine of Southern California and, in November of 1912, he set out for the Coast again. But he suddenly was stricken on the train while it was passing through Missouri and, at St. Charles, he was taken from it, and removed to a hospital. It was there he died on November 26.

Brush's death affected McGraw in many ways. Brush was his friend and his unquestioning supporter in all matters, from the making of deals and the salaries of the players to the frequent jangles in which McGraw was involved with umpires, rival club owners, and league officials. Not again in his lifetime was he to have such a man at his side. Sadness came to him first at the news of

73

Brush's passing. Later he felt resentment at the curbs placed upon him and the petty annoyances thrown his way.

The new president was Harry N. Hempstead, Brush's son-in-law, a man of high character and pleasing ways who, having matured in the clothing business, knew nothing of baseball, anxiously avoided quarrels as McGraw eagerly sought them, and was dedicated solely to the task of guarding the financial interests of his mother-in-law, his wife, and his sister-in-law. For guidance in baseball, he sought the counsel not of McGraw but of John B. Foster, former newspaperman, leading authority on the game, editor of *Spalding's Guide,* and secretary of the Giants. McGraw came to believe, in time, that Hempstead and Foster were in league against him, seeking to strip him of his power, save on the field, and determined that he should have but a small voice, if any, in the conduct of the club's affairs. As the season of 1913 came on, he protested vigorously against the hobbles he wore, addressing himself to Hempstead and Foster, but he might just as well have talked to himself, for neither paid any attention to him. Nor did Mrs. Brush, who was completely confident that the new order was better than the old.

Once upon a time there were two pitchers, a right-hander called Rube Schauer and a left-hander named Ferdinand Schupp. They joined the Giants together as bushers at Marlin in the spring of 1913 and had no effect whatever on the course of the team that year as it plunged to its third pennant in a row—and its third consecutive defeat in a world series. But you will hear more of them later.

McGraw, having a winning combination for two years, added to it in 1913. He had George Burns, who had come to him from Utica two years before as a catcher and, having been converted into an outfielder, sat at McGraw's knee on the bench, learning about baseball from the master and, occasionally, being allowed to play a few innings. Now he was ready for regular duty—and he was to be in the outfield continuously for nine years.

"The almost perfect outfielder," W. O. McGeehan called him. And so he was. He also could hit and was among the best base runners in either league. He was a moon-faced, smiling kid in those days, quiet, serene, and a tremendous favorite at the Polo Grounds.

McGraw also had brought up a pitcher named Charles Tesreau but called "Jeff," a bear of a man from Iron Mountain, Missouri, who, joining Matty and Marquard, also was a standby for the club for many years and ended his days as coach of the Dartmouth College team. Eddie Grant joined up that year too. He was a pipe-smoking Harvard man and an infielder, who came to the Giants by way of Philadelphia and Cincinnati. Four years later he was to be commissioned as a captain in the army and to die in the Argonne Forest. There is a monument to his memory in center field at the Polo Grounds.

Al Demaree, pitcher and cigar-smoking philosopher, was there too, as were Art Fromme, a pitcher from Cincinnati and Claude Cooper, an outfielder who one day, having been traded to the Phillies, was to break a long winning streak for the Giants. And there was Larry McLean, a catcher from Cincinnati and a lusty soul who, one night when he had looked too long on the whisky that was red or the beer that was amber, got mad at Dick Kinsella, broke a rocking chair over his head, and chased him 'round and 'round the fountain in the courtyard of the Buckingham Hotel in St. Louis. Arthur Shafer still was there but he wouldn't be there long. He was the only player ever driven out of baseball by mash notes from feminine fans. A handsome young man and a modest one, he couldn't take the ribald cracks of his hard-bitten teammates as his scented mail, which he never read, piled up in the clubhouse, and at the end of the season he quit and went home to Los Angeles, where he prospered as a businessman.

It was a merry season, that of 1913. McGraw, having long enjoyed his feuds with the Pirates and the Cubs, had begun at least two more. One was with Charles H. Ebbets, president of the Dodgers and the other with Bill Klem, the umpire and his off-field friend. McGraw generously included the entire Brooklyn ball club in his rows with Ebbets, thus assuring the continuation of a relationship that outlived those who fashioned it. McGraw and Klem, who spent many happy hours together once it was candlelight time, were bitter enemies as long as the sun shone —and in McGraw's time, baseball was played only by daylight.

The pennant race was pleasant and exciting. The Giants won 101 games and entered the world series with their old foes, the Athletics, in high hope of winning this time. But they were destined to fail again. Home Run Baker hit a home run off Marquard to win the opening game. Matty shut the A's out in the second. Then the A's won three in a row. And that was that.

McGraw's old pal of Baltimore days, Wilbert Robinson, had been the coach of the Giant pitchers for the last couple of years but some time during the season—neither ever would discuss the matter—there had been a break between them that would never be healed. So when the series was over, Robbie took off his Giant uniform for the last time. Shortly afterward he was engaged as manager of the Dodgers, or Robins, as they were to be called during his tenure at Ebbets Field. That was just fine, as far as McGraw was concerned. It gave new zest to the hate he had thrown on Brooklyn just when it seemed about to wane because the Dodgers were chronic dwellers in the second division and it was getting a little hard to stay mad at a lot of guys who were down.

11

The Team That Fell Apart

⊖ AFTER the ascent, the decline. Gradual to begin
with. Then dazzling sharp.

But first there was McGraw's return, in December of
1913, from a trip around the world by some of the Giants
and some of the White Sox, devised and engineered by the
manager of the Giants and the president of the White
Sox, the old Roman, Charles A. Comiskey. They had been
to Yokohama . . . Tokyo . . . Manila . . . Brisbane . . . Mel-
bourne . . . Sydney . . . Colombo in Ceylon . . . Cairo . . .
Rome . . . Nice . . . Paris . . . and London, where Tommy
Daly, a White Sox catcher of small reknown otherwise, hit
a home run in the presence of George V of England.

Back in New York, McGraw's first official act was to
demand from Hempstead and Foster their reasons for the
trading of Herzog and Grover Hartley, a catcher, to Cincinnati for Bob Bescher, an outfielder and, in a time when
base stealing was important, one of the best base stealers
in either league. McGraw had read about it somewhere in
his encirclement of the globe. He confronted them with a
clipping of the story.

"It says here," he thundered at Hempstead, "that Herzog
had your consent to talk to the Cincinnati club, before the

deal was made, about the possibility of his being made manager of the Reds. So he had your consent, did he? Well, he didn't have my consent, and you didn't, either!"

Foster, trying to take the heat off Hempstead, said, "But you didn't use him regularly last year and you wanted Bescher and ... and ..."

"And we thought," Hempstead said, "that ..."

"You thought!" McGraw said, his voice rising. "You! The two of you! The next time a deal is made on this ball club, I'm going to make it!"

Sound and fury—and only that? Maybe. In spite of McGraw's grudging admiration for Herzog as a ball player, he still hated him, and he did want Bescher. There would be a time when he wanted Herzog back, hating him though he did, and would get him. But that would be in 1916 and this was the winter of 1913. Now he was trying to fight off the invasion of Hempstead and Foster on a ground that had been his own, and this was a challenge he felt he had to meet. He never forgot that deal. He never could square accounts with Hempstead for it. But he did with Foster. He had to wait six years, but when the time came, he threw his Sunday punch.

The season began well enough. The Pirates set the pace, but by the first of June the Giants were in first place. They knocked off the Pirates, the Reds, the Cubs, and the Cardinals. They were almost home free. And then, all of a sudden, there were the Boston Braves.

George Stallings managed the Braves. Johnny Evers, McGraw's old enemy, was at second base. A kid named "Rabbit" Maranville was at shortstop. There was a catcher named Hank Gowdy, who had been with the Giants as a first baseman and had been turned into a catcher by

McGraw; a pitcher named Dick Rudolph whom the Giants got from Toronto in 1911 and sent to Boston the same year; and two other pitchers, "Big Bill" James, a right-hander, and George Tyler, a left-hander.

The Braves had come lagging out of the gate and on the Fourth of July, they still were in last place. Then they made their move. It was a close-packed race and they began to pick up one club after another until only the Giants were ahead of them. Early in September they overhauled the Giants and rolled on to the pennant as the country acclaimed Stallings "The Miracle Man," and McGraw cursed himself and his players for the overconfidence that he felt was the major factor in their defeat.

He was wrong there, as he was to discover the following season. Three years of hard driving from April to October had burned a lot of energy out of the Giants, aging some of them before their time, taking the older players for a ride from which some of them never did fully recover. Curiously, McGraw seemed so unaware of this that the only important addition he made to his club over the winter was Hans Lobert, a veteran, but still one of the best third basemen in the league, whom he bought from the Phillies. But Lobert suffered a crippling knee injury early in the season and wasn't much good after that, and injuries to Burns and Doyle further slowed up the 1915 team.

That which hurt most of all, however, was that Matty and Marquard ground almost to a complete stop. Matty, who had won twenty games or more every year, beginning with 1903, and in three of those years had gone over the thirty-game mark, won but eight games in 1915 and lost fourteen. Marquard, a twenty-game-or-better winner for three years, had slowed up in 1914 and showed so little this year that in August McGraw asked waivers on him and he was claimed by Brooklyn. Meanwhile, Tesreau, who had the best record on the staff, had to settle for nineteen victories, and Poll Perritt, purchased from St. Louis, could win only twelve.

Remember Schupp and Schauer? Well, this was their opportunity, with the older pitchers sagging all about them. And they saw a lot of action. But in the records it says that Schupp was in twenty-three games, that he won one and lost none, and that Schauer, in thirty-two appearances, won two games and lost eight. They roomed together and the other players called them "The Hall Room Boys," after two popular comic strip characters of the time, and they generally were in the same ball games. As a rule, Schupp would start and when he was belted out or was so wild he seemed intent on giving a pass to everybody in the ball park, Schauer would be called in.

"You could describe today's game in three words," Bozeman Bulger of the *Evening World* once wrote. "Schupp, Schauer and shambles."

And, in the *Globe* one day, Sid Mercer cracked, "Where the Giants are concerned, it never Schupps but it Schauers."

What with one thing and another, the club didn't get out of the second division all season and was last at the end of it. It was the only club McGraw ever managed that collapsed in his hands.

Meanwhile, relations between the Giants and the Yankees, who had shared the Polo Grounds with them since 1913, were strengthened in January of 1915: McGraw induced his friends, Col. Jacob Ruppert and Capt. (later

Col.) Tillinghast L'Hommedieu Huston, to buy the American League club from Frank Farrell and Bill Devery who, having founded it in 1903, had reached the end of their long friendship and, quarreling constantly, were eager to sever their partnership and get out of a business from which they had failed to draw either fun or profit. Ruppert would have liked to have bought the Giants but they were not for sale, and when McGraw told him of the breach between the Yankee owners and suggested he and Huston buy them out, he was not interested. But McGraw was persuasive and so, with him as intermediary, the deal was closed.

12

Twenty-Six Games in a Row

⊗ THE Federal League, which for two years claimed
major status, but was recognized by the National and
American Leagues only as a menace and was bitterly
fought in a concerted action by the two organizations
that once had fought each other as bitterly, folded in the
winter of 1915-16. The Giants came out of the struggle
virtually unscathed, since the Feds had been unable to
put a club in New York (although there had been one in
Brooklyn) and their only contribution to the war had
taken the form of financial assistance to their less fortunate
colleagues. As a matter of fact, the Giant players had
rather a warm feeling toward the outlaws. McGraw had
got them all raises to keep them from jumping and he,
himself, had refused to do so although he could have had
a five-year contract at $50,000 a year as manager of either
the Brooklyn or the Chicago club.

Now that the conflict was over, McGraw was prepared
to profit by the peace to the extent of picking up the better
Federal League players on whom the other National and
American League clubs had no claims in the form of reserve clauses in the contracts they had broken. The available players had been allocated to Harry Sinclair, oil

millionaire and turf figure, who had been one of the ill-fated league's backers in the second year of its existence, the notion being that by selling them to the highest bidders, Sinclair might get back some of the money he had spent so lavishly.

The player everybody wanted, McGraw most of all, was Benny Kauff, a muscular ex-coal miner from Pomeroy Bend, Ohio, who, with Newark in 1914 and Brooklyn in 1915, had been a spectacular figure, the "Ty Cobb of the Federal League," as he extravagantly was described. McGraw had tried, in 1915, to kidnap him from the Feds and, as Kauff had been willing, he actually had produced the player in a Giant uniform as a dramatic surprise just before a game with the Phillies at the Polo Grounds.

It never was made clear how he managed to arrange that one with Hempstead and Foster, nor how he hoped to get away with it, since the two big leagues were basing their stand against the Feds on the sanctity of the contract, which they claimed was being violated by their opponents. When William F. Baker, president of the Phillies, who was on the scene when McGraw attempted his coup refused to allow his team to play if Kauff were in the line-up, the Giant manager gave up—but only after a long argument, you may be sure—and Kauff went back to Brooklyn.

Now that Benny was on the market, McGraw offered $30,000 for him and got him. At lesser figures he also got Fred Anderson and Bill Rariden, a battery that had been with the Newark club. He was urged by "Germany" Schaefer, veteran player and diamond comedian, who had been with Newark, to bid on Eddie Roush, his teammate there.

"He's a better ball player than Kauff," Germany said.

84

"He's not as colorful as Kauff but he can play rings around him."

McGraw shook his head. He had Kauff to play in center field between Burns in left and Davy Robertson, young and fast and a good hitter, in right. He didn't need Roush. Eddie and Bill McKechnie were in a small group of leftovers when the bidding was done.

Schaefer kept after McGraw, "Get Roush."

McGraw, worn down by Germany's persistence, asked Sinclair how much he wanted for the player, and Sinclair, who didn't know any more about him than McGraw did, said he thought $10,000 would be about right.

"I'll give you $7,500," McGraw said.

"I'll take it," Sinclair said.

Kauff, who refused to sign a contract with the Giants until he received $10,000 of his purchase money—he wanted it all from Sinclair but the Giants put in $5,000 of it to break the deadlock—was a late arrival at the 1916 camp in Marlin. So was Roush, who never liked spring training, preferring to remain on his Indiana farm as long as possible.

Kauff's arrival created a mild sensation. He wore a derby hat, a fur-collared overcoat, a gray suit, a glaring striped silk shirt, and patent leather shoes, and was liberally sprinkled with diamonds. His wardrobe, which included seventy-five silk shirts, was contained in four trunks and three bags. Roush, looking like the farm boy he was, had two suits and enough shirts to hold him until his laundry came back.

Benny, an extremely likable young man who, in a harmless fashion, believed everything his press agents and sycophants said about him, bragged that he would hit .300 blindfolded in the National League and didn't need much training to get ready for bums like Grover Cleveland Alexander. Roush, completely obscured by the glamour boy, and crowded out of the outfield, hardly got his name in the papers that spring. One who was there with him remembers only that the day he stepped off the train he played a full practice game, hitting, fielding, and running as though he had been in training for weeks.

Now that he had Kauff in center field, Lobert back on third base, Anderson to help out with the pitching, and Rariden to replace Chief Meyers, who had been sold to Brooklyn during the winter, McGraw seemed to think he had a winning team again. One reason was that he had small regard for the Phillies, pennant winners the year before, and could see no other club as championship timber. Once the season was under way, things happened swiftly to cause him to change his mind—and his team.

The first blow fell the day before the season opened. In an exhibition game with Yale at New Haven, Lobert, running out a triple, slid into third base and suffered a recurrence of the injury to his left knee that had put him out of action the year before. Though one could not know then that he never would play again, it was obvious that he would not play for a long time, and the only replacement for him was young Fred Brainard. Since Brainard was not ready for regular duty in the big leagues, McGraw sent for Bill McKechnie, last of the unemployed ex-Federal Leaguers, who had trained with the Browns while looking for a job, and Bill was at third base the day after the Giants opened the season in Philadelphia.

Otherwise, the team was very much as it had been when

it came in last in 1915. Merkle was at first base, Doyle at second, and Fletcher at short. Burns was in left field, Robertson in right, and now Kauff in center. Rariden instead of Meyers was back of the plate. Helping him, occasionally, to bear the catching burden, was young Bradley Kocher, a rookie from Louisville. Anderson was added to a pitching staff still headed by Matty and including Jeff Tesreau, Rube Benton, who was with the team part of the time in 1915, Perritt, Bill Ritter, and the Hall Room Boys.

In three weeks of campaigning against the Phillies, the Braves, and the Robins, the Giants won two games and lost thirteen. This was the beginning of the most unusual season a ball club ever had. A season in which McGraw would perform feats of legerdemain, picking his team to pieces and putting it together again with new parts gathered along the way. The pennant could not be won that year. But what McGraw accomplished then made a pennant possible in 1917.

The Giants and McGraw left New York early in May of 1916 in a state of shock. Within two weeks, they would be the most exciting club in either league, and McGraw, now fully aware of what could be done with them, proceeded to do a magnificent job.

That first western trip opened in Pittsburgh, where the Giants won four games. On the next stop, which was Chicago, they won three. They won three in St. Louis, moved on to Cincinnati and won three. By now they had bagged thirteen games in a row and heading East, they pulled up in Boston—and knocked the Braves off four times. They were out of the depths of the league by now and driving for first place. From Boston they went to Philadelphia, and there, in the morning game on Memorial Day, the streak ended.

This was where Claude Cooper came in. Remember Claude, a young outfielder with the Giants who, one day, would do them harm? Well, this was the day. It was a slam-bang ball game. Going into the eighth inning, the Giants got two men on and, with two out, Merkle lined a ball toward the left field bleachers. It had to be a home run! But it wasn't. It had to be an out. Cooper, a left-handed thrower, got to the bleacher wall just as the ball was about to whistle over it. The ball was to his right but the wall was low and Cooper, actually leaning into the bleachers, made the catch with his gloved hand.

That was all. The Giants couldn't score in the ninth.

But they had set a record, still unequaled, by winning seventeen consecutive games on the road. Now, they believed, they were on their way. But they weren't. Back at the Polo Grounds following the series in Philadelphia, they floundered badly against the western clubs moving in on them. McGraw knew now what he had to do. When the Giants, going west for the second time, reached Cincinnati, he called on Garry Herrmann.

"You're not satisfied with Herzog as your manager, I know," he said. "I don't like him, personally, but I need him and I think we can make a deal. I'll give you two good ball players for him—and a manager to take his place."

"Who's the manager?" Garry asked.

"Mathewson," McGraw said.

Herrmann was startled.

"Mathewson?" he asked, unbelieving.

"Yes," McGraw said. "I don't like to part with him. You know he is my friend. But he can't pitch any more, Garry.

Christy Mathewson

Charles A. Stoneham and John J. McGraw.

And he'd like to be a manager. I know, because we've talked it over. I need help in the infield. You can have Matty if I can have Herzog."

"Who are the other players?" Garry asked.

"Roush and McKechnie," McGraw said. "I haven't had much of a chance to use Roush but I know he's a ball player. McKechnie is steady. He can help you."

Garry didn't have to think it over very long. There was a movement on the part of some of the Cincinnati fans to persuade him to supplant Herzog as manager with "Heinie" Groh, the third baseman. He didn't want Groh and, as McGraw had said, he wasn't satisfied with Herzog. Matty would solve that problem. Roush and McKechnie might come in handy.

"You got a deal," he said to McGraw.

"Not yet," McGraw said. "I'll have to talk to Herzog. I don't know whether he wants to play for me again or not."

"Go ahead, talk to him," Garry said.

That night McGraw and Herzog met in the hotel room of a mutual friend, Sid Mercer of the *Globe*, traveling with the Giants. There were just the two of them there, in this hideout picked by McGraw, but Herzog later repeated the brief conversation between them. It began with McGraw saying, "There is no use kidding ourselves. I don't like you and you don't like me but ..."

And ended with Herzog saying, "There isn't any need for us to be friends. But you like me as a ball player and as far as I am concerned, you're the greatest manager in baseball. I don't need to tell you that I'll give the best I've got to your ball club."

So Herzog came back to the Giants for the second time, and Matty departed. He was to return as a coach three years later but he never pitched another game for them. Whether he was the greatest pitcher is, of course, a matter of opinion. But to the Giant fans of that era there never was any question of his right to be placed above all others.

He won 372 games for the Giants. (He won the only game he pitched for the Reds, so that he and Grover Cleveland Alexander are tied at 373 for the most games won by a National League pitcher.) In 1908, his top year, he was in fifty-six games and won thirty-seven, the modern National League mark. He pitched two no-hit games, one against the Cardinals in 1901, the other against the Cubs in 1905. Many pitchers have a better won-and-lost record in world series games but he is the only one who ever pitched three shutouts in one series and four all told, and none ever equaled his mark of 101 two-thirds innings.

McGraw would miss him not only as a pitcher but as a companion, for no other player was as close to the manager as he was, and together they had grown to greatness in New York. Only his wish to try his hand as a manager had caused McGraw to send him to Cincinnati, for it had been McGraw's thought that when the big fellow no longer could pitch he would stay on in New York as a coach. It was a happy day for McGraw when he came back in 1919.

Herzog was placed at third base but he did not remain there long. McGraw made another deal, this one with the Cubs, to whom he sent Larry Doyle and a young utility infielder named Herbert Hunter in exchange for Heinie (The Great) Zimmerman, off the Bronx sandlots, a graceful and colorful figure, and the best third baseman in the league. With the Great Zim aboard, Herzog was moved to second base.

All this made Arthur Fletcher very happy. With Doyle, who had slowed up, on one side of him and McKechnie, who was steady, as McGraw had told Herrmann, but who couldn't cover much ground, on the other, Fletcher had been run ragged. Now he could work better. Only one more change had to be made in the infield, and McGraw made it. Merkle had come to a pause in his long career as a major league first baseman—he went on at reduced speed for eight more years—and McGraw traded him to Brooklyn for Lew McCarty, a wide-shouldered, heavily muscled young catcher who could pound the ball when it was his turn to hit. To take up Merkle's old stand at first base, a kid named Walter Holke was brought back from Rochester, where he had been farmed out. Now, the critics said, the Giants had the best infield in baseball.

McGraw, now looking to his pitching staff, broke up The Hall Room Boys, sending Schauer to the minors and buying Harry Sallee, tall, slim, veteran southpaw, from the Cardinals. This move may have seemed unimportant at the time but it wasn't. It may be an illogical conclusion but the facts, if they do not prove anything, at least indicate that, separated from Schauer, Schupp became a pitcher.

Pause, for a moment, and look at the young man. Although he had been with the Giants for three years, he still was only twenty-four. Ever read *Huckleberry Finn?* Here was Huck as he might have been if he had grown up to be a ball player. Out of Louisville, with a drawl, a chuckle, and when he really was amused, a belly laugh. Living from day to day, not caring what the next day had to offer. Fairly tall, willowy, left-handed, with a lot of speed and a curve ball that broke away out to here, or away in here, right under the batter's fists. But not knowing, always, when he let the ball go, where it was going. And not inclined to worry over much where it went. Then, overnight, he had it and his pitching was a tremendous help to the team in running up the greatest string of consecutive victories in the history of the game—twenty-six between the seventh and the thirtieth of September, all scored on the Polo Grounds.

Schupp started it when he beat the Robins. The following day Tesreau beat the Phillies. Two days later Perritt took a 3 to 1 decision over the Phillies in the first game of a double-header. The Phillies mocked him, told him he was lucky and that it would be a long time before he would beat them again.

Seething, he said to McGraw, "Let me pitch the second game, Mac!"

"Who do you think you are, McGinnity?" McGraw asked.

"No," Perritt said. "But I can beat these bums all day."

He was a tall, lean, easy-going, squirrel-shooting country boy from Arcadia, Louisiana. McGraw never had seen him worked up as he was now.

"All right," he said. "If that's the way you feel, go ahead. But don't overdo it. If your arm gets tired or begins to hurt, tell me and I'll put somebody else in."

Pitching as effortlessly as he had in the first game and even more effectively, Perritt came off with a four-hit shutout.

The performance set the Giants on fire. Schupp, Tesreau, Perritt, Benton, Sallee, Bill Ritter, who almost never had started a game, George Smith, just out of Columbia University, rolled back the Reds, the Pirates, the Cubs, the Cardinals, and the Braves. There was a lull but no break in the record run on the eighteenth, when the second game of a double-header with the Pirates was called at the end·of the eighth inning because of rain with the score tied at 1-1. Seven of the victories were spun by Tesreau and six by Schupp who, from a virtual nobody, had become a hero at the Polo Grounds and an astonishing figure in the eyes of the experts, since they long ago had written him off as of no account. Having taken part in thirty games, he was credited with nine victories and charged with three defeats, and had the almost incredible earned run average of 0.90.

The streak was broken in the last game of the season at home. The following day the Giants were playing the Robins at Ebbets Field and McGraw angrily quit the bench before the game was over, charging them with not having tried to win. This was hotly denied by the players, and Pat Moran, manager of the Phillies, who were engaged in a breakneck race with the Robins for the pennant, demanded an investigation by John K. Tener, president of the league. But McGraw refused to say anything more; there was no investigation and the whole thing was forgotten within forty-eight hours.

13

A Brawl . . . A Repudiation . . . A Pennant

⊝ THREE years of frustation for McGraw were followed by a pennant in 1917, when the team he had fashioned through the sometimes exciting, sometimes wearing months of 1916 really clicked. It was a year he would always remember, for many reasons. He would see for the first time a boy who was destined to become one of his greatest players. He would be a party to a spring exhibition tour dotted by fist fighting, in the open and behind closed doors. He would find himself in the middle of the most serious brawl with the baseball authorities he had generated since the "Hey, Barney!" affair. He would revisit Wellsville, New York, which he had not seen since he left it as a boy in 1890 to barnstorm through the South and Cuba. Winning another pennant, he would lose another world series.

In the camp at Marlin in the spring the Giants were joined by two veterans and two rookies. The veterans were George Gibson, the iron man catcher who had been released by the Pirates after seven years of heavy duty in Pittsburgh; and Jim Middleton, a pitcher who, having spent all his years in the minors, had been brought up after an impressive season in Louisville. Both rookies were infielders. One, Pete Kilduff, was ready for the majors and was retained. The other was not, and was farmed out to Rochester. His name was Ross Youngs, or Young as it appeared in the batting order and the averages.

When camp was broken, the Giants and the Detroit Tigers set out on a tour north that took them first to Dallas, and it was there the fighting broke out. It began when Tesreau unintentionally hit Ty Cobb with a pitched ball the first time he went to bat. Since the Giants had been taunting Cobb because he appeared on the field just at game time, calling him such things as a ham and a swell-headed stiff, Ty thought big Jeff deliberately had nicked him and angrily threatened reprisal. Tesreau, good-humored and not at all afraid of Cobb, laughed at him, then added, "But if you try any funny business with me, I'll knock your brains out."

Herzog at second base and Fletcher at shortstop threatened to ram the ball down Ty's throat if he tried to rough anybody on their ball club, and Ty, taking up the challenge, raced for second on Tesreau's second pitch to the next hitter. McCarty's throw to Herzog had him beaten but, riding in high, he ripped Herzog's legs with his spikes.

By the time Ty and Charlie were pried apart, the field was swarming with players, cops, and spectators. The gladiators were ordered from the game and, although Herzog went peacefully, Cobb said bitterly to Hughie Jennings, the Detroit manager, "If I have to leave this field, I'll leave the series."

Jennings, knowing he meant it, tried to intercede for him with the umpire but with no success. Cobb stalked from the park and was driven to the Oriental Hotel, where both teams were staying and where they dressed for the game.

McGraw, who had been in the midst of the tangle on the field, hurling imprecations at Cobb, caught up with him in the hotel lobby when the teams returned after the game. There in the hearing of the players and other guests who milled about them, he frightfully abused the Georgian, calling him a quitter, daring him to play the following day. Cobb somehow managed to restrain himself, although, pale with anger, he said, "If you were a younger man, I'd kill you."

Then he walked away, ignoring the insults McGraw hurled after him.

"I'll be up to your room at ten o'clock," Herzog told him, as he was at dinner. "I'll bring one of our players with me and you can have one of yours. You can have Harry Tuttle to referee."

Tuttle, brawny and a good rough-and-tumble fighter, was the Tigers' trainer.

Herzog chose Zimmerman as his second. Not many of the other players knew there was going to be a fight, but Benny Kauff heard of it. Benny wanted to go with Herzog too.

"I'll fight him," Benny said. "I'll murder him."

"No," Herzog said. "This is my fight. And you can't come because I said I would bring only one player and that's all he's going to have."

Cobb and Tuttle were waiting for Herzog and Zimmerman. So were eight other Tigers.

"All right," Herzog said. "If you start anything, Heinie will lick the lot of you.

"Take off your coat and shirt," he said to Cobb.

Herzog's first punch was a right to the jaw that sent Cobb to his knees but Ty got up and hammered him around the room until Tuttle called a halt.

Herzog showed up the next morning with two black eyes, puffed lips, and a wrenched shoulder. He blamed the shoulder injury on a cop who had yanked him away from Cobb on the field and he didn't seem to mind the bruises on his face.

"Anyway," he said, "I knocked him down."

That seemed to have squared him for the spike wounds.

This was a Sunday. News of the disorder at the ball park and the battle at the Oriental appeared in the morning papers. The overflow crowd in the afternoon hadn't paid to see another ball game but another fight. But it had to settle for the ball game. Herzog, because of his bad shoulder, couldn't play, and Cobb wouldn't.

Cobb went as far as the next stop, which was Wichita Falls. He put on his uniform, took batting practice, and even posed for fans who wanted to take his picture. But again he refused to play. The mayor and other civic leaders pleaded with him to change his mind, telling him that hundreds of fans from all over that part of the state had driven in to see him.

"I'm sorry," he said, "but there is no use asking me any more."

The Giants watched him silently as he walked from the field.

That night he left the tour, having obtained permission to finish his training with the Reds. His departure, however, did not put an end to the fighting. Fletcher and Bobby Jones, the Tigers' third baseman, swung on each other on the field at Wichita, Kansas, and the Great Zim threw his bat at Willie Mitchell, Tiger pitcher, who dusted him off in Manhattan. The teams were traveling in a special train and, as a precaution, McGraw and Jennings, his old pal from the days of the old Orioles, arranged with the railroad to have the baggage car placed in the middle that it might serve as a buffer between the Pullmans, three on either end, occupied by the players. This at least assured peace on wheels. At Kansas City, the teams split up. There were no fond farewells. McGraw and Cobb didn't speak to each other for more than ten years.

The pitching strength of the Giants was considerable. Schupp really had come into his own and, as he had been for a brief spell in 1916, was a sensation around the league. When they asked him what had wrought the great change in him, he said, "I got control. I don't know how I got it because I am pitching just like I always pitched. But I got it."

Hooked up with him were two other first-rate southpaws, the veterans Slim Sallee and Rube Benton, and the right-handers, Tesreau, Perritt, and Anderson. But nearly all the pitchers, and especially Sallee, seemed to have trouble with the Phillies, and the Phillies were their most dangerous rivals. Sallee dreaded the sight of the Phils' bandbox ball park with its inviting right field wall.

"Next time Mac puts me in there," he said to the infielders one day, "get some shin guards and tie on your gloves."

McGraw's move to combat the threat of the Philadelphia hitters was to bring back Al Demaree whom he had sent to the Phillies in 1915 and who now was with the Cubs. McGraw got him in exchange for Kilduff, the young infielder who had shown up so well at Marlin. Demaree was smart and a control pitcher, and he knew how to pitch to those who, only a short time before, had been his teammates. Also, he could teach the other Giant pitchers how to do it. The move was effective. Demaree was a handy guy to have around on a ball club that was pennant bound.

It was in June, with the club wheeling along in first place or close to it, that McGraw got into trouble. On the eighth of the month, in Cincinnati, following a hot and rowdy ball game, McGraw punched Bill Byron, the "Singing Umpire," who had worked back of the plate. The attack occurred on a runway leading to the clubhouses and the umpires' dressing room, and Byron's upper lip was split by a short right hand. Before McGraw could hit him again, he was dragged away by Giant players.

Back at the Hotel Havlin, the Giant manager was neither regretful over what had happened nor apprehensive over the possibility that John K. Tener, former governor of Pennsylvania and now president of the National League, would discipline him.

"It had nothing to do with the ball game," he said, "and it did not take place on the field. I hit Byron because he insulted me. We had had some words and he said something about me talking big for a fellow who was run out of Baltimore. When I challenged him on that, he said, 'They say that's what happened.'

"I said, 'They say! Would you say it?'

"And when he said yes, he'd say it, I hit him. That's all there was to it and I don't see any reason for anybody to get excited about it."

Byron would not talk to reporters.

"I can't," he said. "It's all in the report I sent to Governor Tener. You'll have to get it from him, boys."

In New York Harry Hempstead was so alarmed by the news from Cincinnati that he caught the next train for Chicago, where the Giants opened the series the following day. He still was in a state of alarm on his arrival. He was a mild-mannered man, who abhorred violence, and he was justifiably fearful that Tener might throw the book at McGraw and so hamstring the Giants. McGraw first tried to laugh him out of his fears and, when that didn't work, said sharply, "Stop worrying or keep out of this. It's my business, not yours."

No word came from Tener until June 13, when the Giants were in Pittsburgh. Then, adjudged guilty of assault on an umpire, McGraw was fined $500 and suspended for sixteen days.

McGraw, who had been reasonably tractable for the past few years, barring, of course, his incessant quarrels with Bill Klem, his outburst against Cobb in Dallas, and his sporadic flings at rival managers and umpires, now launched an attack on Tener that matched those which a dozen years before he had leveled at Pulliam. Having castigated Tener for taking Byron's word against his and lumped the president and all his umpires as incompetents, he denounced Tener as a tool of the Philadelphia club— remember, the Phillies were the ones the Giants had to beat to win the pennant this year.

"Baker of Philadelphia put him in power," he said, "and he has run the league from Philadelphia ever since. This isn't the first time he has been unfair to New York."

He said much more and loudly insisted that nothing he said was off the record.

"I want it printed in every newspaper in New York!" he yelled.

His wish was gratified beyond his expectations. The story was printed in every paper in the country. Pressed to amplify it, he refused. It was all there, he said. Tener would know what he was talking about. Pleased with himself, confident he had had the last word, he was in a happy frame of mind as he started for Wellsville, where an exhibition game had been booked to fill an open date between Pittsburgh and Boston. It was a great day for him, this return in triumph to the scene of his obscure struggles as a boy. But that night he quietly left the club. He had been summoned to appear in New York before the league's board of directors and explain his charges against Tener.

Now when he was in trouble, it wasn't like the old days. Then he had had the solid and aggressive support of Brush, a fighter like himself. Now he was in the hands of Hempstead and Cornelius J. Sullivan, the club's attorney, two frightened men. At their insistence, he signed a statement prepared by Sullivan, which repudiated the Pittsburgh story *in toto*.

This satisfied the directors, who announced that the case was closed. But it wasn't. It was broken wide open when the newspapermen who had written the story reiterated it and the Baseball Writers Association of America demanded a showdown. Tener acceded to the demand and appointed John Conway Toole to take testimony, weigh it, and advise him as to his findings. At the hearing, McGraw was represented by John Montgomery Ward and the writers by Martin W. Littleton. Toole's decision vindicated the writers and Tener fined McGraw $1,000. Sid Mercer, principal witness against McGraw at the hearing, immediately asked Tener to revoke the fine, but this the president refused to do.

While all this was going on, the Giants had taken a firm

grip on first place. They beat off all the other contenders save the Phillies, then took care of them in a series at the Polo Grounds in September.

Victors in the American League were the Chicago White Sox, the same team, almost man for man, that was to be tempted by gamblers' pay and lose to the Reds in 1919. Managed then by Clarence (Pants) Rowland it was, unquestionably, the best team in baseball, and beat the Giants in six games, the Giants' two victories being shutouts by Schupp and Sallee.

It was in the fourth inning of the last game that Zimmerman lost his famous foot race with Eddie Collins down the third base line. Benton was pitching for the Giants; there were no outs and Collins was on third base and Jackson on first. Felsch slapped a high bounder to Benton, who threw to Zimmerman—and there was Collins, flat-footed, yards off third base. Rariden, instead of remaining at the plate, moved up the line, thinking to close in on Collins for a rundown. Benton in the box and Holke at first base merely looked on, and Collins, seeing in a flash that the plate was uncovered, dug for it, brushing past the bewildered Rariden, and easily running away from Zimmerman. It was a blow from which the Giants could not recover.

McGraw defended Zimmerman and blamed Holke for not covering the plate. It was Zim, however, who entered the best defense when he answered his critics with the question, "Who the hell was I going to throw the ball to, Klem?"

14

Schupp Fades and Youngs Returns

AT Marlin in the spring of 1918, Ferdie Schupp couldn't pitch up an alley. The wildness that had held him back for so long and that he had overcome in 1916 was upon him again. He still had his speed and his curve ball but not his control.

McGraw wanted to know if his arm hurt him when he pitched.

"Sometimes," he said. "Not often. Not much."

Had he suffered a fall during the winter?

"No."

Had he been in a fight?

"No," he said, laughing. "You know me, Mac. You know I don't get into fights."

Well, then, could he have hurt the arm in a friendly scuffle?

"No."

When did he first know there was something wrong?

"Not till I come down here. My arm feels strong. I just can't get my control."

McGraw shook his head. So did the several doctors who examined the arm and could find nothing wrong with it, or the muscle manipulators who worked on it. But Schupp was through for the year, although he didn't stop trying.

Within another year he would have left the Giants to wander from club to club, and then drop back to the minors. But no one who saw him at the peak he held so briefly ever would forget him, nor cease to wonder at so strange a case.

Ross Youngs was back that spring from his year in Rochester, where, at McGraw's orders, he had played the outfield. His return was timely, for Davy Robertson, the Giants' regular right fielder, had gone into the Department of Justice as a special agent. Good as Robertson had been, Youngs was better. Twenty years old, short but powerfully built, he could hit, run, and throw, and was an aggressive and resourceful competitor. From Shiner, Texas, he was a track man and football player at West Texas Military Academy, but rejected the offers of athletic scholarships he received from a number of colleges because he was interested only in becoming a big league ball player. He had had a couple of trials with Texas League clubs but the company there had been a little too swift for him at his age. The Giants bought him from Sherman in the Western Association where, in 1916, he had hit .362.

McGraw bought Larry Doyle back in a deal that no one completely understood at the time, for he sent Herzog and Jimmy Smith, utility infielder, to the Braves in exchange for Larry and Jess Barnes. Herzog still was rated as one of the best second basemen in either league and operated smoothly with Fletcher around the bag; while Doyle had slowed down in 1916, hadn't picked up any since, and had fallen off in his hitting. The Cubs had traded him to the Braves just three days before McGraw reached out to reclaim him.

That Barnes would help the Giants was taken for granted, since he was a young man of exceeding promise. But Herzog for Doyle? Why? Had McGraw's intense dislike for Herzog finally colored his judgment? His answer to that approach was a scornful laugh.

"Herzog is slipping," he said. "I saw that in the world series last fall. I didn't care how much of a —— he was when he was good but I won't have a —— on my club who is slipping."

"But what of Doyle?" they wanted to know. "Is he any better than he was when you sent him to Chicago for Zimmerman?"

"Don't worry about Doyle," he said. "He's got a couple of years of good baseball left in him. You'll see."

It was, although no one foresaw it, the last spring for the Giants at Marlin. Had any guessed it, there would have been a sad leave-taking when the club broke camp, for a genuine bond had grown between the veteran players and the townspeople. But when the day came, there were just the usual good-bys, and the assurance given, as it was every year, that Marlin would be rooting for "its" team through the season.

The Giants, having toured north for the first time with the Cleveland club, playing before a quarter of a million soldiers and sailors at World War I army camps and navy bases, were heavily favored to win the pennant. Had Schupp not lost his effectiveness, they might have won it in spite of the departure of Barnes, Anderson, and Kauff for the army and Holke for a defense plant. But, although they moved off to a good start, the handicaps they bore were too much for them and they finished second to the Cubs in a two-club race, that, with the application of the work-or-fight order to baseball, ended on September 2.

15

The Entrance of Charles A. Stoneham

☒ THE Giants were sold by the Brush estate in January of 1919. The purchasers were Charles A. Stoneham, broker on the New York Curb Exchange, race horse owner, and *bon vivant;* Francis X. McQuade, a city magistrate, and John J. McGraw. Announcement of the transaction was made on the morning of January 14 in the offices of the club in the Fifth Avenue Building. No figures were made public on the price paid for the stock. Guesses ranged anywhere from $2,000,000 to $5,000,000. Stoneham had the controlling interest. It was believed only small blocks were held by McGraw and McQuade. Stoneham was the new president, McGraw the vice-president and manager, and McQuade the treasurer.

The sale of the club came as a surprise to the fans, but there were many to whom it was no surprise at all. Mrs. Brush, her daughters and her son-in-law, Harry Hempstead, shocked by the government's shutdown on baseball the previous September, took a dim view of the future of the sport as an investment and became restive. Even the signing of the Armistice on November 11 failed to brighten their view, for they visioned a long and costly uphill fight to restore baseball to the popularity it had enjoyed before our armies had begun to roll across France.

McGraw first pleaded with them to hold fast, telling them that once the war was over, things would be as they always had been, or better. But when they refused to respond, he made a swift decision. He would dig up the capital necessary to buy a majority of the stock and arrange it so that he would share in the profits when the turnstiles spun at the Polo Grounds again.

After all, HE was the Giants. Brush had supplied the money, but pennants aren't won with money alone. He was the one who molded the teams and directed them. He was the one who had put the great crowds into the Polo Grounds and in all the other parks where the Giants played. He had made millions of dollars for Brush and his heirs and, since Brush's death, although the money he still put into the till made fat dividends possible, he no longer had a voice in the councils of the club. He felt that Hempstead and Foster were in league against him and he knew they had the support of Mrs. Brush. This, then, was the time for him to make his move.

To his surprise, he discovered that the moneyed men among his friends, whose financial support he sought to enlist, were no more confident of baseball's immediate future than were the present owners. Joe Vila, Sports Editor of the *Evening Sun,* to whom he confided his plan, suggested George Loft, candy manufacturer, owner of a racing stable, and member of the New York State Racing Commission. Loft, although no baseball fan, was interested in the Giants from a money-making angle but—and here McGraw's hopes, raised but a moment before, fell with a crash—he would not be interested unless he could buy all the stock and not just the controlling block held by the estate. McGraw knew that was almost impossible, for most of the minority holders were friends of his, who took pride in their ownership, were optimistic over the future, and were of no mind to sell. Not one to surrender even in the face of the seemingly impossible, he tried to persuade them to change their minds, but was meeting with virtually no success when, of a sudden, Stoneham was brought into the picture.

How, and by whom? On the day the sale was announced, McQuade said that he alone was responsible for bringing off the deal. Some years later, testifying under oath, McGraw said that he and McQuade, who had joined him in the quest for a buyer, had been introduced to Stoneham by E. Phocian Howard, owner and editor of a sporting weekly called the *New York Press*. On cross examination, McGraw denied he met Stoneham through McQuade who, in turn, had met Stoneham through a retired police captain named Peabody, but admitted that Peabody had sued him and McQuade for payment of an allegedly promised bonus for getting them together with Stoneham, and that the suit had been settled out of court with Stoneham paying the captain.

However it had been managed, Stoneham was the new owner and president of the Giants. He had little in common with the late John T. Brush, being a sharp-witted and sometimes ruthless trader in the hurly-burly of the curb market by day, and a fun-loving, free-spending, gambling, go-around guy by night; whereas Brush, a conservative businessman, ill through most of his adult life, and a semi-invalid in his last years, was understandably dour and had few pleasures other than those which accrued from making money and seeing the Giants win. But in this respect Stoneham was very like Brush: He believed in and admired McGraw; he would make any deals McGraw suggested, regardless of the amount of money involved, and he would support McGraw whenever the manager was under fire. There would be a time when there was a wide breach in their relations, never to be completely healed but this was January of 1919 and all was serene in the office on Fifth Avenue.

McGraw had entered upon a new phase of his career and in it he achieved greater triumphs than he ever had known. One of the first things he did in his capacity as vice-president of the club was to suggest to John B. Foster that he seek employment elsewhere before the year was out. He had got even at long last for the indignities, real or fancied, that he felt had been put upon him, however indirectly, by the secretary.

Meanwhile, there had been, but a short time before, a rather disturbing case in baseball that was to have a curious repercussion in the ranks of the Giants. Christy Mathewson, having been commissioned in the Chemical Corps of the army and been sent to France, left behind him a. charge that during the abbreviated season of 1918, Hal Chase, the Reds' first baseman, had not given his best efforts on the ball field. Chase had long been suspect, and now his manager had laid a charge against him which, no matter how guardedly it was couched, was an accusation that he had thrown ball games. A trial was ordered before John Arnold Heydler, who had succeeded Tener as president of the league, and was held in New York in December of 1918.

A deposition was sought from Matty, still overseas, but none arrived. The testimony of several other Cincinnati players was not sufficiently convincing to warrant a conviction, and Chase was, in a manner of speaking, acquitted. But every one looked upon it as a Scotch verdict and few thought ever to see him in a major league game again. To every one's astonishment McGraw traded Rariden and Holke to Cincinnati for Chase and, when Matty returned from France and resigned as manager of the Reds, promptly hired him as a coach.

It was, to say the least, a situation difficult to defend, but McGraw defended it. He said Chase had been restored to good standing by Heydler and was as eligible as any other player in the league, that he had lost interest in Holke and Rariden, and that since Matty was free of the Reds, where could he find a better man to serve as his aide than Big Six? His hearers blinked but said nothing. As for Matty and Chase, neither would comment on the other's presence on the club. Nor did they speak to each other.

The first day at the training camp, Larry Doyle's bat slipped out of his hands and struck Matty, standing close by, in the pit of the stomach, toppling him. Doyle and other players rushed to his assistance. Chase, waiting his turn at the plate, didn't move. His face was inscrutable.

"At least," a newspaperman said, "he had the grace not to laugh out loud. But from now on Larry can get anything he wants from him."

The major leagues, obviously uncertain how rapidly the fans would return to the ball parks from which they had been shut out the summer before, had voted at the winter meetings to proceed cautiously, wherefore they had adopted a schedule of 140 games, instead of the usual 154, and limited the training season to four weeks. It was McGraw's feeling that Marlin was too far to go for so short a stand, since the club would spend only two weeks in camp and two on the road home.

In his selection of a new camp he struck a nostalgic note. He accepted an invitation from an old friend of his to train in Gainesville, Florida, where he had quit the barnstorming All-Americans on their return from Cuba and set out on his own twenty-nine years before.

He wanted so very much to win this year, this first year in which he was a part owner of the club. He had a good team, he thought. Chase, Doyle, Fletcher, and Zimmerman in the infield; Burns, Youngs, and Kauff in the outfield; Mc-Carty and Mike Gonzales back of the bat, Gonzales having been got from St. Louis in a swap for Schupp, the lost south-paw; Barnes and Benton, back from the army, to head up the pitching staff; and Fred Toney to help out, to pitch and win when the going was rough.

Kauff was glad to be back. Glad as his mates were to see him. They'd seen him only once since he'd left to go into the army. That was on their last visit to Cincinnati in 1918. He was stationed at a nearby camp. On a Sunday morning the train bearing the Giants stopped at a station where a soldier ball team got on. Kauff was with them. He wasn't wearing a regulation uniform. This that he wore was tailor made, obviously.

"I can't wear this uniform in camp," Benny said. "But, hell, who sees me when I'm on a trip?"

"Some uniform," Doyle said. "I know you're only a private but you look like a major."

"A major!" Benny said. "Who wants to be a major? I asked about majors. Do you know what majors get? Only $7,000 a season!"

When the train reached Cincinnati there were cabs waiting to take the Giants to the Havlin—and cabs waiting to take the army team to the Havlin too. And in the dining room, there were these army kids, sitting table-to-table with the Giants at breakfast.

"I didn't know the army treated you like this," a newspaperman said to one of the soldiers.

The soldier almost choked on his ham and eggs.

"The army!" he said, when he could speak again. "You don't think the army is doing this, do you? Benny is doing this. Right out of his own pocket. The train tickets. The taxicabs. The hotel. We got rooms upstairs where we can put on our baseball uniforms. Benny pays for all this. The army pays for nothing."

Fred Toney, who had been bought from the Reds during the 1918 season, was a great bear of a man out of the Tennessee hills. He was a good pitcher too. There were days when he was almost a great one. In 1917 he and Jim Vaughn of the Cubs pitched nine innings against each other without allowing a hit. The Reds made a run off Vaughn in the tenth but the Cubs could make neither a run nor a hit off Toney in their half of the inning. No one else ever pitched a ten-inning, no-hit, no-run game.

Arthur Devlin, who had served McGraw so well at third base for so many years, now did him another good turn. He was coaching the baseball team at Fordham and one day shortly after the Giants had opened the season, he suggested to McGraw that he have some one scout his shortstop, Frank Frisch.

"I could bring him down here for you to look at," he said, "but I'd rather you'd have somebody look at him in a game. He plays with the New York Athletic Club team too. We

112

don't play again until next Wednesday but he'll be at Travers Island Sunday."

Then he said, "This is a real ball player, Mac. A major league ball player. Right now."

McGraw sent George Gibson to look at Frisch. On Monday Gibson said, "Devlin's right. The kid is a big league ball player. You won't have to send him out."

A couple of days later Frisch signed a Giant contract, but announcement of this was withheld until the college season ended in June. He reported to the club when it was in Pittsburgh on its first western trip and made his first appearance in a game as a pinch runner in Chicago. He did not start a game until September, but he played a few innings here and there and worked out every morning the club was at home. It was in these workouts that McGraw discovered he could play second or third base better than he could play shortstop.

The Giants, during this period in the education of young Frisch, were giving every indication that they were going to win the pennant, but as July wore on, Barnes alone of the pitchers was winning consistently and, to bolster his staff, McGraw traded Davy Robertson to Chicago for Phil Douglas. Robertson, released by the Department of Justice when the war was over—he had been hunting spies, draft dodgers, and deserters—had been a bench warmer since his return as Youngs grew steadily in stature as the right fielder. Now McGraw could spare him, and it was possible that Douglas was just the pitcher he needed.

There was a wagging of heads around the league. Douglas had been in and out of the majors since he first entered them with the White Sox in 1912. He had been in Des Moines, San Francisco, Spokane, and St. Paul. The White

Sox had given up on him after once sending him out and bringing him back, and he'd been with Cincinnati and Brooklyn before the Cubs had picked him up at the waiver price. There was no way to prove it by his record but he was a truly great pitcher. The hitch was that he liked to drink so well that there were times that's all he did. Six feet, four inches tall, with heavy, stooped shoulders, thin legs, and big feet, he had been called "Shuffling Phil" by Charlie Dryden, and the name had stuck. He had had little or no schooling back in Rome, Georgia, but nobody ever knew more about pitching than he did. Besides, he had a bristling fast ball, a curve ball, a tantalizing slow ball, a spit ball, and an uncanny change of pace. If, they said around the league, McGraw could keep him in line, he easily might be "the difference." But other managers had tried and failed and so might McGraw.

"He'll be no harder to handle than Bugs Raymond was," McGraw said, "and I got a lot of good pitching from him before he folded. I'll get a lot out of Douglas too."

So he would, but not right away, for Doug had been on one of the benders he called his vacations and hadn't yet recuperated.

Now the Reds were driving hard at the Giants, loosening their grip on the lead. Now it was August and they were in Cincinnati for a three game series, and the Reds trailed them by but a half game. The Reds won the first game and were on top of the league.

That night McGraw made a deal over the telephone. He bought Arthur Nehf from the Braves for $55,000. Even at that price, Nehf was a bargain, for he was the best left-hander in the league, and although he could not save the

Giants that year, he would be the bulwark of their pitching staff for years to come.

The Reds won the second game and, although the Giants won third, they still were in second place and the situation was really grave because the harassed manager and his players suspected they were being cut down from within. Chase, they thought, was just a shade off on plays he should have made easily. Zimmerman was in an unaccountable slump. Heinie complained that a concrete abutment at one end of the old press box at the Polo Grounds made a bad background for balls hit straight down the third base line. No one stopped to think that he had no difficulty seeing the ball in practice, and McGraw had the abutment painted green. Had Chase reverted to type, to cheat not only his teammates but the one man who had befriended him when he was about to be cast out of baseball? Was Zimmerman, whom they all liked so much and whose skills they had respected, capable of treachery? They didn't know but there was a lot of muttering in the clubhouse.

They made one more stand against the Reds, this one at the Polo Grounds in September, when the teams hooked up in three consecutive double-headers. The Reds won the first, the Giants the second, and the Reds the third. It was on the second day of the series that Frisch started his first game, McGraw resting Doyle and posting the youngster at second base in both games. When the series was over, McGraw knew he had lost the pennant—and gained a player who, in time, might know greatness.

The end of the season was not far off when there came a day on which Chase did not appear.

"He's sick," McGraw told the newspapermen. "He hasn't been feeling well for a long time."

Two days later Zimmerman was missing.

"He's tired," McGraw said. "His eyes have been bothering him. He's been complaining that he can't judge the hops on a ground ball as it comes down to him. I told him to knock off for the rest of the season."

Neither ever played another game in organized baseball. A year later, during one of the several investigations resulting from the revelation that White Sox players had rigged the 1919 world series, McGraw said that he had dropped the players because they had thrown ball games and, moreover, had tried to bribe Toney and Kauff to do the same. Zimmerman, who had gone to work in New York, hotly denied it. Chase, playing in an outlaw league along the Rio Grande, said nothing.

16

Rough Prelude to Triumph

IN retrospect, it is easy to see that 1920 had to be a year of sudden spurts—and stops as sudden—of disappointments, of changes made, of waiting for another year to bring the triumph McGraw felt he had missed in 1919 only because of the perfidy of two of his players. But it didn't seem that way in the spring. Maybe that was only because there was an air of optimism in the Giant camp every spring.

This year the club returned to Texas to train, since the customary 154-game schedule and longer training period had been restored in view of the rousing first post-war season. San Antonio, not Marlin, was the site chosen, Marlin, as McGraw realized in the year he had been away from it, having become outmoded as a base in an era when the exhibition schedule was being stepped up as a means of providing revenue to cover constantly increasing expenses. San Antonio always had been a good baseball town, and no better accommodations could have been found for a ball club anywhere in the state than the spacious, comfortable Hotel Menger on the Alamo Plaza.

With Zimmerman and Chase gone, Frisch was assigned to third base and George Kelly to first. Kelly, six feet four, long-armed, long-legged, lean, and awkward, was from San

Francisco, a nephew of Bill Lange, old-time star and friend of McGraw's. Bar a hitch in the army during the war and a short stretch on loan to the Pirates, he had been with the Giants since 1915, playing occasional games at first base. He wouldn't be as eye filling as the graceful Chase, nor as efficient as Chase had been when he was trying. But he was an earnest kid and he could hit a long ball, and McGraw was willing to go along with him. Doyle still was at second base and Fletcher at shortstop, with Youngs, Burns, and Kauff in the outfield. McCarty was there too, but he had been moved back and soon would be moved out, and the catching would be divided by Frank (Pancho) Snyder and Earl Smith, both having joined the club in 1919. Snyder was a veteran obtained from the Cardinals, and Smith a rookie up from Rochester. The pitching strength rested in Nehf, Barnes, Toney, Douglas, and Benton.

Early disillusionment awaited McGraw. The team started badly, and the season was only a couple of weeks old when Frisch complained of a bellyache, learned it was appendicitis, and went off to a hospital. Fred Lear, a veteran, but mostly of the minor leagues, took his place but wasn't quite adequate. Meanwhile, Kelly was floundering, the crowd was howling at him, and some of the critics were asking in print when the Giants were going to get a first baseman.

McGraw took the unhappy youth into his office in the clubhouse one day and said, "I just want you to know I'm the only one around here you have to care about. I'm running this ball club, not the fans back of first base nor Chase's old pals, the gamblers back of third, nor the reporters in the press box. We don't need another first baseman. You just take it easy and quit worrying."

Kelly felt better after that and played better, but Frisch

had taken to the hospital about all the speed in the infield. Now McGraw, who had been so hopeful a few weeks before, was looking for help and found it in Philadelphia in the person of David James (Beauty) Bancroft. "Banny," as a busher from Portland in the Pacific Coast League in 1915, had sparked the Phillies to the pennant. He still was far and away the best shortstop in the league—fast, agile, a good hitter, a quick thinker, and a hard-bitten competitor. McGraw got him in exchange for Fletcher and a hefty young right-handed pitcher named Wilbur Hubbell.

The necessity for replacing Fletcher depressed McGraw. For eleven years, or since he had come up from Dallas, Fletcher had been his stand-by. No player had been more typical of the Giant spirit which, after all, was the spirit of McGraw. No player had been more steadfast in time of trouble nor—for all his gentleness off the field—more eloquent with his fists in time of strife. He had survived constant changes in the infield. He had played a major part in the winning of four pennants. But he had slowed up and the Giants needed someone with the zing of a Bancroft.

They picked up briefly when Banny joined them, lagged again, then were beset by personal troubles. Kauff, accused of being a member of an automobile stealing ring, was tried and acquitted, but the experience just about wrecked him as a player and McGraw sent him to Toronto, taking a young outfielder named Vernon Spencer in return. Matty, whose health was failing, left the club and went to Saranac. McGraw became involved in an alcoholic evening during which he was slugged by an actor named Bill Boyd in the Lambs Club, and one of his companions, John C. Slavin, also an actor, wound up with a fractured skull on the sidewalk in front of his home in the dawning. Precisely in what circumstances Slavin came upon his injury never was determined, although there was talk, soon forgotten, of indicting McGraw for assault, and McGraw subsequently settled out of court a suit for damages brought against him by his friend. Meanwhile, he belted out a third actor, this one Wilton Lackaye, who was hit on the chin so hard that as he fell he cracked an ankle. Nothing ever came of that either, and McGraw, who had been nursing his own hurts, returned to the dugout—but never to the coaching line.

Once more the Giants gathered speed, for Frisch was back too, and, as the season waned, they made a run at the Robins. But they had dawdled too often and too long and had to settle for second place. Yet, Nehf and Toney each had won twenty-one games and Barnes had won twenty. Youngs had hit .351. Burns still was the almost perfect out fielder. Banny had hit .299 and already was accepted as the best shortstop the Giants had had in years, better even than Fletcher had been at his peak, better, maybe, than any the Giants ever had had. Frisch whose motto was "To hell with technique, get the ball," was spectacular at third base. No fault could be found with Snyder and Smith, the two hard-hitting catchers. Kelly was improving. A few more changes . . .

Frank Frisch

Art Nehf   Ross Youngs

New York Giants

Carl Hubbell

17

First of Four Flags in a Row

⊖ LARRY DOYLE was missing from San Antonio in the spring of 1921. He, like Matty and Fletcher, had been a special favorite of McGraw's. He was the one who had said, "It's great to be young and a Giant."

But that had been a long time ago and he had been away once and come back. Now his major league days were over and he would never be seen in a Giant uniform again.

With his leaving there was a new shift in the infield. Frisch was returned to second base, and at third base there was Joe (Goldie) Rapp. Goldie was only twenty-six years old, although he looked older, and this was his first time up in the big leagues after seven or eight years in the minors. McGraw had been advised that after a solid season in St. Paul in 1920, he was ready. It turned out, unfortunately, for himself and all others concerned, that he wasn't, and never would be. Not for that spot. Not on that team. He wasn't fast enough and he couldn't hit big league pitching, and it didn't take McGraw long to find out a mistake had been made.

McGraw wanted "Heinie" Groh from Cincinnati. He had had Heinie back in 1911-12-13, but Heinie was a boy then and there was no room for him on the team that was rushing to the pennant in those years. He had sent him to Cincinnati and there he had prospered. Now that Zimmerman no longer was around, Heinie was the best third baseman in the league. McGraw wanted him, and he was holding out. But McGraw didn't get him. Commissioner Kenesaw Mountain Landis said he couldn't have him. In answer to Garry Herrmann's complaint that McGraw, by coming right out and saying he'd like to have the player, virtually was tampering with him, in violation of one of the game's basic rules, Landis ruled that Groh must remain with the Reds for at least the season of 1921. So Heinie signed with the Reds and McGraw, in a quick switch from Cincinnati to Philadelphia, got Johnny Rawlings, a second baseman and Casey Stengel, an outfielder in exchange for Rapp, Lee King, an outfielder, and Lance Richbourg, a young first baseman he had signed out of the University of Florida two years before when the Giants were in Gainesville.

At the time, Stengel had given off no signs of ever becoming a successful major league manager, being a light-hearted, free-wheeling, old-time ball player who, while never a dissipater, took his fun where he found it. He had broken in with the Dodgers in 1913, had had a couple of years with the Pirates, and now he was with the Phillies, a hopelessly bad ball club, managed by Bill Donovan, who wasn't a bad manager by any means but who couldn't possibly win with the players he had.

The day the trade was made, the Phillies lost another ball game and they were in the clubhouse when Stengel heard Donovan ask where he was.

"My locker had been next to Bill's," Casey was to say later, "but I couldn't stand listening to the poor fellow moan after every game, so I moved into an alcove. I heard one of the players say,

" 'He's dressing back there.'

"Donovan said, 'Is that so? Well, he'll soon be dressing further away than that.'

" 'Oh-oh!' I said to myself. 'Peoria.'

"Then I come out and I said to Bill, 'Were you looking for me?'

"And he said, 'Yes. You and Rawlings have been traded to the Giants. You can report to McGraw any time tomorrow that you want to.'

" 'I'm leaving right away,' I said. 'I don't know how Rawlings feels about it but I will be there to greet Mr. McGraw the first thing in the morning. I am not taking any chances on him changing his mind.' "

Arthur Nehf said the following night, "I was on the field this morning, sitting on a box against the bleacher wall, right next to the gate. Casey, coming through, didn't see me and didn't know there was any one near him. He slapped himself hard on the chest, on the arms, and on the legs, and he said, " 'Wake up, muscles! We're in New York now!' "

Casey served the Giants well, within his limitations as an aging ball player, but Rawlings was the one McGraw wanted most at the moment. Johnny had been around too: a year in Cincinnati, two years with Kansas City in the Federal League, four years in Boston, and a year and a half in Philadelphia. He was small and lithe, as Bancroft was, they both had broken noses, and at least once they were mistaken for each other. (In the gloom of the runways leading to the dressing rooms under the stand at Forbes Field, after a game one day, Banny let loose a stream of insults at Bill Klem. Bill reported to President Heydler, "Mr. Rawlings

123

called me names no gentleman should call another." And Rawlings was fined $150—which, incidentally, McGraw paid.) Rawlings was a clever fielder, a .280 hitter, and a particularly dangerous one in the clutches. He had slowed up somewhat but he would do for now. McGraw put him on second base and sent Frisch back to third.

It was very soon after that that McGraw turned to Philadelphia again. This time he came up with Emil (Irish) Meusel, outfielder, for whom he gave Curtis Walker, also an outfielder; Walter (Butch) Henline, a catcher; and how much money only he and Stoneham and William F. Baker, president of the Phillies, and their bankers knew. Irish Meusel was the older brother of Bob Meusel who, the year before, had come up as a third baseman out of the Pacific Coast League to the Yankees and had been converted into an outfielder too. Irish, also out of the Coast League, had had a brief whirl with the Senators in 1914 and had been shipped back to the coast. He had hit the big wheel again with the Phillies in 1918 and now he was with the Giants. The brothers Meusel had a date, arranged, no doubt by destiny, a date that was to carry over each year for three years, as you shall see.

Now McGraw had the team he wanted. Kelly, Rawlings, Bancroft and Frisch in the infield; Meusel in left field, where he was accustomed to play; Burns, who could play any field, in center; and Youngs in right; Snyder, Smith and young Aleck Gaston to do the catching; and Nehf, Douglas, Barnes, and Toney to carry the pitching burden.

These were the Giants who, marking time as the changes were made and the new arrivals assimilated, trailed the Pirates into August and, on August 19, were seven-and-a-half games back as the leaders moved into the Polo Grounds

124

for a five-game series in which they planned to clinch the pennant. They were happy and gay, the Pirates were, before the double-header that day that opened the series. Hadn't the Giants lost three out of four to the Cardinals? This, they thought, would be a soft touch. But it wasn't. These were the Giants. Compact now and roused by McGraw, they swept the series, with Nehf, who beat the Pirates seven times that year, winning the first game of the series and the last. These were the Giants who went on from there, as the demoralized Pirates folded, to take the lead and, in a final fling through the West, to win the pennant.

There would be other bright years in the long history of the Giants, as there had been before. But this quite possibly, was the brightest. The infield and the outfield had been re-formed by McGraw under fire. Ground had been lost and hopes dimmed. But in their darkest hour, after they had lost that series with the Cardinals and then faced the Pirates, who held a seemingly overwhelming lead, they had smashed through as only champions do.

The triumph of the Giants was equaled by that of the Yankees, who won the pennant in the American League and so, for the first time, New York had a world series of its own. "The World Series on the Subway," some one called it, or "The Nickel World Series." With the decision going to the winner of five games in a possible nine, the series would be played in its entirety on the Polo Grounds, where the Yankees had been tenants of the Giants since they abandoned their own park in 1913.

The clubs had met in post-season series before, once in 1910, again in 1914, but these had been meaningless. This, though, not only was the real thing but something special.

A terrific rivalry had sprung up between them with the coming of Babe Ruth to the Yankees the year before and, for the first time, the Giants were running second in popularity as the mobs stormed the park to see the Babe hit the ball out of sight. This series would be, too, a test of strength between McGraw and the Babe. Miller Huggins, who managed the Yankees, was a great man in his own right but he had not yet been recognized as such and he was completely obscured in the minds of the fans in this clash of the titans.

There was a superb balance of strength between the clubs. Each had a fine pitching staff, the Yankees matching the Giants' Nehf, Douglas, Barnes, and Toney with Waite Hoyt, Carl Mays, and Bob Shawkey. The Giants had the stronger defense, but the Yankees had an obvious edge on the offense, with the original "Murderers' Row"—Ruth, Bob Meusel, Wally Pipp, and the Giants' old Nemesis, Home Run Baker. The main question was whether McGraw's pitching strategy could nullify the power of the Yankees' bats.

McGraw, openly nettled when reporters asked him how he intended to pitch to the Babe, snapped, "Why don't you ask him? The same way we did in exhibition games when he was with the Red Sox. But don't ask him how he hit against us. He might not like it.

"Ruth!" he went on scornfully. "Why all the excitement about Ruth? We've been pitching all along to Hornsby and he's a three-to-one better hitter than Ruth."

Mays, outpointing Douglas, shut the Giants out in the first game as the Yankees won, 3 to 0. Nehf yielded only three hits in the second game, but Hoyt, who opposed him, gave the Giants but two, and errors behind Nehf decided the outcome in the Yankees' favor, 3 to 0. No team that had lost the first two games of a series ever had won it, and the suspicion that the Giants were licked seemed to be confirmed when the Yankees knocked Toney out and scored four runs in the third inning of the third game. Then there was a swift turn, for the Giants hammered Shawkey to the showers, assaulted his successors, and, with Barnes holding the Yanks in check, won, 13 to 5.

Douglas and Mays resumed their tussle in the fourth game and although Ruth hit a home run—his only one of the series—the Giants won, 4 to 2. Hoyt again took a decision over Nehf, 3 to 1, in the fifth game. Ruth was out of action with an injured elbow when the Giants won the sixth and seventh games, and now they came to the eighth, and a spectacular wind-up.

Going into the ninth inning of the third meeting between Nehf and Hoyt, the Yanks were trailing, 1 to 0, an unearned run having fallen to the Giants in the fourth. Now, in the ninth, Ruth batted for Pipp and was an easy out on a grounder to Kelly. But Aaron Ward walked, and Baker slashed a ball toward right field for an apparent single. Rawlings, going far to his left, somehow stopped the ball, sprawled, came up—and threw to Kelly, retiring the hitter. Ward, apparently thinking the ball had gone through, had rounded second base and now headed for third, and Kelly cut him down with a bullet throw across the diamond to Frisch, completing a double play and ending the series.

Rawlings had played a remarkable series, handling forty-eight chances without an error, and had hit .333. To the surprise of the experts, the Giants had outhit the Yankees, with Snyder topping the winners with an average of .364. Nehf, although he was beaten twice, had pitched magnificently, allowing only thirteen hits, or one less than Matty had given up in his three shutouts back in 1905.

McGraw had got no more than a standoff with Ruth, however. Although the Babe had made only one home run, he had made five hits for a mark of .313 and, of course, if he hadn't been sidelined through two complete games and had only one time at bat in another, there is no telling what he might have accomplished.

But the Giant manager was not concerned with Ruth now. He had won another world series, at long last. He was in a mood to celebrate and so, of course, was Stoneham. There was a party at the old Waldorf that night which lasted well into the next morning.

Now that the Giants were on top of the world again, McGraw was determined that they should stay there and, before the year was out, he made a deal calculated to further strengthen them. Heinie Groh, having got off Landis' hook by playing out the season in Cincinnati and, at the same time, having worn out his welcome there, could be had by anybody who would pay the right price for him—and McGraw reached out and got him. For Groh he gave money —just how much no one would say—Mike Gonzales, the Cuban catcher, and one of his old favorites, George Burns. Seldom an exciting player but an exceedingly talented one, for ten years Burns had been the key man in the outfield. He was the last of the dashing crew that had raced breathlessly to those now half-forgotten pennants in 1912 and 1913. McGraw, parting with him, felt as he had when parting with Matty, Doyle, and Fletcher.

There was one more deal he made that caught the flaring headlines. He paid $75,000 to the San Francisco club for Jimmy O'Connell, a twenty-one year old kid from Santa

Clara College who, playing first base and the outfield for the Seals that year, had hit .337 and was hailed on the Coast as a sure-fire major league star. Because of his youth and the fact that he had played professionally for only two seasons, McGraw arranged to have him remain in San Francisco, and to play only in the outfield, for another year.

18

Everything Happened in 1922

ONCE more, as the Giants assembled at San Antonio in late February of 1922, there was a revamping of the infield. McGraw felt that Rawlings, who had had such a fine season the year before and had been a standout in the world series, would be a handy man to have around. But not as a regular this time. And so, as every one had supposed he would, he benched Johnny, shifted the mobile Frisch back to second base, and put Groh on third.

Meusel again was in left field, and Youngs in right. First call as replacement for Burns in center went to Ralph Shinners, who had been purchased from Milwaukee. To back him up, there were Stengel and Bill Cunningham, brought up from Seattle the year before, but little used. Claude Jonnard and Jess Barnes's kid brother, Virgil, were added to the pitching staff. This was the team that many who followed it closely thought was McGraw's greatest.

It has been said that, in Dick Kinsella, McGraw had a one-man scouting staff and it is true that Dick was the only one who was engaged on a professional basis. But through the country there were friends of the manager who, when they saw a promising young ball player, immediately thought of him in terms of his possible usefulness to the

Giants. Now, on the way north this spring, McGraw heard for the first time, from two of his friends, of two young men who would have a great influence on the course of the Giants in years to come. It happened in Memphis where, in those days, the Giants were accustomed to stopping for at least a week end and sometimes for four or five days.

First to call on him in his room at the New Peabody was Norman Elberfeld, the "Tobasco Kid" of the early vintage Yankees and, at the time, manager of the Little Rock club of the Southern Association. He had a young fellow in his club, he said, that he was sure McGraw would like. A kid named Travis Jackson.

"He didn't hit much last year," the Kid said, "but he'll hit better as he goes along. And he can hound the ball around shortstop and you never saw a better arm. Have him watched. If you like him, you can have him at the end of the season."

Then there was Tom Watkins, owner of the Memphis club.

"There's a fellow named Bill Terry in this town," Watkins said, "that you should get. He's a big, left-handed pitcher, an all-around ball player, and a good hitter. He used to pitch for Shreveport and he was one of the best pitchers in the league when he quit."

When McGraw asked why Terry had quit, Watkins explained, Bill had married young and was raising a family. He didn't like to be away from home, he wasn't happy as a minor league ball player, and, seeking better pay and greater security, he had gone to work on a year-round basis with the Standard Oil Company.

"But he pitches or plays first base for the Polarines, which is the plant team," Watkins said. "He's the best hitter on the team. If you'd like to talk to him, I'll send him up."

"Fine," McGraw said. "Send him up tomorrow."

The first meeting between McGraw and the man who was to succeed him ten years later was at least mildly unpleasant. That the first impression each got of the other was lasting seems certain. As manager and player they never were friendly.

McGraw immediately was taken by Terry's appearance but not completely by his attitude. After they had talked for a few minutes, McGraw asked, "How would you like to come to New York with me?"

"What for?"

"To play with the Giants, maybe."

"For how much?" Terry asked.

The question started a slow burn in McGraw.

"Do you understand what I am offering you?" he asked. "I'm offering you a chance to play with the Giants—if you're good enough."

"Excuse me if I don't fall all over myself," Terry said. "But the Giants don't mean anything to me unless you can make it worth my while."

"If that's the way you feel about it . . ."

"This is how I feel about it, Mr. McGraw," Terry said. "I'm doing all right here. I quit the Southern League because I got tired of tramping around the country with a minor league ball club. I was married and had a baby and I wanted to settle down. I liked Memphis and I came here and got a job. I have a nice home and I'm in no hurry to leave it, or the job. If I can make much more money going to New York, I'll go. You can't get me excited just by talking to me about the Giants. And remember this, I didn't come up here to ask you for anything. I came because Tom Watkins said you wanted to see me."

"All right," McGraw said, probably because he couldn't think of anything else to say to this busher who talked to him as no other busher ever had. "There's no hurry. I'll think it over."

Bill got up to leave. He smiled at McGraw and shook hands with him.

"It's nice to have met you," he said. "You can reach me in care of Standard Oil."

Three weeks later McGraw wired his offer to Terry: $5,000 a year, plus a guarantee that if he needed further minor league seasoning, he would be sent out only as the property of the Giants, and would be recalled when he had demonstrated he was ready for the majors. Terry accepted. McGraw looked him over on the Polo Grounds and sent him to Toledo as a first baseman. The fact that he was rejected as a pitcher after so short a trial hurt him. He held that against McGraw always, although he earned fame and fortune (perhaps $200,000) as a hard-hitting first baseman.

Jackson, meanwhile, was placed under surveillance by Kinsella. All reports from Dick being highly favorable, he was bought that summer for delivery in the spring of 1923.

Ralph Shinners, counted upon by McGraw to be his regular center fielder, began splendidly and was hitting over .300 when, in a game in Philadelphia, he was hit in the head by "Columbia" George Smith, the former Giant. The doctors who examined him in the hospital to which he was removed from the field told McGraw he was gravely hurt, that his sight might be permanently affected. Whether or not the prognosis was correct, Shinners was ineffectual at the plate when he returned to the line-up and spoke of frequent headaches and McGraw farmed him out to Toledo. He would be back again the following year but he would not last.

Ralph, however, did not leave New York the first time without taking such revenge as he could on the one who cut short his major league career. No one particularly noticed it, since, while he was in uniform again, he had not returned to the line-up, but this day at the Polo Grounds, with the Giants playing the Phillies and Smith starting the game, he was in the Giants' bull pen. Not doing anything. Just sitting there waiting ... hoping ...

Along about the fourth inning, that for which he had been waiting and hoping occurred. Smith was knocked out of the box. Now, whether Smith had meant to hit Shinners in the head, nobody knows. More likely, he merely had tried to drive Ralph back from the plate. But to hear the ball players tell it, he had taken dead aim at the busher who was hitting over .300. Shinners had heard it, and as Smith neared the clubhouse in center field, there was Shinners waiting for him.

Shinners knocked him down and jumped on him, and all of a sudden there was a third party on the edge of the fight. McGraw was trying to kick Shinners when the cops broke up the brawl. Seems he had guessed what was about to happen when he saw Shinners get up from the bull pen bench and start in to meet Smith, and he had got there the short way, under the right field stand and out on the field through a gate he commanded a surprised cop to open for him.

In July the Giants, although driving steadily, were having pitching trouble. Specifically, Phil Douglas was taking more frequent and longer "vacations." Now, there was on the Boston club, a pitcher by the name of Hughie McQuillan. He was a handsome, dark-haired, blue-eyed, laughing guy from Queens, which is a part of New York, and he had a fast ball and a curve ball and all the rest of it that a pitcher needs, especially when he is in trouble. But he was so temperamentally constituted that he could lose interest in a ball club that was down in the race and, as the Braves were about as far down as they could go, he was showing very little interest in them indeed. Stoneham, not knowing the young man's predelictions but looking only at his record, was dubious when McGraw suggested they buy him.

"Never mind his record," McGraw said. "He'll win for a good club. He'll win for me."

"Get him," Stoneham said.

George Washington Grant, who owned the Braves, proudly exhibited a certified check for $100,000 that he received from Stoneham in exchange for the pitcher, but the transaction didn't seem to please any one save Grant, Stoneham, and McGraw. Branch Rickey, whose Cardinals were running second to the Giants, understandably bellowed with rage; Grant was hammered all over Boston for selling his only good pitcher to strengthen the Giants; and even in New York there was sharp criticism of this attempt to buy a pennant. McGraw paid no heed to any of it.

He was more concerned about Douglas than he was about the shots being fired at him for the purchase of McQuillan. "Big Shuffling" Phil had been acting up and eluding, or turning on and terrifying, detectives hired by

McGraw to trail him. McGraw was sorely tempted to get rid of him but didn't because he still was a very good pitcher. Finally he engaged a keeper for him. Doug didn't like the idea at first but he liked the keeper, who's name was O'Brien, and soon became reconciled to the arrangement.

"That feller that goes around with me," Doug called him.

O'Brien—he was a private eye from Chicago, by the way—soon formed a great liking for Doug and, moreover, knew how to handle him. If Doug wanted a couple of beers or even an occasional rye when they were out walking of an evening, or returning from a movie, O'Brien always knew where there was a good speak-easy. But he never let Doug get out of hand and, after a while, Doug was securely bound to temperance by an unwillingness to do anything that would cause trouble for his friend. Ironically, it was this happy relationship that led to eventual tragedy for the unfortunate pitcher.

McGraw, thinking perhaps O'Brien would become too lenient with his charge, dismissed him, and in his stead assigned Jess Burkett, a former great hitter, minor league manager, and confidant of his, to watch over Doug. Now, Phil had nothing against Burkett but he was disturbed and resentful over the firing of his pal. Inevitably he lost Burkett in a crowd on Broadway one night and was not seen again until four days later when, in the grip of a dreadful hangover, he shuffled into the clubhouse at the Polo Grounds. McGraw berated him frightfully, winding up with, "Don't bother to dress! Go home and sleep it off, you big bum! But be here tomorrow or I'll fix you so you'll never pitch for anybody again!"

The players, going on the field, left Doug alone in the clubhouse. How long he remained, no one knew, but he was gone before the game was over. So was a bottle of lemon extract from the trainer's closet. But he was back the following day and, when the Giants left for Pittsburgh, he seemed to have recovered entirely from his spree and was in a cheerful and confident frame of mind. That was on the night of August 15. The next morning the newspapermen were called to McGraw's suite in the Hotel Schenley. To their surprise they found Judge Landis seated at a desk in the living room. He looked very stern, but when he spoke there was sadness, not anger, in his voice.

"Gentlemen," he said. "I have just placed the name of Phil Douglas on the permanent ineligible list."

McGraw, staring out a window, was silent, as the reporters, shocked by the Judge's statement, questioned him.

"I called Douglas and asked him if he had written this," he said.

He held out a letter written on the Giants' stationary.

"He confessed that he had," the Judge continued. "There was nothing else for me to do."

The letter had been written that day in the clubhouse when Douglas had been left alone. It was addressed to Leslie Mann, a St. Louis outfielder. It was a proposal on Douglas' part to go fishing for the rest of the season if the St. Louis players would "make it worth my while." Mann promptly had turned the letter over to Rickey, who had placed it in the Judge's hands.

An hour or so later, Dave Bancroft went up to McGraw's suite.

"I've got Doug in my room," he said. "He's crying. He wants to know if you'll see him."

McGraw shook his head.

"No," he said. "It wouldn't do him any good, or me either. I feel sorry for him but there is nothing I can do to help him. Tell him I have arranged for his transportation home. The tickets are at the porter's desk. And give him this."

He handed Bancroft a hundred dollars.

Bancroft rode to the train with Douglas. He said Doug still was crying. None of the Giants ever saw him again, but they spoke of him often. They had no reproach for him in his attempt to sell them out. They said he didn't know what he was doing when he wrote the letter and, having written it, had no recollection of it.

Having thus lost one good pitcher, McGraw soon got another, not by trade or purchase this time, but simply by giving a break to one who was down on his luck.

The pitcher was Jack Scott, a big right-hander from Ridgeway, North Carolina. He had been with the Braves and the Reds and, in the off seasons, raised tobacco. Early that spring his sheds, in which the drying leaves were hung, had burned, and he'd had no insurance. In May he injured his pitching arm, and the Reds released him. He had tried to borrow money to build new sheds but there was a tobacco war raging and money was scarce in Ridgeway. Broke, out of a job, and with only the ashes of his last year's crop on his farm, he showed up at the Polo Grounds and asked McGraw to give him a chance.

"Hard luck's been on my back long enough, Mr. McGraw," he said. "It's got to get off. Let me work out

138

with you for a couple of weeks and I know I'll be able to pitch again."

Impressed with his earnestness, McGraw staked him and made arrangements for him to work out mornings on the Polo Grounds—the Giants were leaving the following day for a spin on the road, and the Yankees would be playing there in the afternoons. When the Giants returned, Scott said he was ready, and so he was. McGraw signed him to a contract for the balance of the season, and he was effective as a relief pitcher.

While all this... the purchase of McQuillan, the departure of Douglas, and the arrival of Scott... was going on, the Giants were disposing, one by one, of their contenders—the Cardinals, the Pirates, and the Reds. On September 25, they clinched the pennant and on October 4, moved against the Yankees in another world series.

This resulted in a complete triumph for them. Nehf, opposing Joe Bush in the first game, was behind, 2 to 0, when he was taken out for a pinch hitter in the seventh; but in that inning the Giants scored three times and Bill Ryan, following Nehf, fended the Yankees off and the Giants won, 3 to 2. The second game was locked at 3-3 at the end of the tenth inning, with Barnes in the box for the Giants and opposed by Bob Shawkey, when Umpire Hildebrand, back of the plate, called a halt because of darkness.

There is a legend that the sun was shining brightly when Hildebrand decided it was too dark for the players to follow the ball. That isn't quite true. But there was sufficient light to have permitted the playing of at least another inning. The players were bewildered; the crowd howled in anger; reporters rushed to Landis' box. He plainly was as surprised as any one but he rallied quickly. "I stand by the umpire's decision," he said firmly.

He left the field with the crowd at his heels, hooting him, calling him an old faker, and throwing wadded newspapers at him, thinking he had ordered the calling of the game. When he reached the shelter of his suite at the Hotel Roosevelt, he announced that the receipts from that game would be divided among the major New York charities, and closed out the incident by privately frying Hildebrand's ears.

The third game was dramatic. So was its immediate aftermath. To every one's surprise, McGraw started Scott against Waite Hoyt, and Scott shut the Yankees out with four hits. Ten minutes after the game, Ruth and Bob Meusel, who had dressed hurriedly, appeared in the Giants' clubhouse. The Babe was glowering. Meusel, trailing him in, seemed a little embarrassed, as though he wasn't quite sure what he was doing there.

"Where's Rawlings?" Ruth demanded, looking about him.

"Right here," Rawlings said. He was seated in front of his locker, putting on his socks.

Ruth towered over him.

"Listen, you little ———," he said, "if you ever call me that again, I'll beat the hell out of you. I don't care how little you are."

"What's the matter?" Rawlings asked, looking up at him calmly. "Can't you take it?"

"I can take it," Ruth said. "But I won't take that."

Earl Smith, one of the toughest men in latter-day baseball, walked up to Ruth, an amused smile on his face.

"What did he call you?" he asked.

"He called me a ———," Ruth said.

Smith spat a stream of tobacco juice on the floor.

"That's nothing," he said, and walked away.

Jess Barnes said, "You shouldn't mind that after what you called me when I was pitching yesterday."

"I didn't call you anything yesterday," the Babe said.

"You're a ——— ——— liar!" Barnes said.

Ruth took a step toward him. Barnes, who also had dressed, ripped off his coat. A couple of Giants moved between them. Then the door opened and Hughie Jennings, who had joined the Giants as a coach, came in. He was startled at the angry scene.

"What are you doing in here?" he asked Ruth.

"I came in to see Rawlings," Ruth said. "He can't ...

"Get out of here!" Jennings said. "And you too, Meusel. You have no business here. Get out before McGraw finds you here."

McGraw was in his office at one end of the big room and the door was closed.

Ruth started for the exit. That afternoon, he had plowed into Groh at third base, knocking him down.

"And remember, when we get out there tomorrow," Groh said, "we're playing baseball, not football, you big slob."

Ruth stopped and turned.

"Listen, fellows," he said. "I'm sorry this happened. I don't mind being called a ——— ——— ——— or a ———, but from now on, none of that personal stuff!"

The Giants howled. The drama had become a comedy. Ruth, bewildered by the laughter, went out, followed by Meusel, who hadn't opened his mouth.

McQuillan took a pasting in the first inning of the fourth game but survived it mainly because Cunningham went almost to the clubhouse to catch a towering blow by Ruth, then hung on, and won, 4 to 3, as the Giants got to Mays. Nehf, making his second start, beat Bush in the fifth game, 5 to 3.

The Giants had won the series in four games, barring the tie. Their pitchers had held Ruth to two hits and an average of .118, Scott, the castoff, had pitched a shutout. The old Waldorf rocked that night as Stoneham and McGraw celebrated with their friends.

19

Still Another Series on the Subway

◎ NOW it was 1923 and Jimmy O'Connell, Travis Jackson, and Jack Bentley were in the group at San Antonio—O'Connell, the "Golden Boy," who had cost $75,000; Jackson, the skinny kid from Little Rock, who cost perhaps one tenth of that; and Bentley, the one-man gang from the International League, for whom the Giants had paid the Baltimore club $65,000.

O'Connell, tall, light-haired, loosely built, had an easy style at the plate and lashed the ball about the field in practice. He was a smiling, friendly kid and everybody liked him. Jackson, dark, shy and likable too, could, as Kid Elberfeld said, hound the ball around shortstop, and showed surprising power at the plate. But the one who attracted the most attention was Bentley, a big, wide-shouldered, dark, good-looking fellow with a ready wit, a booming base voice, and the poise of a champion.

"I never saw anybody," Arthur Nehf said, "who looked more like a major league ball player—or acted like one is supposed to act."

In his own right and in the field he had just left, Bentley was a fabulous character and the greatest drawing card the International League had known for years. Taking part in every game the Orioles played in 1922, he won thirteen and lost two as a pitcher, had an earned run average of only 1.73, and played 141 games at first base. His batting average was .350 and he made twenty-two home runs and thirty-nine doubles, driving in 128 runs and scoring 109. (There was a tailor in Baltimore who advertised that he would give a suit of clothes to every home player who made a home run. After Bentley had collected eight suits, he suggested a compromise to the tailor. He would take one suit for every four home runs, which naturally made the tailor happy. "I didn't want to break the poor fellow," Bentley explained.)

McGraw wanted the big fellow as a pitcher, for Nehf not only was the only left-hander on the staff but was under a considerable strain, starting, and often finishing, every important series. And McGraw was irritated when Bentley held out until he received part of his purchase price, so that he was late starting and reported overweight. McGraw fixed him for that. He had him bundled in woolen and rubber shirts, running constantly around the park, not only in San Antonio but everywhere else the Giants played, from there to the Polo Grounds. By that time Jack was in shape.

So was the rest of the team. Jackson worked in neatly at shortstop or third base whenever McGraw wanted to give Bancroft or Groh a rest, and Ryan, in his third season with the club, had become a combat-toughened pitcher and a real asset. Terry was brought up to New York but McGraw decided he needed another year in the minors and packed him off to Toledo again.

Strong as they had been in the past two years, perhaps even stronger, the Giants won the pennant for the third time in a row. O'Connell, possibly because he tried too hard, was not up to expectations, but when Bancroft was stricken with pneumonia Jackson moved in at shortstop and played as though he had been in the major leagues for years. Bentley won thirteen games and, used also as a pinch hitter, was the best the Giants had had since the time of Moose McCormick; while Ryan won sixteen games and lost only five.

The Yankees also won their third pennant, and while the rest of the country might have wearied somewhat over this cornering of the world series by New York, the town was more excited than it had been before. This series would be for blood, and everybody knew it.

The ascendency of Ruth and the rocketing of the Yankees in public favor, so that they had become the dominant team in a city that once had belonged exclusively to the Giants, had shattered the once beautiful friendship between McGraw and Stoneham on the one hand and Colonel Jacob Ruppert and Colonel T. L. Huston, owners of the Yankees, on the other. In the summer of 1922, notice had been served rather abruptly on Ruppert and Huston that their lease at the Polo Grounds would not be renewed for 1923, whereupon the "Battling Colonels" went directly across the Harlem River from the Polo Grounds and there, in the Borough of the Bronx, reared the Yankee Stadium in an incredibly short time. Now half the series would be played there and McGraw wanted terribly to give the Yankees a beating to remember him by.

So bitter were his feelings toward the men whom, seven years before, he had induced to buy the Yankees, and so hateful was the Stadium in his sight that he refused to allow the Giants to dress there when the Yankees were the home club, having them dress at the Polo Grounds and transporting them across Central Bridge in taxicabs. He grudgingly consented to use the visiting clubhouse at the Stadium as a place where the players might change their sweat shirts, but that was all. Awkward as the arrangement was, he was completely satisfied with it.

The series opened at the Stadium and the Giants won, 5 to 4, on a home run by Casey Stengel. John Watson, obtained by the Giants from Boston in midseason, started that game but Ryan finished it for him, while Bush pitched for the Yanks. Herb Pennock, in his first year with the Yankees, outpointed Bentley in the second game, played at the Polo Grounds, 4 to 2. Back at the stadium, Nehf shut the Yankees out and Stengel hit another home run to beat Sam Jones, 1 to 0, but the Yankees won the next two games, knocking Scott out and beating Bentley.

The climax of the sixth game, which the Giants' needed to tie the series and which was played at the Polo Grounds, almost wrecked McGraw. The Giants were leading, 4 to 1, with Nehf pitching, going into the eighth inning, but there Nehf's arm cracked and before McGraw could get him out the Yankees had tied the score and had the bases filled—with only one out and Ruth at bat. Ryan, hurled into the breach, struck the Babe out, but Meusel singled through the box, driving in two runs. And that was it, for the Giants couldn't score in their half of the inning, or in the ninth.

It was one of the heaviest blows McGraw ever had to take. But he proved he could take it. When friends called on him at the Waldorf to condole with him, where once they had helped to celebrate his victories, he threw a party that transcended any that had gone before.

Shortly after the series, McGraw announced that he had agreed to trade Bancroft to Boston that he might become the playing manager of that club. He was aware, he said, that Banny had many years as a player ahead of him and he would not otherwise have thought of parting with him, but he could not deny him this opportunity to advance himself. With Bancroft went Stengel and Cunningham. In return, the Giants got Billy Southworth, outfielder, and Joe Oeschger, a pitcher. Jackson, of course, McGraw said, would be the Giants' shortstop in 1924.

20

The Dolan-O'Connell Case

⊖ NINETEEN TWENTY-FOUR. A year to be remembered in Giant history. A year in which the Giants
won a fourth consecutive pennant, as no other club had
done up to that time. A year in which, because of them,
baseball rocked under the impact of a scandal as it had
in 1919, when the White Sox turned black overnight. A
year in which, with another pennant won, another world
series defeat was suffered.

That spring McGraw allowed himself to be persuaded
by his friend, John Ringling, to take the club to train at
Sarasota, Florida, where Ringling had established the
winter quarters of the circus and where an almost im-
plausible real estate boom, in which he also was interested,
was in progress. McGraw obviously was not aware of
what he was getting into, nor was Ringling, who knew
nothing of baseball and was motivated only by the thought
that the presence of the Giants in Sarasota would help to
ballyhoo his circus and his real estate.

Consequently, when the task force from New York arrived—sixty strong, including newspapermen, women, and
children, McGraw, who was at the head of it, discovered
Ringling had made reservations for it in a cement-block

heap that passed for a hotel and that could accommodate, at most, twenty persons. McGraw was furious. Having snarled at Ringling, he set out in person to find quarters for these suddenly displaced persons and came up with two hotels, the Mira Mar for the regulars, newspapermen, women, and children and the Watrous for the rookies. It was not an arrangement to his liking. The hotels were separated by a long block and every night saw him charging back and forth, making sure his athletes were observing the eleven o'clock curfew.

Once the billeting of the players, their families, and the correspondents had been attended to and the weather, which was miserable in the beginning, had settled down, the training proceeded in orderly fashion and the outlook for the impending season was bright. Bill Terry, who not only had had a good season in Toledo but had wound up managing the club, was back to stay. Kelly still was a fixture at first base, but McGraw was looking ahead to a time . . .

"Why don't you try me in the outfield?" Terry asked him one day.

"And have you get hit on the head?" McGraw countered. "Just hold still. You're going to be a big league first baseman some day."

"I played the outfield in Shreveport," Terry said.

"This isn't Shreveport," McGraw said.

Oeschger had been added to the pitching staff, Southworth to the outfield crew, and there were in the camp three rookies of extraordinary promise. One was Perce (Pat) Malone, a pitcher purchased from Altoona; the second was Lewis (Hack) Wilson, an outfielder from Portsmouth; the third was Freddy Lindstrom, an infielder from Toledo. McGraw released Malone outright to Toledo at the end of the training season because, while Pat had plenty of stuff, his mind seemed to be more on fun after dark than anything else. But Pat would haunt him, in a manner of speaking, for he came up with the Cubs later and helped to beat the Giants out of the pennant in 1929. McGraw would keep Wilson, get good use out of him, and then lose him. But he was to have Lindstrom for as long as he was manager of the Giants, and, in that very first year Lindstrom would prove that, although he was but eighteen years old, he already was a man.

The club broke on top, faltered after a while, and wavered under a stern challenge by the Robins who, early in September, made a menacing run at them. Wilson and Southworth were spelling each other in center field. Sometimes, against certain pitchers, McGraw put Kelly out there and sent Terry to first base. Groh had developed a bad knee and was out of action frequently. When he was out, Lindstrom played third base. McGraw, having grown tired of arguing with Earl Smith ("A ⸺ ⸺ anarchist!" McGraw said time and again) had sent him to Boston and brought back Hank Gowdy, whom he had sent to the Braves away back in 1911 and now Hank was helping Snyder with the catching.

Through the trying days and into the ultimate time of victory, there were seven men who carried the club: Nehf, Ryan, and Bentley in the box; Snyder back of the plate; Frisch at second base; Youngs in right field; and Kelly, whether at first base or in the outfield.

But before the victory could be achieved, there was the numbing, inexplicable thing that has been filed away, but

150

not forgotten, bearing the label, "The Dolan-O'Connell Case."

Alvin James (Cozy) Dolan was a Giant coach and McGraw's bodyguard. He was from Oshkosh, Wisconsin, and, as a third baseman, had been with the Reds, the Yankees, the Phillies, the Pirates, and the Cardinals. He was a big man, with heavy shoulders, gray hair, a broad face, a broken nose, and twinkling eyes that were very blue. At the time of the trouble, he was forty-two years old.

Three years before he had appeared in the Giants' camp at San Antonio and asked McGraw for a job. Later he was to say, "I meant nothing to Mac but I was so hard up I was desperate. He staked me and put me to work. Do you think there is anything I wouldn't do for John McGraw? I'd kill a man for him."

Nearly everybody liked him, but the ball players did not. They suspected that, in his devotion to McGraw, he was not above spying on them and carrying tales to the manager. One morning at the Polo Grounds, Earl Smith accused him of being a stool pigeon and gave him a terrible beating as the other players looked on in silence.

Now it was late September of 1924, and the Phillies moved into the Polo Grounds for a series that opened on a Saturday. Arthur Fletcher had become manager of the Phils and, late that night his shortstop, "Heinie" Sand, reported to him that, before the game, Jimmy O'Connell had tried to bribe him, promising him $500 if he "would not bear down" against the Giants, hard-pressed by the Dodgers. Early the next morning Fletcher called John Heydler, and the league president joined him and Sand at breakfast, where Sand repeated the story he had told his manager. Heydler immediately put through a call to Landis in Chicago, and Landis arrived in New York on Monday morning. His presence there was unknown save to Heydler, Fletcher, and Sand.

Once more the player repeated to the commissioner the story he had told first to Fletcher, then to Heydler.

"Jimmy O'Connell came to me before the game. He asked me, 'How do you fellows feel about us?'

" 'What do you mean?' I asked him. And he said, 'About us winning the pennant. Who would you rather see win—us or the Robins?'

" 'I told him we didn't care who won. It was all the same to us.' And then he said, 'Well, if you don't bear down too hard against us this afternoon, it will be worth $500 to us.'

"I said, 'You ought to be ashamed of yourself to say anything like that to me. What's the matter with you? Are you crazy? Get away from me and don't ever say anything like that to me or to anybody else.' "

Landis asked, "Did any of the other Giant players speak to you?"

"No."

"Were any of the other Philadelphia players approached, so far as you know?"

"No."

"Have you any idea why O'Connell should have picked you—as he apparently did—as the only Philadelphia player he might safely approach with a proposition such as this?"

"No."

"Is he a friend of yours?"

"Not particularly. I've known him for quite a while. I was in the Coast League with him. I've always liked him."

152

Landis next summoned Stoneham and McGraw. Their first reaction was one of resentment against Heydler for not having notified them of Sand's charges against one of their ball players before calling Landis in. Neither ever forgave Heydler for that.

McGraw said to Landis, "How do you know Sand isn't lying?"

"I don't know," Landis said, "but I propose to find out. I want to talk to O'Connell... alone, by the way, gentlemen."

The appearance of O'Connell before him and the story he told shocked and saddened Landis. In straightforward manner Jimmy confirmed what Sand had said. He had offered Heinie $500 not to bear down. He didn't have the money and he had no idea where it was coming from. He added, "Cozy Dolan told me to do it."

"Did any of the other Giants know of this?" Landis asked.

"Well," O'Connell said, "nobody said anything to me before, but when I was at the batting cage later, Kelly asked me what Sand had said and I told him. Frisch and Youngs spoke to me, too."

"And what did they say?"

"They talked as if they knew all about it."

Landis asked, "Do you understand that, as a result of what you are saying, you will be expelled from baseball?"

"Yes, sir," O'Connell said.

Landis next called in Frisch, Youngs, and Kelly. They denied they had spoken to O'Connell about his conversation with Sand and, confronted by the hapless young man, reiterated their denial. Last came Dolan. Landis read O'Connell's testimony to him and asked, "Did you tell

153

O'Connell to offer Sand $500 not to bear down against the Giants?"

"I don't remember," Dolan said.

Landis was startled.

"You don't remember!" he said.

"No, sir," Dolan said.

"This is Monday," Landis said slowly. "Do you mean to sit there and tell me you don't remember whether or not you told O'Connell to offer a bribe to Sand on Saturday— two days ago?"

"Yes, sir," Dolan said.

" 'Yes, sir' what?" Landis roared.

"I don't remember," Dolan said.

Landis, a veteran of years on the bench and accustomed to handling recalcitrant witnesses, couldn't break him down.

"I don't remember," Dolan kept saying. Or, "I don't recall."

So well guarded had the inquiry been that not until Landis announced his findings did the newspapers and the general public learn of it. Dolan and O'Connell had been banished from baseball for life. Frisch, Youngs, and Kelly had been cleared of any knowledge of the plot, and Sand commended for reporting the attempt to bribe him.

The story rolled and echoed across the country. Ban Johnson from his office in Chicago demanded that the world series, the Giants having won the pennant in the National League and the Washington Senators in the American, be called off. Why? Because he hated both McGraw and Landis, McGraw from the Baltimore days and Landis from the time he was brought in to supersede the National Commission, of which Ban had been the most influential member. Because, with the betrayal of baseball by the White Sox only five years before still fresh in his mind, he honestly was fearful for the future of the game, to which he had devoted his life.

Meanwhile, there were others who were asking questions. What was this all about? If Dolan had told O'Connell to offer a $500 bribe to Sand, whose idea was it? And whose $500? Dolan's? Why was O'Connell, a decent kid, so eager to do Dolan's bidding? Why, if anybody was going to try to put the fix on a ball club, would he select only the shortstop? Why not the pitcher, the catcher, the first baseman? Why did O'Connell say that Frisch, Youngs, and Kelly had spoken to him after he had spoken to Sand? Frisch? Youngs? Kelly? They were three of the key men on the ball club. They had denied having spoken to O'Connell and Landis had believed them. Landis had believed everything else O'Connell had said. Who had put the names of Frisch, Youngs, and Kelly in his head? Why?

And Dolan. Dolan had played dumb. Must have played dumb.

"I don't remember," he had said.

Remember? How could he forget? As Landis had said, it was only two days before. Dolan was McGraw's man. Hadn't he said he would kill a man for McGraw? Couldn't McGraw...? Even McGraw's enemies, who were practically legion, laughed at that. They didn't like McGraw, but he was honest. He would fight you and revile and beat you if he could. But always honestly.

There was one who came up with a theory.

"Suppose," he said, "somebody went to Dolan and said, 'Listen, Cozy. There is somebody I know...and somebody you know...who wants...'

"And suppose Cozy thought . . ."

Suppose . . . suppose . . . suppose. There is no answer to any of it. There wasn't then; there isn't now. All that is known is this: Dolan tried to see McGraw and McGraw angrily refused to see him. A few months later William J. Fallon, one of the great criminal lawyers, announced that he was planning to bring suit in Cozy's behalf against Landis to force the reinstatement of Dolan in baseball. Dolan was broke. Fallon's fees were high. A reporter asked Fallon who had sent Dolan to him. Fallon, who was one of McGraw's closest friends, said, "John McGraw."

"Why?" the reporter asked.

"Well, Fallon said, Dolan was a clown and a slob. But he had been faithful to McGraw and he is in trouble, and McGraw wants to help him . . . and so . . ."

"So what?"

"So nothing, I'm afraid," Fallon said. "I've had long talks with Dolan. He thinks Landis is going to reinstate him anyway, although you and I know he is not. After pleading with me to help him, he has become afraid that if he brings suit against Landis, he never will get back into baseball."

On that note, O'Connell having accepted his fate with resignation and gone home to California, the matter ended.

Meanwhile, there was the world series. All over the country, the Senators were the sentimental favorites. They never had won a pennant before; they were led by Stanley Harris, the "Boy Manager"; and, for the first time, Walter Johnson appeared in a world series. The teams opened in Washington, with Nehf pitching against Johnson. That night, Nehf said, "Walter was so nervous before the game

156

I felt sorry for him. He knew that millions of people were pulling for him. When we shook hands for the photographers, his hand trembled."

The game went twelve innings, Nehf winning, 4 to 3. But at the end of six games, the series was tied. It ended in dramatic fashion in the twelfth inning of the seventh game, played in Washington. Both managers had shuffled their pitchers through the game. At the finish, Bentley was opposed by Johnson, twice beaten in the series.

Miller, the Senators' third baseman, led off in the twelfth and was thrown out by Frisch. Muddy Ruel, who had made only one hit in the series, seemed an easy out on a pop foul between third base and the plate, but Gowdy, starting for the ball, threw his mask directly in front of him, stepped in the mask, stumbled, got free of it, stepped in it again, and lost the ball. Ruel then doubled to left. Jackson fumbled Johnson's grounder; McNeely grounded toward third base—and as Lindstrom reached for the ball, it struck a stone and bounded over his head, Ruel scoring with the winning run.

The hero of the series, from a Giant standpoint, was Lindstrom. Groh was unable to play because of his flapping knee joint, and Freddy, at an age when most boys are just getting out of high school, met the exacting test superbly hitting .333 and making four hits off the great Johnson in one game.

Two days later, following another of McGraw's win-or-lose post-series parties, the Giants and the White Sox sailed for a tour of Europe. Casually planned, it was as casually conducted. They had bad weather; they reached Dublin a month sooner than they had been advertised to appear, and they attracted virtually no attention anywhere save London. There they played at Stamford Bridge before King George V and the late king, then the Duke of York; Frank Kellogg, American ambassador to the Court of St. James's; and George Bernard Shaw, whose description of the game in a London newspaper baffled the players.

21

New Heroes for Old

◎ AT Plant City, Florida, in the spring of 1925, a husky
young man named Fred Fitzsimmons, pitching for the
Indianapolis club, had the Giants throwing their bats
away in an exhibition game. He had pitched all winter in
Cuba and was well ahead of the hitters, who had been in
training for only a couple of weeks, but he obviously was
a first-rate prospect. McGraw, becoming interested in him
that day, bought him in midseason. The second guessers
said that if he had bought him sooner, the Giants might
have won the pennant. It is doubtful. They had run at
high speed for four years and there was bound to be a
letdown. They were in the lead part of the way, and in
the race all the way, not going down before the rush of
the Pirates until late September.

Shortly after the return of the club to the Polo Grounds
from its first western trip McGraw fell ill. For the first time
since he assumed command of the Giants in 1903, it was
rumored that he would not be seen in the dugout again.
He had been absent for two weeks, and the rumor, printed
in at least one newspaper, was that the state of his health
would cause him to retire. But he came back snorting the
day the story appeared.

159

"Resign? What would I do? Play the horses?" he demanded.

By way of demonstrating that he was feeling better, although it wasn't planned that way, he had another of his historic rows with Bill Klem that afternoon. This one took place at the door of the umpires' dressing room under the grandstand, where McGraw had gone to upbraid Klem for having called the game at the end of the third inning because, in his judgment, a flash storm had made the field unfit for further play. As the Giants were leading, 4 to 0, McGraw naturally wanted the game continued and protested that Klem was exceeding his authority by calling a halt just because of a little rain like that.

"I'll find out from Heydler if his umpires are going to be allowed to ruin baseball!" he yelled. "I'll take care of you, you —— —— dummy!"

But all he could get from Klem was, "You'll see Mr. Heydler! I'll see him! I'll see that you never come to this room again! I'll stop you, or you'll stop me!"

That was Bill's current refrain. Of course, neither ever stopped the other.

It was near the end of the season that Melvin Thomas Ott first walked through the players' gate at the Polo Grounds. He was sixteen years old and was not only nervous at the thought of approaching McGraw but had just had the terrifying experience of riding up from Thirty-fourth Street on a Sixth Avenue elevated train, which he had expected to topple from the structure at every turn of the wheels.

McGraw had been expecting him. He had heard about

him from a friend, Harry Williams, Louisiana lumber baron. Mel had caught for the high school team in his home town, Gretna, and, having quit school in June to seek fame and fortune as a ball player, had received a brief trial with the New Orleans club but had been turned away with the advice that he grow up before trying again. Some one had sent him to Williams, who had a team of his own on his plantation and, having watched him for a few weeks, Williams had written to his friend, McGraw, about him.

"He isn't a major league ball player yet," Williams said in his letter. "But I am convinced he will be some day. This I know, he can hit."

McGraw not only agreed with him about Mel's hitting when he saw the boy hammering the ball into the right field stand at batting practice the next morning but realized that here was one who, some day, might be a great player. Where? Back of the bat? Not necessarily. In the infield, the outfield? He'd find out. He'd keep him right where he could see him all the time too.

The following spring, at Sarasota, Casey Stengel, newly appointed manager of the Toledo club, in which the Giants held a controlling interest, said, "Let me have that boy for this season, will you, Mac?"

"No," McGraw said. "No minor league manager is going to have a chance to ruin him. And that goes for you too."

The team that, with few changes, had won four pennants and two world series, then had dropped back to second place, was wearing out. Frank Frisch ... Travis Jackson ... Freddy Lindstrom ... Bill Terry. They were all right, of course. But some of the older players ...

Arthur Nehf was worried at Sarasota in 1926. A control

pitcher, he always could sweep the plate or its corners with his curve, or fire his fast ball through the middle if that was the thing to do. Now, after he had been at work for a week, he couldn't make the ball behave. There was a curious numbness in the thumb and two first fingers of his hand, a curious pressure on his feet.

"As though somebody else was standing on them too," he said with a wry smile.

Without saying anything to anybody, he consulted a doctor.

"Neuritis," the doctor said.

"Will I be able to pitch?"

The doctor shrugged.

"I don't know," he said. "I am not a sportsman."

After the workout that day, Nehf said to McGraw, "I'm afraid I have some bad news for you—bad for you and worse for me."

"Why, what's the matter, Art?" McGraw asked, suddenly alarmed.

"I can't pitch. I have neuritis."

McGraw seemed relieved.

"Oh!" he said, "that's nothing. Lots of ball players have had neuritis but that didn't stop them from playing ball. Take it easy. Go see a doctor. Start treatment here. Stay in the sun as much as you can."

Nehf shook his head.

"You'll be all right," McGraw said.

He didn't know what to think. Art was a worrier sometimes and inclined to exaggerate any minor ill that afflicted him. Still, this thing really seemed to have him down. Suppose he couldn't pitch? It would be rough on him, and as rough on the Giants. Nehf had been their stand-up, stickout pitcher since he joined them in 1919. Well, you never could tell.

McGraw was more concerned about Youngs. In 1925, for the first time since he had been with the Giants, Ross had failed to hit .300 or better, his average having fallen to .264 from .355, his highest, in 1924. He said he had been ill much of the time following his return from Europe the winter before. Now, this spring, he didn't look well and he was sluggish.

"I guess I'm getting old," he said, laughing. "It takes me more time to get in shape."

McGraw sent him to the doctor who now was treating Nehf. The doctor said to McGraw, "Youngs is not a well man."

His voice was grave.

"It sounds serious," McGraw said.

"It could be," the doctor said. "When he gets to New York I want him to put himself in the care of a physician. If he plays this year . . ."

Well, there it was. Youngs was sick. It was Bright's disease. There was a chance it might be checked. Diet. Constant attention. He could play, but not every day. McGraw was greatly upset. Only Matty had held a place in his affections such as Youngs held now—and Youngs alone. In October of 1925, Matty had died at Saranac.

When the Giants reached New York, McGraw engaged a male nurse to be with Youngs constantly, at home and on the road.

"I used to laugh at Phil Douglas and his keeper," Youngs said. "Now I've got one."

You might say the Giants never got off that year. Less than a month had passed before McGraw knew that unless he gave them a rude shaking up, they'd never get anywhere. He asked for waivers on some of them. The club was in St. Louis when, on the night of May 11, he announced that Nehf had been claimed by the Reds and that both leagues having waived on Groh, Heinie had been released outright.

Nehf had started only two games and hadn't won either of them. Groh had been in twelve and his batting average was .229. McGraw, much as he disliked jettisoning them, was proving to the others that, no matter how good they had been in the past, they must deliver now or they'd soon be gone too.

There was an unfortunate repercussion in Nehf's case. Jack Hendricks, manager of the Reds, didn't know Arthur had neuritis when he claimed him. On discovering why McGraw had asked waivers on the pitcher he appealed to Heydler to cancel the transaction, but the league head refused to do so on the ground that he should have looked before he leaped. Hendricks was no more bitter about it than Nehf was. He felt that unwittingly he had been made a party to a fraud and refused to speak to McGraw when they met. The breach between them was healed six years later, however, in a rather interesting fashion, as you shall see.

The passing of Nehf and Groh did not have the effect that McGraw had hoped it would have on the other players. As they rocked along at an exasperating pace . . . third . . . fourth . . . fifth . . . fourth . . . fifth . . . he was beside himself. The chief object of his wrath was Frisch. It wasn't because Frisch was lagging. A great ball player and a fierce competitor, he was hitting well over .300 and playing his usual game at second base. But he was the captain of the team and the captain always was the one singled out by McGraw, the one on whom much of the blame was poured for sins of the others. Frisch had taken it in 1925, as the Giants had struggled futilely to stave off defeat by the Pirates. But this year he took so much he reached a point where he couldn't take any more. He made a decision one night in St. Louis on the second western trip. The next morning he got up early, packed his bag, and took a train for New York.

McGraw and the other players were unaware of this until they reached the ball park shortly after noon. Outwardly McGraw was calm at the news.

"You play second base today," he said to Kelly. "You play first, Terry."

But all the while he was wracked by the knowledge that, for the first time in his life, one of his players openly had rebelled against him. One of his favorite players too. One, somebody once had written, and he silently had agreed, who was more like him than any other player he'd ever had. He told the newspapermen he didn't know why Frisch had left the team and that any decision he might make would have to wait until he could see Frisch in New York. But they knew better. They knew, as well as if he had told them, that while Frisch might finish that season in a Giant uniform if he cared to, he would not start another.

For the first time in ten years, the Giants failed to finish in the first division. They were fifth when the last put out had been made.

In December a rumor that had been going the rounds for a week or more was confirmed. The Giants had traded Frisch and pitcher Jimmy Ring to the Cardinals for Rogers Hornsby.

Hornsby, greatest right-hand hitter the National League had known since Hans Wagner, had won the pennant as manager of the Cardinals that year and had beaten the Yankees in the world series. No other player on either St. Louis club, including George Sisler of the Browns, ever had been as popular. But when, following his spectacular triumphs in the season just passed, Sam Breadon, who owned the club, offered him but a one-year contract, he rejected it, wanting one for three years. Breadon refused to give it to him and after a period of name calling on both sides, Breadon braved the wrath of the fans—and it descended upon him ten-fold—by sending Hornsby to New York.

22

The Giants Meet Hornsby

⊖ FEW, if any, of the Giant players knew Rogers Hornsby, except by sight, until they met him at Sarasota in the spring of 1927. Does that sound strange? Well, the Cardinal players didn't know him any better—those whom he had managed through most of 1925 and through all of 1926; or those in the years before, going back to 1915, who had grown up around him.

Going as far back as 1919, there was Ferdie Schupp who, when somebody asked him what sort of fellow Hornsby was, said, "I don't know. He comes into the clubhouse and gets into his uniform and goes out and plays the ball game. When the game is over, he takes his shower and dresses and goes out and we don't see him again until the next day. Nobody knows where he goes or where he lives or what he does between ball games, because he don't talk to anybody except during a ball game, and then he don't talk much."

The only ones who knew him in the Giant camp that spring were the newspapermen. Even they saw little of him, save on the field, during the first couple of weeks, for his wife and small son were with him. When Mrs. Hornsby and the boy left for their home in St. Louis, however, they were his companions after dark. He didn't smoke or drink but he would sit around with them until eleven o'clock. Most of them had known him for a long time and liked him.

His status in the camp was not an ordinary one, although that bothered him not at all. Only the year before he had managed the world champions. Now he was just another ball player, playing for McGraw. Yet McGraw had appointed him captain of the team and when McGraw was away from the camp as, for the first time, he was frequently because he had become involved in a real estate deal that apparently needed a lot of explaining, Rog was in command of the squad. He took seriously the authority delegated to him by McGraw. Just as he did without question all that McGraw demanded of him, so he expected the other players to do without question all that he ordered in McGraw's absence. This led to resentment on the part of some of the players, and to a blunt question one day on the part of Freddy Lindstrom.

"So you think you know more than the Old Man, do you?" Lindstrom asked, when Hornsby had told him how to make a play at third base.

"I didn't say anything about that," Hornsby said. "It just happens he wants it done one way and I want it done another, and as long as I'm in charge I'm going to have it my way."

Lindstrom didn't like that, nor did any of the others. But no one wanted to argue further with Hornsby, who was cold and hard and determined, and didn't care whether they liked it or not.

There were other new faces in the camp that spring, and some familiar ones were missing. Burleigh Grimes

168

who, as a Dodger pitcher, had battled the Giants hard and often, was with them now, and it was a comfort to have him on their side, because it meant they didn't have to hit against him any more and run the risk of having their caps turned around or their heads bashed in by fast balls if they crowded the plate. Gone were Irish Meusel, who had been sent off to Brooklyn, and George Kelly who, this spring, was training at Tampa with the Reds, so that Terry finally had inherited first base.

Eddie Roush, regained from Cincinnati after eleven years, during which he had become one of the top outfielders in either league, had not reported. He joined up later, when his salary demands were met, but there was one who would not be back, ever. From San Antonio, word was received that Youngs's condition steadily had worsened and that he now was confined to his bed.

Outspoken as always, Hornsby said one night when the team was in Tampa and had lost an exhibition game with the Red Sox that afternoon, "Our outfield stinks. They got to get Roush in there to keep those clowns from knocking their heads together under fly balls and if they don't go and get him, no matter how much they have to pay him, they're crazy. McGraw hasn't asked me for advice but if he does I'll tell him what I just told you."

A short time later, during a twelve-day stay at St. Augustine, McGraw surreptitiously left for New York. When Hornsby learned of the manager's departure, he said to one of the newspapermen, "What did he go to New York for, to tell Stoneham to sign Roush?"

"That's what we think," the newspaperman said.

"You can go bet on it," Hornsby said.

It would have been a good bet. Roush caught up with

the team on the road and got in a few days work before the season opened. His presence tightened up the outfield and the infield was well manned, but the pitching was uncertain. McGraw had tried unsuccessfully to buy Adolfo Luque from the Reds and even had given the fairly ancient Rube Marquard a trial, but the Rube couldn't make it. Now, however, as the opening of the season was almost upon him, he was concerned with another and more urgent matter.

Hornsby had not yet disposed of a considerable amount of stock in the Cardinals which he had purchased a couple of years before. As every one was aware, he could not keep it and play with the Giants and, of course, he did not want to keep it. He merely was holding still, waiting for an offer from Breadon. In fact, he had held so still that his untenable position had been generally overlooked. It was brought sharply to mind when Breadon, who had been waiting for Hornsby, weakened under the strain and asked him how much he wanted for it.

"One hundred and sixteen dollars per share," Hornsby said.

Breadon curtly reminded him that he had paid only forty-five dollars a share.

"That was before I won the pennant and the world series for you," Hornsby said. "I have had the stock appraised. It is worth $116. That's what I'll take."

Breadon swore he wouldn't pay it. Hornsby said it didn't matter to him whether Breadon bought it or not. Heydler said unless somebody bought the stock, Hornsby would not be permitted to play with the Giants. He promptly was attacked by McGraw. In a prepared statement—prepared, probably, by Leo Bondy, the club's attorney—he said:

> There is no rule in the league's constitution or by-laws to keep Hornsby from playing with the Giants. Heydler can't invent new rules. It takes a unanimous vote to change the by-laws and you can bet the Giants won't vote for any such change.
>
> The deal with St. Louis was made in good faith. We delivered two players. In return, we got Hornsby and we are going to play Hornsby. We are obliged to go through with our contract with him. This isn't a question of baseball but of property rights. The trouble is that Heydler spoke too soon.
>
> If necessary, we will go over Heydler's head to the league's board of directors. If that is done and we fail to get satisfaction there, we are prepared to go into the courts.

Behind all this huffing and puffing, McGraw was most anxious. He knew Breadon and Hornsby—how bitter were their feelings toward each other and how stubborn they could be. If one of them didn't weaken before the opening of the season, he knew, regardless of his statement aimed at Heydler, that Rog would not be permitted to play with the Giants. And the opening was less than a week away. Seeking to loosen Hornsby up, he sent Bondy to see him. It was a chilling experience for Leo, who hadn't met Hornsby before.

"While I was talking," Leo said, "he simply stared at me. I never was so uncomfortable in my life. And when I had finished, he said, 'Why don't you mind your own business?' "

Heydler, beating McGraw to the punch, referred the matter to the directors. Breadon, a member of the board, disqualified himself. The others—Garry Herrmann of Cincinnati, William F. Baker of Philadelphia, and Wilbert Robinson of Brooklyn—had an immediate solution, which immediately was knocked down by Stoneham: Let the Giants pay the difference in the price offered by Breadon and that demanded by Hornsby. Further alarmed by the directors' approach Stoneham and McGraw told Bondy to draw up an application for an injunction restraining Heydler from barring Hornsby from the Giant line-up, just in case.

The injunction never was necessary. The directors had another idea. They turned the matter over to the league as a whole, with the suggestion that, since Hornsby's presence on the Giants was important to every club in the league, each of them, save St. Louis, should contribute to the amount necessary to satisfy the player. One or two of the owners argued against it but it was accepted finally. Hornsby was at second base when the Giants opened the season at Philadelphia on April 12 and everybody was happy, especially Hornsby.

23

An Unhappy Time

IT was a wearing year for McGraw. He and Stoneham and McQuade, who had formed such a happy union back there in 1919, had been quarreling on and off for the past year or so. Now the quarrels were becoming more frequent, the things they said to one another harsher, and a fourth party had taken a hand in the game. James J. Tierney, the secretary, had become a person of tremendous influence in the club, and McGraw awoke one day to the realization that, where once Tierney had been a neutral cast among the three belligerents, he had taken his place solidly on the side of Stoneham. This not only weakened McGraw's position but caused him to writhe inwardly because, no matter how often he denied it now, he had picked Tierney for the post.

His first choice as successor to John B. Foster when John "resigned" in 1919 was Joseph D. O'Brien, who had been secretary once before and, in the interim, president of the American Association. This time O'Brien lasted two years. Then, having incurred McGraw's displeasure in some fashion, he summarily was moved out and replaced with Tierney, who had an unusual background for a baseball executive. As a young man, along about 1912, he arrived in New York from his home in upstate Granville to take up a career as a teacher of mathematics and, going to live in Harlem, he had become acquainted with Fletcher, Murray, Herzog, and other Giant players of the time. After a while he shared an apartment with three or four of them and, on visits to the Polo Grounds, met McGraw. A few years later, he left the classroom for the Secret Service and, in 1920, was a captain commanding the Pittsburgh district when he renewed his old acquaintance with the Giant manager. They would see each other every time the Giants were in Pittsburgh and sometimes Jim would accompany the team to Pittsburgh or Cincinnati, so that he was a familiar figure to the latter-day players and the newspapermen who traveled with them when McGraw made the surprising announcement that he had been persuaded to leave the secret service to become secretary of the Giants.

Now, in 1927, there had come this break between them. Tierney never joined in the wrangling between McGraw and Stoneham, never had anything to say to even his closest friends that would reflect on McGraw. But he almost constantly was in Stoneham's company, and McGraw openly denounced him, accusing him of disloyalty and of coloring Stoneham's mind. McQuade never had liked Tierney nor had some of Stoneham's other intimates, but when they were critical of him, Stoneham would say, "Jim is the best friend I have on my ball club. I don't care whether you like it or McGraw likes it or anybody else."

The situation in the front office, the failure of the Giants to remain above fourth place for more than a few days at a time through the first half of the season, and a nagging sinus condition affected both his health and his temper, and by July he was so dispirited that when the team set out on its second western trip, he turned his command over to Hornsby and remained in New York. He was back in the dugout through the long home stand that followed, but when the team was about to make its last swing of the season through the midlands, he again put Hornsby in charge and went on a scouting trip. Hard driven by the acting manager, who was blazing at the plate, the Giants achieved second place on this trip and threatened briefly to overtake the league-leading Pirates, but they couldn't hold to the pace and, as the season dwindled, slipped back to third.

It was a relief to McGraw when the race was over. Yet another blow fell upon him soon thereafter. Ross Youngs died at San Antonio on October 22.

On the afternoon of January 10, 1928, Jim Tierney made an almost incredible announcement to the newspapermen whom he had asked to gather at the Giants' office. Rogers Hornsby had been traded to the Braves for Frank (Shanty) Hogan, a catcher, and Jimmy Welsh, an outfielder.

The reason? There wasn't any. That's what Tierney said. That's what Stoneham said too. The newspapermen wanted to know where McGraw was and learned from Tierney that he had left for Havana that morning. Picked up by correspondents en route to Cuba, McGraw said, "I have nothing to add to the statement given out in New York. Any further information will have to come from Stoneham or Tierney."

In St. Louis Hornsby said the trade was as much of a surprise to him as it was to the reporters who questioned him, and added, "I hit .361, played second base, and managed the club on two western trips. What does a fellow have to do to stay in New York?"

Back in New York, the newspapers and the fans ridiculed the attempt by Stoneham and Tierney to make it appear that this was a perfectly natural deal and that it was made without any hidden motive. It was pointed out that if it had met with McGraw's approval, the manager would not have fled the scene nor, when caught up in flight, have failed to defend it, no matter how absurd it was on the surface. And that if Hornsby knew why he had been dispatched to Boston, he would have said so. The assumption was that Stoneham was the one who had marked Hornsby for dismissal and that McGraw had not been powerful enough to compel his retention. Old rumors of friction between them were revived and there was at least a touch of plausibility to a story told by a reporter who had been with the team continuously through the past season.

"Stoneham fired Hornsby," he said. "He never liked Rog and I don't think Rog liked him, although I never heard him say anything about Stoneham, one way or another. He just ignored him. Then, one day in Pittsburgh, Rog called him a ——, right in the lobby of the Schenley. I heard him. Stoneham had got excited about the club, thinking it was going to win the pennant and came out to Pittsburgh, and this day the Giants lost a close one. After the game, he was in the lobby and Hornsby came in from the ball park, and he asked Rog why he didn't use Cummings as a pinch hitter. Hornsby just looked at him and said, 'Are you trying to tell me how to run this ball club?'

"That kind of took Charlie back and he said, 'Why, no. I just thought ...'

"And before he could say any more, Hornsby said, 'I don't care what you thought, you ———. If you don't like the way I'm running the club, get somebody else to do it.'

"He walked away and the chances are that right there Charlie made up his mind Hornsby never would play another season with the Giants."

It could be that was it. Stoneham and Tierney would say nothing more. When McGraw returned from Cuba in the middle of February he went direct to Hot Springs, Arkansas, where he had ordered his battery men for preliminary training. He refused, on his arrival, to discuss the trade and the insistence of one reporter that he explain it broke up his first conference.

24

Southpaw from Beaumont

⊘ THE training base was moved from Sarasota to Augusta, Georgia, in the spring of 1928, and McGraw, having recovered from the effects of the punishment he took the year before, was in better health and better spirits than he had been in for a long time. As usual, he thought he was going to win the pennant and, as usual, there was some reason for him to think so.

True, he had lost Hornsby and, in his stead, must play Andy Cohen at second base. Cohen, a graduate of the University of Alabama, had joined the Giants in 1926 and played in a few games at shortstop or second base and had been farmed out in 1927. It would be no easy thing for him to follow the great Hornsby, of course, but he would have the help of Terry, Jackson, and Lindstrom. Roush would be in center field and Ott would take over as the regular right fielder after two years of schooling. Frank (Lefty) O'Doul had been drafted from San Francisco and would play left field—and hit, too, McGraw vowed. Welsh would understudy all three. Hogan, big and strong and a long-ball hitter, had shown promise as a catcher in Boston.

"He'll do all right if I can keep him from eating himself out of the league," McGraw said, and went about devising curbs for the young man's terrific appetite.

Grimes, who had won only twelve games in 1927 while losing thirteen, was a holdout this spring, and McGraw, greatly disappointed in him, traded him to Pittsburgh for Vic Aldridge, also a right-hand pitcher who hadn't been able to reach terms with the Pirates. Fitzsimmons was a consistent winner and McGraw had no doubts about him, and seemed to sense, as every one else in the camp did, that Larry Benton, a right-hander obtained from Boston the year before, was headed for a rousing season.

Cohen had a great break-in at the Polo Grounds on the opening day of the season, his hitting and fielding winning the game, and was carried off the field on the shoulders of excited fans. When he continued to get two hits a day for the next two or three days, the sports editor of the *World* got excited about him too, and began to print a box on the main sports page showing how much better he was doing than Hornsby was in Boston. The box had been running for three or four days when Hornsby arrived with the Braves.

"That's a lousy trick that paper is playing on poor Cohen," he said. "I ain't hitting now but when I start I'll lose him."

And, inevitably, he did. For a while it appeared the Giants might get lost too, for they were knocked back to fifth place after a brave start. But they came on again as May lengthened into June.

June of 1928. It was the month in which the Giants acquired one of the greatest pitchers any ball club ever owned and if they didn't precisely get him by chance, chance figured largely in his transition from a discouraged castoff of the Detroit Tigers to a star at the Polo Grounds.

He was Carl Owen Hubbell, born in Carthage, Missouri, reared in Meeker, Oklahoma, and discovered—for the Giants, that is—pitching for the Beaumont club of the Texas League in Houston by a man who should have been in attendance at the Democratic national convention, to which he was a delegate from Illinois. The truant was Dick Kinsella, who saw no point in sitting through a dull afternoon session when he could be at the ball game. He hadn't planned to scout anybody but it was natural that his eye should be caught by this lean southpaw and his interest aroused when he learned this was Hubbell, for although he never had seen Carl, he knew of him.

Although he was only twenty-five, Hubbell had been up twice with the Tigers. The first time, Ty Cobb was the manager; the second time, George Moriarty. Each was convinced he would not succeed in the majors. Later, Hubbell was to say, "I had just about got around to believing them when Kinsella recommended me to Mr. McGraw. I figured they must know something when they both turned me down and it looked to me like the other managers must have figured the same way. I never expected to get up here again."

Kinsella wasn't sure the Tigers had released him outright, since Beaumont was a Detroit farm club. Once he had established that there were no strings on the pitcher, he made some discreet inquiries and learned that Cobb believed the screwball, Hubbell's big pitch, would ruin his arm, and that Moriarty, on hearing this, agreed with it. He called McGraw that night.

"I like him, Mac," he said, "but there's one thing you ought to know about. Cobb didn't keep him because he said the boy would throw his arm out with his screwball."

"That's a joke," McGraw said. "When Matty was pitching it, they called it a fadeaway and it never hurt his arm. If there isn't anything else wrong with him, I'd like to hear more about him."

"I'll follow him around for a while," Kinsella said.

Forsaking the political arena, Dick tucked himself in behind the Beaumont club and made the grand tour of the Texas League. Then he called McGraw again.

"He's got it, John," he said.

McGraw bought Hubbell for immediate delivery. Just a few days before he had got another pitcher—Joe Genewich, from the Braves, giving up Virgil Barnes, two younger pitchers, Ben Cantwell and Bill Clarkson; and Al Spohrer, a catcher for him. And, for relief purposes, had recalled Scott from the minors. Benton was having the kind of year everybody had thought he would in the spring, and Fitzsimmons was winning regularly. Only Aldridge had failed, but it seemed now that the addition of Genewich and Hubbell would take care of everything, for Genewich was one of the best pitchers in the league, and Hubbell, from the outset, proved that Cobb and Moriarty had been wrong.

The team was hitting behind good pitching and on August 19, took the league lead from the Cardinals. But three days later they went into a slump. McGraw, stunned at first by the quick switch in fortunes, now lashed them so savagely that he lacerated the nerves of some of the players. When he realized this, he pulled himself up short, even to the extent of remaining in the clubhouse when one very badly frightened pitcher was working. However, before quiet had been restored, Aldridge was in Newark.

No longer jumpy at the very sight of the manager, the

young men hammered their way forward again and, by September 27, were but half a game back of the Cardinals. Visions of a pennant were dancing in McGraw's head again. And then came the crash. That very day.

The Giants were playing a double-header with the Cubs at the Polo Grounds and, in the first game, Hubbell was pitching against Nehf who, released by Cincinnati, had been signed by Chicago. Umpiring back of the plate was McGraw's old sparring partner, Bill Klem. The Cubs were leading, 3 to 2, when the Giants went to bat in the sixth inning. Andy Reese, a young infielder, singled to center and reached third when Leslie Mann doubled to right. Lindstrom fouled out. Then came the crusher.

Hogan hit to Nehf, who threw to Beck at third base, hanging Reese up on the line. Reese feinted toward third, then whirled and started for the plate, and crashed into Gabby Hartnett, the Cubs' catcher, who had come up the line to close the trap on him. Gabby, rocked by the collision, threw his arms around Reese, and while the struggling pair were still locked, Beck tagged Reese. Klem called the runner out.

McGraw exploded. The Giants milled about Klem, furiously claiming that Hartnett had interfered with Reese. The crowd howled. Klem angrily brushed the players from him, trumpeted his defiance of McGraw, and ordered that play be resumed. McGraw promptly notified him that the Giants were playing under protest. Nehf got the side out without a score, and the Cubs went on to win.

Genewich shut the Cubs out in the second game but, in Boston, the Cardinals beat the Braves.

President Heydler heard McGraw's protest in his office the next morning and denied it. He had been at the game but said he did not base his decision entirely on his own view of the play. He said a careful study of pictures he had got from the news photographers bore out, in his mind, Hartnett's testimony that he had clutched Reese only to keep from falling and, within the meaning of the rule, had not been guilty of interference. McGraw was almost incoherent. He also had a set of the pictures and he had them framed and hung on the wall of his office as evidence of the job he said Heydler did on him.

Suddenly the fire seemed to have gone out of the Giants. They lost the next two games, the Cardinals won, and the pennant went to St. Louis. McGraw was reminded by his critics that Hornsby had led the league in batting and Grimes had won twenty-five games for the Pirates, and that if he had kept both of them the pennant would have flown at the Polo Grounds instead.

25

The Lag Continues

ⓢ ONE spring in Augusta was enough. The players complained they couldn't work up a sweat in the cool, bracing air. So, in 1929, they returned to San Antonio.

McGraw had made only one important deal between seasons. It didn't seem reasonable when he made it and it panned out badly. He sent Lefty O'Doul to Philadelphia for Fred Leach, also an outfielder. In Philadelphia they believed they had got the better of the swap and they had. O'Doul was no great shakes as an outfielder and, far from having illusions on that score, his own view of himself was reflected in a story he told. He said the owner of a midtown saloon in which he'd never been sent him a bouncing check which bore a forgery of his signature and asked him to make good on it.

"I went around to the saloon that night and asked the man if he'd ever seen me. When he said he hadn't, I proved to him that I was Lefty O'Doul. Then I said, 'When the guy who gave you this stiff said he was me, you should have taken him out in the back yard and hit him a fungo. If he caught, you would have known he was a phony.'"

But he was a winning ball player, a first-rate hitter, and a hustler. He had been only a fair pitcher with the Yankees and the Red Sox and couldn't stick with either, but his hitting made him a big leaguer. Leach, quiet, almost morose at times, and constantly homesick for his family in Jerome, Idaho, had looked good with the Phillies, but the Phillies were very bad. However, McGraw hadn't judged him that way and now he was in left field, with Roush in center, and Ott, on the first leg of his journey to greatness, in right. It was assumed that Cohen, with a full season behind him, would be an improved second baseman. Bob O'Farrell, who had succeeded Hornsby as manager in St. Louis and been demoted to the ranks after one season, had been with the Giants through most of 1928, although Hogan still was the first-string catcher. The pitching staff, built around Hubbell, Fitzsimmons, and Benton, seemed adequate. Benton, who had won twenty-five games the year before, seemed likely to win twenty, at least.

The blue print for a pennant—after all, they'd lost by only two games the year before—was there. Or so it seemed. But Leach failed to hit .300 for the first time; Cohen was hurt often and when he was in the line-up he didn't show the expected improvement; Genewich crumpled his right shoulder making a play at first base; Roush ripped his abdominal muscles in a spill in the out-field; and Benton was not the pitcher he had been. Hubbell, who pitched a no-hit game against the Pirates on May 8, won eighteen games, and Fitzsimmons won fifteen. Ott hit forty-two home runs. Ott carried the team most of the season but he could carry it only as high as third place.

McGraw was having bad luck with his trades. In Philadelphia, O'Doul hit .398 and led the league.

Individual players did well in 1930. Terry, by this time regarded as as fine a first baseman as the Giants ever had, led the league in hitting with a mark of .401. Lindstrom, ranked second only to "Pie" Traynor of the Pirates as a third baseman, hit .379. Ott hit .349 and made twenty-five home runs. Hogan and Jackson each hit .339, and Leach, .327. Hubbell and Fitzsimmons again pitched well. But the club finished third.

Benton, who had again not come close to achieving the form he held in 1928, was traded to Cincinnati in May for a player the Giants needed very badly—a real big league second baseman. Cohen and Reese both having foundered at the bag, McGraw now had Hughie Critz, small and slender but an amazing fielder. Jackson, who had been trying to play second base and shortstop at the same time, was pretty nearly tuckered out when Critz arrived. Now it could be said once more that the Giants had an infield as fine as any on the circuit.

Roush had refused to sign. His days as a Giant were done, and after he remained out of baseball for a year he was sold to the Reds. To replace him, McGraw got Wally Roettger from St. Louis in exchange for George (Showboat) Fisher, an outfielder, and Eddie Farrell, who had come to the Giants straight from the University of Pennsylvania five years before, and had been sent to Boston, and brought back in 1929.

Near the end of the season, Johnny Vergez, a third baseman, was purchased from the Oakland club of the Pacific Coast League. News of this evoked surprise. What need had the Giants for another third baseman when they had Lindstrom?

"I am going to play Lindstrom in the outfield next year," McGraw said.

That was another surprise, and Lindstrom didn't like it.

In 1931 there was some improvement, the Giants finishing second to the Cardinals. In the closest race for the batting championship in the league's history, Terry barely was beaten out by Chick Hafey of the Cardinals and barely beat out Jim Bottomley, also of the Cardinals, only seven-tenths of a point marking the difference between first place and third. Hafey hit .3489; Terry, .3486; and Bottomley, .3482.

Lindstrom was unhappy in the outfield. McGraw started him in center, then moved him to right, putting Ott in center. Lindstrom said, "I am a center fielder playing in right field when I should be on third base."

Soon he was back in center field but he was out of the line-up frequently with minor injuries, and McGraw intimated he was malingering.

As the season lengthened, McGraw's health was poor again and his nerves were rubbed raw. In July he raged at the umpires from the dugout in St. Louis until he was ordered to the clubhouse, and the following day he publicly excoriated John Heydler just inside the gates of Sportsmans Park. The reason for the outburst was that Heydler, although he had arrived in St. Louis that morning, and receiving the umpires' report of the jam the day before, had not called McGraw to ask him for his side of the story but, instead, had sent a wire to him at the park notifying him he was fined $150.

"That's a fine thing you did to me!" McGraw yelled at Heydler, as fans, on the way to their seats, stopped, open-mouthed at the spectacle of the Giants' manager's tongue lashing the president of the league. "You didn't even have the decency to call me up when you are in the same town and find out what I have to say, did you? You're still standing behind those lousy, rotten umpires of yours just as you stood behind Klem!"

"Klem?" Heydler asked. "When?"

"When? When? You know ——— ——— well when! In 1928, that's when!"

He was almost choking with rage now. He cursed the fans who had gathered about him and drove them away. He turned to Heydler again and abused him and the umpires. Heydler, pale and shaking, tried to stop him.

"Now, John," he said. "Now, John!"

"Don't you 'Now, John' me, you Dutch ———!" McGraw snarled. "You ———"

But he could go no further. His breath came with difficulty. He turned to a reporter who was with him and said, "Tell Bancroft to take the club. I'm going back to the hotel."

Heydler looked after him as he left the park.

"I'm afraid," he said, "that McGraw is a sick man."

On his return to the Hotel Chase after the game Bancroft, who had rejoined the Giants as a coach, went to McGraw's room to report. It was still daylight but the shades had been drawn and McGraw sat alone in the darkened room. He was calm now but all his strength seemed to have gone out of him.

"It scared me," Banny said, "seeing him sitting there like that."

The quarreling that had been going on in the front office was brought out in the open in December of 1931, when a suit filed by Judge McQuade against Stoneham and McGraw came to trial before Justice McCook in the Supreme Court in New York. Although it had been printed the year before that there was such a suit, no one expected to see it reach the courts, but there it was.

McQuade charged that in 1928 he had been voted out of office as treasurer by a dummy board of directors made up of Stoneham stooges and that this was a violation of the contract entered into by the three of them in 1919, by which each was bound to exert his utmost efforts to retain the two others in office as long as they owned the club. He now sought reinstatement and back salary at the rate of $10,000 a year for three years.

There were many witnesses, but the testimony of the three principals was, of course, most interesting. It gave the public at least a sketchy notion of the scenes that must have been played behind closed doors. McQuade said Stoneham had rigged his dismissal from office because he had insisted Stoneham repay loans made from the club. Stoneham stoutly denied this, and he and McGraw said they had got rid of McQuade because he was a disorderly figure in the office and around the ball park. Stoneham denied that the directors did his bidding, and two of the directors, Ross F. Robertson and Dr. Harry A. Ferguson, denied it too. There were tales spun of brawls in New York, New Orleans, and Havana, of the times McQuade threatened Stoneham and Stoneham threatened McGraw.

Isaac N. Jacobson, representing McQuade, said in summation, "The defendants have sought to make facts fit the case, not the case fit the facts. They have gathered up everything that has happened in these last nine years and blamed it all on McQuade. All of these men are of a type

189

—all greedy, all fighting men—and a rough element was in control of the club."

Arthur Garfield Hayes, counsel for the defense, countered with equal violence. He called McQuade a liar, a perjurer, and a disloyal associate.

Justice McCook rendered a split decision. He refused to restore McQuade to the office of treasurer on the ground that to do so inevitably would lead to more fighting, which conceivably would adversely affect the interests of the minority stockholders, but ordered the club to pay McQuade the $30,000 in back salary that he sought. The club took the second part of the decision to the Court of Appeals, which ruled in its favor. And so McQuade was out of the job and out of pocket too.

26

Spring in California

⊖ STONEHAM and McGraw came to grips with another determined opponent in January of 1932, when Terry returned his contract unsigned and with a demand that he be sold or traded to another club. In a letter addressed to Stoneham, and in subsequent interviews with reporters in Memphis, he charged that he was being unfairly treated in that an attempt was being made to cut his salary 40 per cent, and that he was "thoroughly disgusted."

Almost invariably, Stoneham assigned the task of lining up the players each year to McGraw but he was so aroused by Terry's belligerent attitude that he issued a sharp reply through the newspapers and press associations in New York, and since it was one of the few times he wished to be quoted on anything, it received wide circulation. It was as follows:

> In reference to Terry's statement at Memphis, it is true that he has returned his contract. It will be necessary for Terry to sign with the New York club on fair terms, or what the Giants believe to be fair terms.
>
> Terry has been treated better by the New York club as to salary than any other player who ever wore a

Giant uniform. He has made trouble about signing every year since he was a rookie. Terry received in 1931 within $1,500 of what Bottomley and Hafey received together, nothwithstanding that all three finished in a tie [*sic*] for the batting championship of the league. He received thousands more than other great National League players.

Since 1925, his first regular season with the Giants, in which he received a liberal salary, his increase has been more than 200 per cent. Further, because of holding out every spring he has been a detriment to the club.

We tried to trade him last year and no one wanted him because of the high salary he was commanding. Now he will not be traded or sold.

McGraw, who could blister a holdout when he was of a mind to do so, was strangely silent on this one, even when Terry nonchalantly brushed off Stoneham's blast. But he must have got Stoneham's consent to see what he could do with a different method, for when he went to New Orleans in early February for the minor league meetings, he asked Terry to meet him there. However the invitation was worded, Terry accepted it and within a very short time after they had met, Terry, seemingly pleased with himself and with all the world at that moment, let it be known that he had signed his contract. Did the last thousand dollars he demanded come in the form of a personal check from McGraw? That's what was said at New Orleans.

The Giants and other clubs had worn out San Antonio as a profitable training site, and McGraw, looking elsewhere, hit on Los Angeles where the Giants had trained in 1907. Although he could not know it then, for over the winter his health had improved, it was to be his last training trip. Looking back on it in the brief time left to him, he must have remembered it with a great deal of pleasure.

For him it was, among other things, a reunion with old friends. Mike Donlin, who was a character actor in the movies . . . Tilly Shafer, who owned a haberdashery patronized by film stars . . . Fred Snodgrass, a hardware merchant of distinction in his home town of Oxnard . . . Chief Meyers, apparently living the life of Riley in nearby Riverside . . . James J. Jeffries, living on a small rancho in Burbank . . . Tom Sharkey, who fought twenty tough rounds with Jeffries in San Francisco in 1898 and twenty-five at Coney Island in 1899 . . . and Tod Sloan, one of the great jockeys of all times.

Snodgrass, coming in from Oxnard one day, brought with him a young outfielder named Joe Martin for inspection, and McGraw liked him and kept him and called him "Smokey Joe" Martin after his friend, a famous and gallant chief in the New York Fire Department. And there was a day when Art Nehf walked in, and he had with him a ball player too, Hank Leiber, a big blond outfielder whom, one day, they would know at the Polo Grounds. This was the first time they had met amicably since Nehf had gone to Cincinnati and now peace was made between them. Actually, it had been a one-sided war all the way, for McGraw never was angry with Nehf and never could understand why Art felt as he did.

Nehf, who had quit baseball after the 1929 season, had entered the insurance business in Phoenix, Arizona, and within a very short time had become almost incredibly successful. As a diversion, he managed a team in the city league, and Leiber, who had played at the University of Arizona, had been his best player. Believing that with some minor league schooling he would make the majors because of his power at the plate, Art wanted McGraw to have him.

"It's curious," he said, that afternoon at the ball park, "the grip that McGraw gets on you. No one could have been nicer to me than Jack Hendricks was when I was with the Reds, nor than Joe McCarthy was when I was with the Cubs. But when I had a ball player I knew could make the big leagues, I had to give him to McGraw although I hadn't spoken to Mac for six years."

It was a spring in which McGraw, who always "went for broke"—as the Japanese-Americans in California say, meaning to shoot the works with only the main prize as the target—had every reason to believe that after a lapse of eight years the Giants would win the pennant with the team assembled in Los Angeles. Time would prove that he was right. It wouldn't be this year, and when it happened, he wouldn't be the manager. This was the team, he was sure it was. But before the year was out, he would be defeated. The team would go on.

There was a kid named Leonard Koenecke, up from Indianapolis, in left field, with Lindstrom in center, Ott in right and Joe Moore and Chick Fullis for relief. There were Terry, Critz, Jackson, and Vergez in the infield and Hogan and O'Farrell to do the catching. Hubbell, Fitzsimmons, and the veteran Adolfo Luque, whom McGraw had tried in vain to buy from the Reds five years before, were the solid three around whom the pitching staff was built. There was brawny LeRoy Parmelee but he was wild and wouldn't be ready for another year, and Hal Schumacher, who would hang on this year, as he had last, and who would be ready the next year, too.

They beat the Cubs and the Pirates and the Coast League clubs. They were so good that the writers with them claimed the pennant for them. McGraw, who had made no claims since 1906 and made none now, obviously was pleased with what he saw. And yet, one day in Oakland, there was an incident that, could any one have known it, foretold the fate of this team in 1932 and put the finger squarely on one of the two figures who was to do most to bring that fate about.

McGraw was seated in the center field bleachers, contentedly soaking up the sun as he watched the team mop up the Oaks. Mrs. McGraw, seated in a box close to the Giant dugout, wanted to know if he was going to remain for the whole game or take an early ferry across the bay to San Francisco. The obvious way to find out was to ask Lindstrom, who played closest to where McGraw sat, to ask him at the end of an inning. When she called to Lindstrom, he didn't hear and when he finally had been directed to her, she laughed and said, "Freddy! Why don't you pay attention?"

And Freddy, in mock horror, said, "Good God! Are you giving signs, too?"

Well, there it was. Yet those who heard it, while understanding, didn't realize the state of mind of one who spoke in jest. McGraw constantly, in one way or another, was throttling the initiative of his players. No matter what the situation in a game, they must watch constantly for signs. What to pitch. When to hit. Or when to take. When to move in, or out.

Now it was the opening of the season, and the Giants couldn't win. And whether it was the stunning setbacks they received or the harshness of a New York spring after the almost perfect weather in California and on the way home that was responsible, suddenly McGraw was ill again, and his illness, although it did not keep him out of the dugout, caused him to sulk or blaze in turn, to rasp at the players or to treat them with contempt, to yell at them in the clubhouse or to curse them through gritted teeth in the dugout. And the one he picked on most, as once he had picked on Frisch, was Lindstrom.

Lindstrom took it in silence for a while, as Frisch had done. Then he began to talk back and there came a day in the dugout at the Polo Grounds when McGraw's voice rose in angry criticism of a play he had made in the half inning just ended.

"That's right!" Lindstrom said. "Yell at me! I'm lousy! I don't know anything! You're the only one that knows anything!"

He laughed shrilly, almost hysterically.

"You're the only one that knows anything! The rest of us are a lot of dummies! We know it! You've told us often enough! You're the king—and the king can do no wrong!"

He walked to the cooler and got a drink of water and sat down. There was silence in the dugout. Once McGraw seemed about to say something but he didn't. He sat there, staring out at the field.

The Giants, rained out of the last game of a series in Boston, were on their way to Philadelphia, having taken an early afternoon train. McGraw got off at Stamford, having planned to spend the night at his home in Pelham, a New York suburb and a station stop between Stamford and the city. The threat of revolt rode the rails that night, and the players, having had dinner where they pleased in New York and met again at the Pennsylvania Station, were in no better mood than they had been when they left Boston. They were not plotting anything but they had reached a point where they were muttering and mumbling behind McGraw's back the things that only Lindstrom said to his face.

Now on the run from New York to Philadelphia, Lindstrom caught sight of the trainer, whom they hated.

"There's a snitch with the ball club too," he said, loudly enough to be heard the length of the car. "A copper. A lousy stool pigeon. He'll have a fine story to tell the Old Man in the morning."

What might have happened in Philadelphia, considering the mental state of McGraw on the one hand and of the players on the other, no one ever will know. What did happen was that Lindstrom suffered a fracture of a bone in his left instep during the game and was packed off to a hospital, and the impending revolt did not materialize, for he, although he had not meant to cast himself in such a role and was speaking, he thought, only for himself, he was the one the others regarded as their leader.

So they went on, and moved into the West for the first time, and the situation worsened. McGraw gave no indication that he had any intention of quitting but it was obvious that the club would have to get a new manager or a new crop of ball players.

27

End of a Reign

⊖ NOW they were back in New York and on June 3, when a scheduled double-header with the Phillies was rained out, a notice was posted on a wall in the clubhouse.

John McGraw had resigned. The new manager was Bill Terry.

Only one reporter was there to read it. Tom Meany of the *World-Telegram*. In spite of the rain, the "No Game" sign posted outside the grounds and the grudging dissolution of the small crowd that had come hoping to see a game, Tom went in, thinking to pick up a story of some kind—and happened on the biggest exclusive story in baseball since Joe Vila, a decade before, got the tip on the site for the Yankee Stadium.

McGraw's resignation, a complete surprise to the public, did not surprise those close to the rumbling, potentially explosive state of the ball club. The choice of Terry as McGraw's successor, however, was—those who thought they were on the inside would have said even that morning—unthinkable. Hadn't Terry, as recently as January, been castigated by Stoneham? Had there ever, from the day they first met, been a feeling of mutual respect on the part of McGraw and Terry? Perhaps there had been, but there was no friendlines between them.

At any rate, there was this statement from McGraw:

> For over two years, due to ill health, I have been contemplating the necessity of turning over the management of the Giants to some one else. My doctor advises me . . . and so . . . it was my desire that a man be appointed . . . who has learned baseball under me. We [Stoneham and McGraw] therefore agreed on Bill Terry who, I think, has every qualification to make a successful manager.
>
> While my illness may be but temporary, I want it fully understood that Terry will have full and complete charge of the team . . . I do not intend to retire from baseball but will continue with the Giants, not only retaining my same stock holdings but also as vice president and general adviser and counselor, in business as well as in baseball matters . . . I am turning over a good team to Terry who, I believe, will capably handle it. If at any time he wants my help . . . During my thirty years with the Giants, the fans have been completely loyal to me. I hope they will give to Terry the same loyalty and support.

Terry, that night, said that the first knowledge he had of McGraw's plan to retire and appoint him as manager had come to him the day before and that it had come to him from McGraw. And that that afternoon he had been summoned to a meeting of McGraw, Stoneham, Bondy, and Tierney in Stoneham's office over the clubhouse. That there the new deal had been sealed in hand shakes all around and a toast to the new manager.

"How do you think Mac really felt about all this?" a reporter asked.

"He acted like a man who was glad to get a great weight off his back," Terry said.

There were, of course, stories around the town. That McGraw hadn't resigned willingly. That he had been forced out by Stoneham and Tierney. Had he? There is no answer to that, even as this is written. At the time, those who had been with him in the weeks leading up to his withdrawal from the clubhouse and the dugout believed that, aware as he must have been of the unrest among the players, his first impulse was to roll the iron ball through the ranks; and his second to step down because, old beyond his years, which were fifty-nine, and in poor health, he was ill equipped to start upon an almost complete purge of the athletes. And that after considerable reflection he had decided to obey the second impulse.

It developed that only one player had known McGraw was going to resign and he was bitter when he learned that Terry, not himself, had been appointed as manager. Freddy Lindstrom told his friends the appointment had been promised to him. By whom? That he wouldn't say.

Terry's first move was to fire the trainer and replace him with his predecessor, Willie Shafer, the former lightweight boxer, and a great favorite with the players. His second was to bring Joe Moore back from Jersey City, where McGraw had sent him, and to put him in left field.

The team was in last place. With all its potentialities, it could not shake off the effects of its early plunge and the spirit of unrest that followed. At the end of the season, it was tied for sixth place with the Cardinals. After the last game, Lindstrom said to Terry, "I have nothing against you, Bill, as you know. But after the way I have been lied to, I don't want to stay with this ball club any longer—and I have no wish to be unfair with you. So please sell me or trade me before next season."

That winter Terry arranged a three-cornered deal by which Lindstrom went to Pittsburgh and Chick Fullis to Philadelphia in exchange for George Davis, Philadelphia outfielder, and Glenn Spencer, a Pirate pitcher.

28

After Nine Years

☺ THIS was the spring of 1933 and the Giants had returned to Los Angeles to train. This was the beginning of a new era for them, since for the first time in thirty years they were about to start a season under a manager other than McGraw.

William Harold Terry was thirty-four years old that spring. He was born in Atlanta, Georgia, and had virtually no childhood, for his parents separated when he was very young and he, who remained with his mother, left school to become a wage earner at the age of thirteen.

"When I was fifteen," he once said, "I was doing a man's work. I was unloading freight cars, throwing sacks of flour into trucks."

When he was fifteen he had the mind and body of a man. He was determined to make money, determined that nothing should stand in his way, and he had the strength and vitality he needed to combat the odds against him.

"I played baseball," he said, "because I could make more money doing that than I could doing anything else."

It was when he was fifteen that he first came to the notice of a major league club. A scout for the St. Louis

Browns saw him pitching for a semi-pro team in Atlanta and signed him to a contract.

"I was to go to spring training with the Browns in 1914. I got all ready for it. I even bought a Saratoga trunk, although I didn't have enough clothes to fill it. While I was waiting orders to report, I got my release instead."

So, that spring, he got a trial with the Atlanta club and showed up well enough to be signed and sent to Thomasville in the Georgia State League for schooling. In 1915 he was sent out again, this time to Newman in the Georgia-Alabama League. That fall he was sold by Atlanta to the Shreveport club of the Texas League. It was after two years in Shreveport that he quit organized baseball to go to work with the Standard Oil Company in Memphis and to pitch for the Polarines.

Now, at Los Angeles and about to begin the first season on which he could be judged as a manager, he was at the very peak of his career as a player. Big as he was, he was remarkably fast and, after years of practice and experience under fire, he was a smoothly agile first baseman. Above all, he was a hitter. His home run production was relatively small for he was a low line drive hitter, but over the ten-year span he had been with the Giants he had a composite average of .343. In 1932, he had hit .350.

He was generally popular with the other players although he had formed no hard and fast friendships. He had been rooming with Hal Schumacher, in New York and on the road, when he was appointed manager. That night, Schumacher had not returned to their hotel but had telephoned to Bill from the home of an uncle in New Jersey to tell him where he was and that he would see him at the Polo Grounds in the morning. And Bill had laughed and said, "He got right out of the clubhouse as soon as they put the notice about me up on the board. I guess he is afraid to be seen with the manager."

As manager, of course, Terry was withdrawn from the players and, away from the ball park, he was rather a lonely figure and would remain so, for he did not have friends in every town such as McGraw had, nor the companionship of the newspapermen as McGraw had had. This, however, seemed to concern him little, if at all. Even in Los Angeles, there were feuds brewing between him and some of the reporters.

At any rate, there he was in command of his first training camp and with a team that, as McGraw had said, and as he agreed, was a good team.

"We are not a sixth place club," he had said in September of 1932, "even if that is where we will finish. If we hadn't had an unfortunate start, we might have won the pennant. I am very hopeful for next year."

He had made moves to strengthen the team other than that in which he replaced the discontented Lindstrom with Davis, a first-rate outfielder who, following his graduation from New York University, had had a brief fling with the Yankees and six years of minor league training before he had been brought up by the Phillies in 1932. In a deal with the Cardinals, Terry had got Gus Mancuso, one of the league's best catchers, in return for O'Farrell, Ethan Allen, an outfielder; and pitchers Jim Mooney and Bill Walker. He had bought a young catcher, Paul Richards, from Brooklyn and he had brought Roy Parmelee back from Columbus before the end of the 1932 campaign, sure that, in spite of Roy's wildness, he was ready. From Atlanta, he bought John Collins (Blondy) Ryan, a light hitting but clever, colorful, and spirited infielder who would become a great favorite with the other players and with the fans at the Polo Grounds.

Hubbell, now acknowledged as a great pitcher, was hooked up with Fitzsimmons, Schumacher, and Parmelee, and for mopping up, there were Luque, Herman Bell, and Spencer. Critz was at second base. Ryan or Jackson would play shortstop, and Jackson or Vergez third base. Ott, the "Shetland Pony Outfielder," as Will Wedge of the *Sun* called him, had become one of the all-time great Giant right fielders and the deliverer of prodigious blows at the plate. Moore was in left field and Davis in center. Mancuso was the first-string catcher, with Richards as his stand-in.

Bar an earthquake, there was nothing startling about the stay of the squad in Los Angeles. It occurred one evening, just at the cocktail hour, and the Biltmore Hotel, in which the players were quartered, shook.

"For a moment," John Drebinger of the *Times* said, "I thought it was something in my drink."

The players rushed out of the hotel and into the park across the street. Some of them slept on the park benches all night. Almost all were for leaving town the next day, but Terry calmed their fears.

It was plain from the start that this year the Giants would achieve the destiny marked out for them the year before. They broke on top, dropped back to second the last week in April, slipped to third the last week in May, and then began to move once more in the right direction. They took the lead on June 10, and were not headed thereafter, although the Pirates challenged them strongly a couple of times.

Meanwhile, as they rushed along, Terry was overlooking no opportunity to bolster his reserves. Lefty O'Doul, by now with Brooklyn, had led the league in batting again in 1932, but an early season injury this year had taken him out of action and he hadn't recovered his stride on his return. Terry learned he could get him. This he promptly did, sending his understudy, slugging Sam Leslie, to the Dodgers for Lefty and William Watson Clark, a shopworn but still useful southpaw.

On July 2, at the Polo Grounds, the Giants won two games, each by a score of 1 to 0, from the Cardinals after an amazing show of pitching strength on both sides. The first game lasted eighteen innings, and Hubbell, going all the way, yielded only six hits, struck out twelve batters, and walked none; while Tex Carleton pitched sixteen innings for the Cardinals and, when he gave out, Jesse Haines relieved him and took the rap in the eighteenth. In the second game, Parmelee and "Dizzy" Dean, each noted for his speed, tangled. Parmelee was reached for five hits, Dean for only four.

Ryan, playing mostly at shortstop, was having a terrific season, when just before the team was to go West for the last time, he suffered an ugly spike wound in his left ankle. He remained behind for treatment and to have a special guard made to protect the still open wound, and it was nearly a week later that he was told he might rejoin the team. The week hadn't been a happy one for the Giants. The Pirates were making one of their drives and they were wavering. Before boarding the train in New York, Blondy sent a wire, addressed to the team and reading: WE CAN'T LOSE! AM ON MY WAY!

No braggart, he hadn't meant it to sound as it did. He

simply was affirming an unshaken faith in his teammates and letting them know he soon would be with them. But it got a chuckle all over the country, and Blondy took a ribbing for it in good part and it became a sort of battle cry. Sure enough, when Blondy rejoined them, they picked up and smashed on ahead.

Late in the season, Vergez was hauled off to a hospital for an emergency appendectomy, and Terry, unable to pry a utility infielder loose from another major legue club, came up with Charlie Dressen who, after six years with the Reds, had gone back to the minors in 1932, as playing manager of the Nashville club of the Southern Association.

"The owner of the Nashville club is a friend of mine," Terry explained. "The race down there is about over and he told me I could have Charlie for the balance of the season."

(Charlie, on his return to Nashville, told his players that his experience should be an encouragement to them at times when they were disposed to look upon the future bleakly.

"It's baseball for you," Charlie told them. "In the spring I am managing and playing third base in Nashville. In October, at the age of thirty-five, I am with the Giants in the world series.")

When the season was over and the pennant safely stowed away and a final accounting could be made, it was seen that four pitchers—Hubbell, Schumacher, Fitzsimmons, and Parmelee—had won seventy-one games. Hubbell had one of his greatest years. Winning twenty-three games while losing twelve, he had an earned run average of only 1.66, the lowest since Grover Cleveland Alexander's 1.55 with a dead ball in 1916. He led the league in games won, earned run average, innings pitched (309) and shutouts, (10). Over the stretch from July 13 to August 1, he set a National League record by pitching forty-six scoreless innings.

Terry was the only hitter above .300, with a mark of .322, but Ott, hitting .283, had hurled twenty-three four-base blows upon the enemy.

Curious that the Giants, getting into a world series after a lapse of nine years, again should encounter a Washington team led by another "boy manager"—in this case Joe Cronin who, that year, had succeeded Walter Johnson.

The series opened at the Polo Grounds, with Hubbell holding Washington to five hits and beating Walter Stewart, also a left-hander, 4 to 2. Ott made four hits in four times at bat, including a home run the first time up.

Schumacher was trailing, 1 to 0, in the sixth inning of the second game when the Giants suddenly fell upon the veteran, Alvin (General) Crowder, for six runs. The hit that really won the ball game was a single to center by O'Doul with the bases filled, Lefty being sent up to swing for Davis in the clutch.

The teams now moved to Washington, and President Franklin D. Roosevelt was in a box close to the Senators' dugout as Earl Whitehill, the handsome southpaw, shut the Giants out with five hits, taking a decision, 4 to 0, over Fitzsimmons.

Hubbell moved in again the following day, and won again, this time by a score of 2 to 1 in eleven innings of a real thriller. Terry's home run off Monte Weaver in the fourth put the Giants in front, and Hubbell's fumble of Kuhel's bunt in the seventh led to the tying run for the

Senators. In the eleventh, Blondy Ryan's single to center broke the tie, and when the Senators filled the bases in their half of the inning, Charlie Dressen came in handy. Cronin sent Cliff Bolton, a young catcher from Chattanooga, up as a pinch hitter. None of the Giants ever had seen him before or knew anything about him but Dressen had been looking at him all summer. Calling for time, Charlie dashed out of the dugout and said to Terry, "Make him hit it in the dirt and you got a double play. This fellow can't run as fast as I can."

Bolton slapped to Ryan, who flipped to Critz, who threw to Terry, and the game was over.

The Giants closed out the series in the fifth game, winning 4 to 3, on a home run by Ott in the tenth. Luque, who relieved Schumacher in the sixth, was in a bit of a jam in the home half of the tenth, when, with two out, Cronin singled and Schulte walked, but he struck Kuhel out on three pitched balls.

Ott had a fine series, making two home runs and leading both teams with an average of .389. Hubbell, in his first big test against the American League, had added to his fame.

Above all, Terry had justified the faith of McGraw ... or Stoneham ... or Tierney ... or whoever had chosen him ... by the manner in which he had brought the club through the season and the series. The players, rushing back to New York after the final game, were McGraw's guests at another fabulous post-series party.

209

29

Gibe That Cost a Pennant

IN February of 1934, the major league meetings were
on in New York, and one afternoon, in the lobby of the
Hotel Roosevelt, Terry was talking with some newspapermen. They asked him about his own club, about this club,
about that. Roscoe McGowen of the *Times* asked, "How
about Brooklyn, Bill?"

Brooklyn had finished sixth in 1933.

Terry, in mock wonderment at the question, countered
with, "Brooklyn? Is Brooklyn still in the league?"

It was a fateful moment in the history of the National
League but none present could know that. Everybody just
laughed, and everybody printed the question and answer.

Terry hadn't liked training in California and moved the
Giants' base to Miami Beach. The headquarters of the
squad was the Hotel Flamingo and the playing field was
but a block away. They were all back that spring, the
world champions of 1933 and, with them, some new boys
and some who had been farmed out the year before. Hank
Leiber was there and Harry Danning, a young catcher
from Los Angeles—"Harry the Horse," they were to call
him at the Polo Grounds, taking the name from a Damon

Runyon character. They were at work under the hot sun on the morning of February 25, when the news came.

John McGraw had died in the early hours of the day in the hospital at New Rochelle.

"What would I do?" McGraw had asked, years before when it was rumored that he would resign as manager of the Giants. "What would I do with myself? Play the horses?"

Well, it had amounted to that, after his resignation. He still was vice-president of the Giants, there to give counsel whenever it was asked. But it never was. There were no books, no papers, no letters on his desk in an office overlooking Bryant Park. He was the vice-president in charge of what? His memories?

When the Giants were playing at the Polo Grounds, he watched them from a window in the office on the top floor of the clubhouse in center field. When they were away, he was at Jamaica, Aqueduct, Belmont Park, Empire City. Now he was dead and, on a terrace at the Flamingo, Terry said, after the morning workout, "The day he resigned, he said to me, 'I never will come into this clubhouse again, unless you ask me to do so.'

"Well," Terry said, "there never seemed to be any reason for me to ask him. He had said I was to be the boss of the team and I was . . . and I am. Anyway, we got back from a trip last summer and I was in the office that had been his, and is mine now, and I noticed that the pictures of Matty and Ross Youngs that had hung on the wall were gone. One day I walked into his office on Forty-second Street and there were the pictures, hung over his desk.

"Kidding, I said to him, 'I see you were in my office in my absence.'

"And he said, 'No. I've never been in that office since the day you became manager. But I knew you wouldn't mind if I had these pictures brought down here.'

"And I said, 'Of course not, Mac.'

"I guess," Bill said, "he wanted to have those pictures where he always could look at them."

There was another morning at Miami Beach when Jim Tierney, coming out of the dining room, met two news-papermen going in and said, "We have just traded George Davis to St. Louis for George Watkins."

Watkins, a fair long-ball hitter, but awkward on defense, was the right fielder of the Cardinals. Davis, just as good a hitter, was an excellent fielder. The trade didn't seem to make sense.

"How," one of the newspapermen wanted to know, "did this come about?"

"You'll have to ask Bill," Jim said. "He's down at the field."

A little later, one of the newspapermen said to Terry, "Tell me about the Davis-for-Watkins trade."

"What's the matter with it?" Terry asked.

He seemed to be on the defensive.

"I didn't say there was anything the matter with it," the newspaperman said. "I just asked you to tell me about it."

Terry said, "I traded Davis for Watkins. What else do you want to know?"

"Can Watkins play center field?"

"Pancho Snyder says he can," Terry said. "He had him in Houston."

He didn't seem happy about it.

"Well?" he said.

"Nothing," the newspaperman said.

"Are you mad at me, too?" Terry asked.

"No. Why?"

"All you newspapermen," Terry said. "What have you got against me? I thought you and I were friends."

"We are. That is, as far as I know."

"Did I ever lie to you?" Terry demanded.

"No."

"Did you ever find me unfair in my dealings with you?"

"No. What the hell are you getting at?"

"How long have you known me?"

"What is this?" the newspaperman asked. "You know how long I have known you. Since the spring of 1922."

"Did you ever hear me say that I thought all newspapermen were rats?"

"No. Did you?"

"No, I didn't!" Terry said. "But that's what they're saying. I know one newspaperman who is a rat and I told him so to his face! And I'll tell it to him again! He's lied about me and faked interviews with me and . . ."

"Look. I came down here to ask you about Davis and Watkins. Since you asked me before what was the matter with the trade, I will say I don't like it. But I'm not the manager. You are. I'll say in the paper I don't like it. But I'm not mad at you. Why should I be?"

"I don't know," Terry said.

For the first time, he smiled.

"I'm not mad at you either," he said.

The time would come when the newspapermen covering the Giants would be split on their attitude toward Terry.

There would be childishness and stubbornness on the part of Terry and of those who were opposed to him, and senseless wrangles between those who were for him and those who were against him. None of this would affect the course of the team, but there it was.

As world champions in 1933, the Giants naturally were favored to top the National League again, but soon after the season opened, Parmelee's appendix had to come out; Fitzsimmons, although he pitched well, couldn't win consistently; and the infield and outfield were shot through with illness and injuries. On the other hand, Leiber and Danning came on fast, and Phil Weintraub, a seasoned minor leaguer who could play first base or the outfield, was slugging the ball. Terry would look at him and say, "I wish he was five or six years younger."

Parmelee came back at a time when he was needed badly and pitched effectively. The Giants, after a bad first western trip, began to move up. They moved into first place but they were having trouble from two sources, the Cardinals and the Dodgers.

In June, the Cardinals had been in sixth place and Dizzy Dean, always contemptuous of the American League, had said "If we was in that other league, we could win the pennant."

And Leo Durocher, the shortstop, said, "They wouldn't let us in the other league. They would say we were a lot of gashouse ball players."

Durocher, the Dean brothers, Dizzy and Paul, Pepper Martin, and their manager and knockdown timekeeper, Frank Frisch, were rolling and clawing and fighting now. Up out of the second division and into the first. The Gas

House Gang. On the Giants' heels, and now on the back of their necks. The Giants would win, it seemed. But they'd be breathless at the finish.

And then there were the Dodgers, Casey Stengel's club. Casey wasn't the manager when Terry made that crack about Brooklyn. Max Carey was the manager. But Carey was dismissed before the season began and Stengel, promoted from coach to manager, didn't think the gag was very funny. Or maybe he merely seized upon it as a goad for his sixth place and somnambulant ball club. Real or simulated, the wrath he turned on the unsuspecting Terry revived the old rivalry between the ball clubs, dormant these last ten years or more.

Over the course of the season, the Dodgers missed no opportunity to harass the Giants and the Dodger fans, none to insult and vilify Terry. And ironically, as the Cardinals and the Giants roared down to a photofinish, the Cardinals had but two games to play at home with the Reds, and the Giants two at the Polo Grounds with the Dodgers. If the Cardinals won and the Giants lost on Saturday, the Cardinals could get no worse than a tie even if they lost on Sunday and the Giants won.

Fifty thousand fans were in the Polo Grounds that Saturday afternoon and it must have seemed to Terry they were all from Brooklyn, for never before had a Giant manager been so abused by a multitude in his own ball park. Bill picked Parmelee as his pitcher. Stengel threw in Van Lingle Mungo. Mungo was the fellow who, they used to say, was going to be a great pitcher—next year. Well, he was a great pitcher this day. He beat Parmelee, 5 to 1, and the Cardinals beat the Reds.

Now, on the closing day, there remained the chance the

215

Giants could get a tie. But there was no stopping the Dodgers now. The score board showed the Cardinals were beating the Reds again, as the Giants lost, 8 to 5.

Terry sat at a round table just outside his office in the clubhouse, talking to Tierney and some of the newspapermen. Under the windows thousands of fans trooped through the gathering darkness. Bill was in uniform still. He seemed in no hurry to take it off or to do anything else. They had been talking about the game and then there was a lull and, after a moment, Tierney said, "Oh, well, it might have been worse. We've still got our health."

"Yes," Bill said. "At least they left us that."

A couple of other reporters came in.

"Sorry, Bill," they said.

"Thanks," Bill said.

Then he said, "Some of the fellows here asked me who I figured was to blame for us losing. I told them that when we won the pennant last year they gave me all the credit and now that we've lost, I want to take all the blame. I guess we all made mistakes. Maybe I made more than anybody else. The ball players just did what I told them to."

There didn't seem to be much for any one to say after that and the group broke up. Two of the newspapermen were going down the steps from the clubhouse to Eighth Avenue, and one of them said, "I don't like him as well as you do. In fact, I don't like him at all. But I'll say this for the guy. He has plenty of class and when he gets licked he talks like a man."

30

A Near Miss in '35

⊖ BEFORE the year was out, Terry completed two transactions with the Phillies. In November he turned over Blondy Ryan, Johnny Vergez, George Watkins, and a reported $50,000 for Dick Bartell, shortstop. That the Giants needed a young, hustling, hollering shortstop was recognized at the Polo Grounds. And where would the Giants have come up with another like Bartell, who was twenty-seven years old and, in seven years of National League play with the Pirates and Phillies, had been in the middle of more fist fights than any other player of his time? But in Brooklyn, his acquisition by the Giants was regarded as one more evil thrust by the despicable Terry. Wasn't Bartell the one who had spiked Joe Judge in 1933? Wasn't he the one who had spiked Linus Frey in 1934? They had a name for him in Brooklyn, "Rowdy Richard."

In December, Bill retrieved George Davis. George had been traded by the Cardinals to the Phillies. Now he was back with the Giants.

"I made a mistake last spring," Terry said. "I had to see George play with another ball club before I realized how good he was."

The one who had challenged the trade of Davis for Watkins at Miami Beach asked, "Didn't you have an inkling, almost the moment after you'd sent George away, that you had made a mistake.?

"No," Bill said. "Why do you say that?"

"Because the day the deal was made it seemed to me you were on the defensive when I asked you about it."

Bill shook his head.

"No," he said. "I thought it was all right then. Maybe I was upset about something else."

The year 1935 was one on which the Giants left few marks as they journeyed from April through September. Davis was back but O'Doul was gone, having decided to settle down in his home town, San Francisco, and manage the Seals. Bartell, the new shortstop, hit .262, got into a few fights, and could cause a Brooklyn crowd to bellow merely by sticking his head out of the dugout. Mark Koenig, once of the Yankees and later with the Tigers, the Cubs, and the Reds, was taken on as an all-purpose infielder. And he did all right, playing in 107 games at shortstop, second base, and third, and hitting .283.

Fred Fitzsimmons, the dean of the staff—he was thirty-four in July and this was ten years after McGraw first had seen him in Plant City, Florida—was very hot in the spring but was hurt in July and wound up with only eight victories to show for the season. Clydell Castleman, a young pitcher up from Nashville who looked enough like Terry to be his kid brother, also started well but finished limping. Hubbell won twenty-three games and Ott hit thirty-one home runs. Mel also played third base when, because of sickness or injuries, no one else was available. It was his own idea. One day when Terry was groping about him wildly for somebody, anybody who could play third, Mel said, "I'll play there if you want me to."

218

"If I let you," Terry said, "will you promise me you won't get hurt?"

"Promise," Mel said.

"All right, go ahead."

It was the first time but it wouldn't be the last. He would play there many a day in the next three or four years and, if he looked a little awkward, sometimes, he usually came up with the ball.

It was in 1935 when Terry began to give out as a first baseman. As early as July he was groaning. He still was the best first baseman in the league and he was hitting beyond .330, but he would say, "I wish I had a first baseman. My legs are killing me. Now its the right ankle. I didn't twist it or bump it or anything. It just hurts. I've got to get out of there as soon as possible. I'm not going to wait for the fans to yell, 'Why don't you drop dead, you bum?' I've got too much pride for that."

Since he had no replacement for himself, he stuck it out. He didn't do badly either. He hit .341.

All this while the Giants had been bustling around the top of the league, first or second much of the time, shuttling in and out of the lead with the Cardinals. As late as August, Terry thought the Cardinals were the only ones he had to beat and couldn't see the Cubs. But the Cubs fooled him, as they did every one else. They won twenty-one games in a row as the season waned and, with them, the pennant. The Cardinals were second; the Giants third.

For all that they had been very much in the race all the way and no one would have been surprised if they had won. But the Giants were not an exciting team. The only really aggressive player they had was Bartell. There were complaints in the town that they had lost their color.

31

Death Takes C. A. Stoneham

⊖ THERE would be another pennant for the Giants in 1936 but Charles A. Stoneham would not live to see it, for he died on January 7, sixteen years minus one week, from the day he bought the club and took McGraw and Judge McQuade in with him as partners. Now of the triumvirate only McQuade was left and he no longer was active in the club.

For most of his years in baseball, Stoneham was a vital and forceful figure in the councils of the game, yet so far as the public was concerned, he was but a name, even in New York. Only now and then, such as on the occasion of a season's opening or a world series, could he be persuaded to sit in his box at the Polo Grounds. His favorite vantage point was his office window in the clubhouse. Since he never appeared in the clubhouse proper, the dugout or the press loft, it was possible for a reporter to remain with the Giants all season without seeing him.

Yet he was bound closely to baseball, as much by sentiment as by the money he had invested in it. A fan in his boyhood, he was a fan to the day he died. Had he not been, he could have eased the financial difficulties, which, growing out of his tangled Wall Street affairs, all but crushed him in his later years, by selling the ball club. But that, his friends knew, he never would do, though he might have to beg or borrow to hold it.

It had been his plan, on buying the club, to leave it to his family on his death, and now his son Horace was thirty-three years old and, as soon as the necessary formalities had been concluded, would be elected to the presidency. Everybody said when that happened, Jim Tierney would be through. They were right. When it happened, Tierney resigned.

It was not that Tierney, by cleaving to the elder Stoneham, thus alienating McGraw and McQuade, had alienated Stoneham's son at the same time. Unwittingly, he had done that as long ago as the spring of 1924, which Horace spent in the camp of the Giants at Sarasota. Horace, a high-spirited youth, resented the avuncular attitude which Jim assumed toward him and formed a quick dislike for his father's friend. In the years that followed, while Horace was serving his apprenticeship around the ball club, learning to know every detail of the business he one day would take over, his aversion for Tierney mounted, and it was certain that his entrance as master of the front office would be coupled with the secretary's exit.

And so it was that Tierney, who had become an exceedingly able baseball executive, tendered his resignation and, on its prompt acceptance, walked out of the sport that, starting from scratch, he had learned so well, and retired to his home in upstate New York.

His successor was Edward T. Brannick, who literally had grown up with the Giants. As far back as the spring of

1905, when he was in short pants and living on the West Side of New York, he was hired as an office boy. A year later his duties—which had consisted of keeping the ink wells filled, and the wastebaskets empty, and pasting all he could find about the Giants in the newspapers in a big scrap book—were extended. Every noon when the Giants were at home, he reported at the Polo Grounds as errand boy for McGraw and the players and, during the game, as custodian of the ball bag. In the last capacity, he sat in the dugout next to McGraw and so, of course, became the most envied small boy in all the town.

As he grew into a pleasant, smiling, capable young man, he became in effect, the assistant secretary, and although he did not actually have that title, served as such under Joe O'Brien, John Foster, and Tierney. And, in time, of course, he became so much a part of the organization that no one could think of that organization without him. Yet until now, although he constantly was in line for promotion and although every one thought highly of him, he constantly was passed over. Now at last he was secretary of the Giants, and the baseball writers felt so good about it that they gave him a dinner and made him an honorary member of their association.

Horace, on taking office, had the support and advice—which he sometimes took and sometimes didn't—of Leo Bondy, for years his father's attorney and, since the defeat of McQuade by the board of directors in 1928, treasurer of the club. A shy young man and as great a fan as his father had been, Horace shunned the spotlight, just as his father had. He never had been conspicuous in the Polo Ground stand but now his place became his father's window in the clubhouse and his room in the office on Forty-Second Street, the last one at the end of a small tangle of corridors. Brannick's, or on occasion, Bondy's, became the voice of the Giants. Save at the spring training camps, Horace seldom was seen and even more seldom heard.

32

After a Stumbling Start

⊖ IN that first year of Horace's stewardship, the training site was Pensacola, Florida, and some changes had
been made in the team that finished third the year before
and second the year before that. Hughie Critz had, as they
say in baseball, nailed his shoes to the wall after the 1935
season and from there on would devote all his time to his
extensive cotton business at Starkville, Mississippi. Thus
a nice little man and a greatly underrated second baseman
passed. In his place, Terry had obtained Burgess Whitehead, who had won his letter and his Phi Beta Kappa
key at the University of North Carolina before breaking
into the big leagues with the Cardinals three years before.
He hadn't had much chance to play regularly in St. Louis,
with Frisch still holding down that bag, but he was a big
help to the Giants. Terry had brought Sam Leslie back
from Brooklyn and gladly moved aside to make room for
him as the regular first baseman. Bartell was at shortstop
and Jackson at third. Jackson couldn't play every day, for
his left knee creaked when the weather was cold or damp,
but there were days when he was almost as good as he was
at his best, which was very good indeed. Jimmy Ripple,
fresh from the minors, was added to the outfield corps of

Ott, Moore, Davis, and Leiber. Mancuso and Danning would do most of the catching; Hubbell, Schumacher, Fitzsimmons, and two young fellows, Harry Gumbert and Frank Gabler, most of the pitching.

The training season was uneventful; the opening of the pennant race was bright.

"Whom do you think you'll have to beat this year, Bill?" they asked Terry.

And he said, "The Cardinals."

"How about the Cubs?"

"I don't think they're that good," he said. "I think they played away over their heads in the last month or so of the season. They had to, to win twenty-one games in a row."

A cold spell that hit New York shortly after the opening of the season hit the Giants hard. Leslie was flattened by influenza and Terry had to play first base. Bartell was out for a week. So was Koenig. The infield was scrambled and games were lost that might have been won. The first western trip was rough. But, by June, the Giants, who had looked as though they might fall out of the race, were climbing. By the end of July they were in third place and still climbing. They had won eleven of their last fourteen games. Fitzsimmons was wheeling. Mancuso was the best receiver in the league. In August they rapidly were overhauling the Cardinals and the Cubs, and Hubbell was greater than he'd ever been.

Moving into September, the Giants were in the lead. They had a critical double-header with the Cardinals at the Polo Grounds on September 14. They won the first game, lost the second when Dizzy Dean, as a relief pitcher, stopped them cold as they tried desperately to come from behind in the ninth. On September 24, they clinched the pennant.

The story of the world series was the ofttold tale for the Giants, of disaster following triumph. Hubbell, pitching one of his greatest games, beat Charlie Ruffing, 6 to 1, in the opener. Hubbell had won twenty-six games during the season and lost only six. Going into the series, he had won sixteen games in a row and not the Yankees nor the cold and the damp of the Polo Grounds that day could stop him.

But in the second game Schumacher was knocked out in the third inning, and the Yankees, belaboring Al Smith, Dick Coffman, Gabler, and Gumbert, who came after him, rolled up eighteen runs while the Giants could make but two off Vernon Gomez. President Roosevelt saw this game.

Fred Fitzsimmons held the Yanks to four hits in the third game but was beaten, 2 to 1, and, in the fourth, a home run by Lou Gehrig beat Hubbell. Schumacher, making his second start, won the fifth game, taking a lot of punishment along the way but, like the game guy he was, getting off the floor, inning after inning, until he triumphed in the tenth, 5 to 4.

But the Giants had fought the Yankees off as long as they could, and in the sixth game the Yanks again won by a lopsided score of 13 to 5, as Fitzsimmons crashed.

33

Approach to a Turning Point

⊖ THAT winter the Giants bought the Jersey City club of the International League and Stoneham and Terry selected Travis Jackson to manage it. So ended the major league playing days of another storied Giant and one of the fast vanishing group of "John McGraw's boys."

To take his place, Terry got Lou Chiozza from the Phillies. Meanwhile, he wangled Johnny McCarthy, a slim, left-handed first baseman, away from the Dodgers, and now he said, "This—McCarthy, Whitehead, Bartell and Chiozza—is as good an infield as the Giants have had since I have been with them."

His appraisal provoked a mild comment in the newspapers, his critics reminding him that, not too long before, the Giants had an infield composed of fellows named Terry, Frisch, Jackson, and Lindstrom, that was pretty good too.

But this one looked all right, especially with Blondy Ryan back, this time from Cincinnati, as utility man. Ott, Moore, and Leiber were the regular outfielders, with Davis and Weintraub, also back from Cincinnati, standing by. Danning had improved to a point where there was little to choose between him and Mancuso. Terry thought he had improved the pitching staff by adding to it a young fellow named Cliff Melton. As a matter of fact, he had.

Terry, who had a loose foot where training camps were concerned and would go anywhere if the price was right, picked two for the spring of 1937. He would open in Havana in late February and, after two weeks there, would shift to Gulfport, Mississippi, playing a few exhibition games in Florida on the way. He wanted to get away from the monotony of a long spell in one spot, he said. He did too, but some of the players grumbled. They said it was a little early in the year to start living out of their suitcases.

It was when the Giants were on their way north, playing their annual series of games with the Cleveland club, that a sorry thing happened. Bob Feller was pitching to Leiber and a fast ball got away from him and hit Leiber on the head. Being strong and with great recuperative powers, Leiber was back in the line-up the next day and continued to play regularly, even when the season opened, but by now he was becoming listless and complaining of frequent and severe headaches.

For some reason, Terry scoffed at his complaints and intimated that he merely was looking for sympathy, but the seriousness of Hank's condition was revealed when he virtually collapsed in the clubhouse one day. He was removed to a hospital, where the physicians who examined him said he should not have been playing and that by so doing he had risked permanent loss of his sight and speech.

Terry, with a "How did I know?" shrug, moved Ripple into center field and got Wally Berger, a hard-hitting veteran, from the Braves. With Berger on the bench, he sent Davis to Cincinnati. Leiber did not return to the line-up until August.

Generally favored to win the pennant, the Giants gave the experts who liked them little cause for worry. Hubbell, having won sixteen games in a row the year before, opened this season by pitching a three-hit shutout against the Braves, then won seven more in a row before he was stopped by the Dodgers on May 31. With Melton, Schumacher, and Castleman swinging along with Hub, the club was in first place early in June.

Of the regular pitchers, only Fitzsimmons was lagging. On June 11, Terry called him into his office at the Polo Grounds. Fitz had been as close to him as it was possible for any player to be, and now he had some bad news for the stout-hearted pitcher who had been so much a part of the ball club for more than ten years. He had just arranged a trade with the Dodgers, Fitzsimmons for Tom Baker, a young pitcher.

Fitz was close to tears.

"Have I done anything wrong that makes you want to get rid of me?" he asked.

"No," Bill said. "No. Of course not."

"Then why are you trading me?"

"Only because I think I am helping the ball club," Bill said. "I don't like it any better than you do. I just think maybe this young fellow can win more games for us than you can. It's baseball, Fred."

Fitz walked out of the office. A little later he was back.

"Everything is all right, Bill," he said. "I was upset when you told me I was traded." Later, Fitz was to say, "It was the blackest day of my life. I'll never forget riding across the bridge in a cab that afternoon. More than once I was tempted to tell the driver to turn around and go back. What was I going to Brooklyn for? I was a Giant and for years I had hated the Dodgers and it almost made me sick to think that I had been traded to them."

Another of "McGraw's boys" had gone and would be missed by the fans, but the Giants plunged on. This year Terry was at his peak as a manager. He had won two pennants, been second once, and third once in four full seasons of command. Now he was on his way to a third pennant.

Yet he was not an altogether popular figure. It was written of him at the time by one who was friendly to him and often defended him in arguments with other writers:

> He was then (i.e. as a player) as he is now, a self-contained, self-centered young man, intent upon the achievement of his own ambitions, impatient of those who, intentionally or otherwise, might hold him back or interfere with him. He had a way of doing things that was his own way. He sought no one's advice, was unlikely to take it when it was proffered. . . . He became the best first baseman in the National League and, in time, the manager of the Giants.
>
> The independence of thought which characterized him as a ball player, and which was of tremendous help to him then, has become his principal handicap as a manager insofar as his relations with his public are concerned. His prime interest still is the winning of ball games and pennants. What any one thinks about him as he drives toward his goal doesn't matter to him in the least.

It was this attitude on Terry's part that was responsible in good measure for his troubles with the newspapermen but the situation that existed there was of relatively minor importance. More important was that the fans were beginning to gather, not from anything they read but from first hand observation at the Polo Grounds, that he cared little for them once they had paid their way in, since there never was any warmth or heartiness on his side in his occasional contacts with them, and he could be as brusque with them as he could with an unfriendly sports writer. Important, too, was the fact that Horace Stoneham had an uneasy feeling Bill was looking beyond the dugout to the front office. Horace, too, was beginning to feel the force of Terry's drive.

But none of this really seemed important in this summer of 1937. Terry was doing a masterful job, and the Giants were in first place, out of it briefly, and in again. Battling through July and into August and, late in the month, taking the lead and holding it in a great home stand. Throwing off charges by the Cubs and the Pirates. Winning the pennant in September. Terry's third pennant in five years.

Hubbell, building on his fine beginning, won twenty-two games, the fifth year in a row in which he won twenty games or more. Melton, best rookie pitcher in the league, won twenty. Schumacher weighed in with thirteen. Castleman, a bit of a problem child in the spring and never to be quite the pitcher Terry hoped he would be, won eleven. Gumpert won ten.

The most valuable player? A fellow named Ott. He hit .294 and hit thirty-one home runs. He played in 151 games. In sixty of those games, he was at third base.

In the American League the Yankees, on their way to an all-time record of four pennants and four world championships in a row, had won again. Good as the Giants were, and they had to be pretty good to win in their league, they were overmatched. The Yankees won the first three games. Hubbell, beaten in the opening game, won the fourth. In the fifth game, the Yankees applied the crusher. It was, suddenly, a dismal end to a season that, for Giant fans, had seemed so pleasant so short a time before.

It was more than that. It was the prelude to years of frustration and disappointment. Fourteen seasons would pass before the Giants would win another pennant and there would be a time when interest in the club would be at a lower ebb than it had been since the time of Andrew Freedman. A time in which, with the Yankees on one side of them and the Dodgers on the other, they would run a bad third in New York. It would be a while before this would come to pass. But the humiliating defeat by the Yankees in this world series was, as so easily could be seen in retrospect, the turning point. It was not simply that the Giants had lost the series. There wasn't another club in either the National League or the American that year that could have defeated the Yankees. Yet the outline of the Giants' immediate future was sharply etched for all those who could read to see. Among those who did not read it accurately was William Harold Terry.

So rapid was the switch in the club's fortunes that there was but slight resemblance between the pennant winners of 1937 and the team that Terry somehow managed to drive to third place in 1938. This, one critic wrote as the season drew to a close, was a cross between a minor league outfit and something Bill might have picked up on a corner lot in Queens.

Obviously, Bill found no clue to the approaching dissolution at Baton Rouge, Louisiana, where the Giants, having moved again, trained that spring, although Burgess Whitehead, one of the key men in the 1937 campaign was not there. He had been ill of a nervous disorder most of the winter and his condition as spring came on was such that his doctor said it would be well for him not to think of playing that year. So he went on the voluntary retired list and all season long Terry was trying to replace him and not succeeding.

The temporary loss of Whitehead, however, was but the beginning of the troubles that assailed the infield, called by Terry only the year before as good as any the Giants had had in his time. Bartell was injured, Chiozza had a series of minor mishaps and wasn't particularly effective when he was in action, and Ott played 113 games at third base. Terry's resourcefulness, not only in putting nine men on the field every day but finishing third, may be read in the changes he had to make.

McCarthy and Leslie split the first base assignment. At second base, at one time or another, were Chiozza; Alex Kampouris, whom he got from the Reds in exchange for Berger; Bill Cissell, claimed from the Athletics on waivers; and Mickey Haslin, up from the minors. George Myatt, another rookie, was Bartell's understudy. Myatt or Haslin played third base when Ott or Chiozza didn't. Ripple and Moore were the steadiest of the outfielders. Leiber was in and out. So was Bob Seeds, salvaged from the minors after previous service with the Indians and the Red Sox. Even Chiozza was pressed into service on the picket line.

Leiber, although restored to health and strength—he had played near the end of the 1937 season—was not in a happy frame of mind. His resentment of Terry's attitude when he was injured, and subsequently, seemed to mount every day. Moreover, he was very outspoken about it, repeatedly, and bitterly, saying, "He never came near me, all the time I was in the hospital."

Other players, sympathizing with him, no longer had a completely friendly feeling for their manager.

Meanwhile, Hubbell, although he pitched a one-hit game against the Phillies on May 28, was slipping after years of service of a caliber that had caused someone to call him "The Meal Ticket." He couldn't win, or even pitch, as often as before and he had only thirteen victories to show at the end of the season as against ten defeats. Gumbert won fifteen games, Melton fourteen, and Schumacher thirteen but no one really was moving up to take much of the load Hubbell had carried for so long.

Once more Ott was the strong man. Playing thirty-seven games in right field, in addition to his 113 at third base, he hit .313 and led the league in home runs with thirty-six. The only other .300 hitters on the club were Danning, with .306, and Moore, with .302.

In December, Terry made two moves that, he thought, would go a long way toward checking the deterioration of his team. He traded Bartell, Leiber, and Mancuso to the Cubs for Bill Jurges, shortstop; Frank Demaree, outfielder; and Ken O'Dea, catcher. He bought "Zeke" Bonura, first baseman, from Washington for $20,000 and threw in Haslin and Tom Baker, the young man he'd got in barter for Fred Fitzsimmons, and who had won exactly one game in two seasons.

That winter Hubbell underwent an operation for the removal of bone chips from his left elbow.

Back at Baton Rouge in the spring of 1939, Terry was, the newspapermen thought, overly optimistic.

"Jurges is a better shortstop than Bartell," he said. "Whitehead is back. O'Dea is younger and faster than Mancuso and will be a big help to Danning. Demaree is a good man to have between Ott and Moore."

"When Ott isn't playing third base?" one of the writers said.

"Ott won't have to play third base," Terry said. "Chiozza is bound to have a better year than he did last year and if he needs any relief, we have Tom Hafey."

Hafey, younger brother of the famed Chick, great hitter with the Cardinals and the Reds, came up that spring from the Pacific Coast League.

"And," Terry said, "while Bonura may not be a fielding wonder, he'll add a lot to our power."

Bonura, big and powerfully muscled, had been with the White Sox for four years and the Senators for one. He could hit, but he was slow and clumsy around the bag, and the Senators had no trouble getting waivers on him from the other American League clubs. He was colorful and, Terry thought, would be popular at the Polo Grounds. He was too, and that year he would be the best hitter on the team. But he wasn't the answer to what was wrong with the Giants. There was, most emphatically, the pitching situation, so grave that it was astonishing Terry failed to recognize it as such. Hubbell couldn't be sure that his arm would be sound again, following the operation, nor could any one else, yet Terry was vexed when some of the observers raised the question, although Hubbell was not. Schumacher was wearing out. And what of Melton and some of the other younger men on the staff? Only Gumbert seemed worthy of his manager's complete confidence.

The forebodings of the writers unfortunately were not empty. Chiozza suffered a broken leg after playing in only thirty games—and was followed at third base by Hafey, Kampouris, Myatt, and Ott. Demaree had a fine season and hit .304, but Bonura's ragged fielding just about offset his batting average of .321. Jurges was as good a shortstop as there was in the league, but Whitehead didn't get into a hundred games. Danning had another good year and hit .313, but the team had no help in the box save from Gumbert, who won eighteen games and lost eleven, and Hubbell, who won eleven and lost nine. Not a single other pitcher accounted for as many as ten complete games, won or lost.

The Giants were last in May, spurted up to second in late June, then fell back. For the balance of the season they were not higher than fourth or lower than sixth. At the end of the season they were fifth.

It had been a most unhappy season for Terry. His never too friendly critics were sniping at him from the press box. So, by now, were the fans from the grandstand and bleachers. He was getting more than a little tired of it all and was looking, with increasing yearning, toward the front office. His ambitions in that direction were encouraged by Leo Bondy, but Stoneham remained unimpressed by his qualifications as a general manager. He felt that if Bill had any contributions to make to the rehabilitation of the team—and now he was beginning to wonder—he could make them better from a seat in the dugout than he could from a swivel chair.

34

Lights over the Polo Grounds

⊖ THERE was much that happened in 1940 but nearly all of it was bad and the only development of permanence was the introduction of lights at the Polo Grounds. Both Stoneham and Bondy had scoffed at Larry MacPhail when he introduced night baseball in the National League, but now the need for a check on the dwindling attendance in Harlem was pressing, and if an operation by night was it, they were willing to undertake it.

Once more there was a new backdrop for the spring training. This time it was Winter Haven, Florida, and Terry, refreshed by a winter's rest, was hopeful that his troubles soon might be over. He had unloaded the powerful but inept Zeke Bonura back on Washington and the regular first baseman now was Norman (Babe) Young, a New York boy and a Fordham graduate who had been trained in the minors at Terry's direction and had been broken in gradually the year before.

There was a new second baseman, named Mickey Witek, bought from Newark (a Yankee farm club), and Whitehead was shifted to third, with Jurges, of course at short.

The player who really excited Terry that spring, however, was a young outfielder by the name of Johnny Rucker.

He was from Crabapple, Georgia, and a nephew of the practically immortal George (Napoleon) Rucker of the Dodgers. Out of the University of Georgia less than two years, he had hit .346 with the Atlanta club of the Southern Association in 1939. He was twenty-three years old, never had been out of the deep South, and, naturally, never had seen a big league ball park. But Terry's unbridled enthusiasm for him and the manner in which he smote the ball at Winter Haven, St. Petersburg, Tampa, and the other Florida towns where the Giants played, had a rather appalling repercussion. He was siezed upon by sports writers and magazine and newsreel editors as the "rookie of the year," and, as such, the subject of a ballyhoo that swept the country and, in the end, terrified him.

Young, Witek, and Rucker—they were new and fresh and eager. But there were so many who were a little old, a little worn, a little tired. Joe Moore, for instance. Joe had been at San Antonio with McGraw in the spring of 1931 and at Los Angeles with him in 1932 and, under Terry, he had become one of the best outfielders the Giants ever had. Gaunt and looking, even as a youngster, as if he were held together with strings and safety pins, he was running out of time now and he had a bad knee, too. With Rucker in center field, Demaree had been moved to left and Moore was seeing little action.

"But I'm not complaining," he said. "I need more training to get ready than I used to. When I look around at all these young fellows, it makes me feel old—and then I count the few of us that are left from McGraw's team and that"—with a wry smile—"don't help much either. There are only Terry, Hubbell, Schumacher, Ott, Danning, and me."

238

And the pitching. Again, what of that? Gumbert was the only one who looked good. Hubbell pitched a four-hit game against Cleveland, but only Terry took much comfort from the performance. Schumacher was slogging along and thinking, much of the time, as Moore was, about the old days and the thinning ranks of Giants who had been champions.

Also in the camp was Paul Dean, Dizzy's brother, and called "Daffy," although there was nothing daffy about him. The Cardinals had sent him to Columbus in 1939 and the Giants had drafted him in the fall, hoping he had something left from the days when he was almost as good a pitcher as his brother. But he had very little left indeed, and he was a lorn figure, lost-looking as he toiled on the field by day or walked the streets of the town at night.

The early weeks of the season, however, were somewhat better than most of the critics had expected, even if the Giants did lose the opening game to Boston when Gus Suhr hit a home run off Hubbell with two men on the bases in the eighth inning and Rucker failed to get a hit in four times at bat. That day Terry had said, watching Rucker at batting practice, "We may be looking today at the start of the career of one of the greatest ball players we've ever seen."

That night he said, "Johnny was over anxious today. He'll be all right when the excitement wears off. He had to spend more time with the photographers today than he did in practice."

With Rucker still faltering, the Giants moved along, winning a few, losing a few, giving off flashes of promise, however faint, every now and then. The first night game was played on May 24. The weather was threatening and the crowd was small—about 22,500—but Gumbert pitched well against the Braves and the Giants won going away. The fans who were there seemed to enjoy seeing the Polo Grounds a bowl of light, but Terry didn't. With characteristic candor when almost every one else was praising the premier, he said, "Night baseball stinks."

"It will make money for you," somebody said.

"Nevertheless," Bill said.

The first western trip was good. The pitching was better than expected, Whitehead seemed to have nailed down the third base job, Young was more than adequate at first base, and if Witek was no ball of fire at second, he could hit the ball. So far, Terry had ridden along with his hopes high. Then, on June 23, in a game with the Reds at the Polo Grounds, Jurges was hit in the head by a fast ball pitched by Bucky Walters. It was a terrible blow and Jurges had a severe concussion and was hospitalized for several days. When he was allowed to rejoin the club, he played well enough and seemed to have recovered completely but he hadn't. It would be a long time before he would shake off the effects of the injury. As the season dragged on, Jurges would be slowed down and so, for that and other reasons, would the team.

Rucker, poor fellow, couldn't recover from the strain of the first few weeks, when he was trying to justify in a hurry his picture on the covers of so many magazines and on virtually every newsreel screen in the country. When his batting average seemed locked at .188, Terry benched him, shunted Demaree back to center field, and put Moore in left. Ott wasn't hitting and complained of eye strain.

"I can't read the numbers on the score board," he said. "I see the ball coming out to me in the field but it doesn't look like a ball. It looks like a bunch of fuzz, but I don't care as long as I can judge it and catch it."

He tried wearing glasses. He said they made him nervous and soon discarded them, but he remained in the line-up.

The inevitable crash came in August and it was a sad September as the team wallowed and came to rest at long last in sixth place.

Horace Stoneham, a fan first and an owner second, was disconsolate.

"What are we going to do?" he asked.

"Junk that team and get a new one," a friend of his said. "Do what McGraw did when he first came to the Polo Grounds."

"Where are we going to get the players?" Horace demanded. "It's easy enough for you to say 'Get a new team.' But where? We have practically no trading material and every time we want to buy a player, the price on him is doubled."

His friend shrugged.

"I don't know," he said. "That's your business, not mine. Maybe you should have spent all that money last spring for ball players instead of for lights. You might have had a good team by now. And the lights don't help these guys. It only shows them up."

Horace had no answer. The club was down and drab. Even the feud with the Dodgers was gone and forgotten. The crowds were small, and listless as the ball players.

"Terry," a critic wrote, "reminds me of a fellow I knew in the South a long time ago who fancied himself as a horse trader. He had a pair of spanking bays when he started trading, and he wound up with a team of mules."

35

The Last Time Around for Terry

🙂 IT is nowhere on record that Horace had made up his mind, before the Giants went South in the spring of 1941—this time to Miami—that if he couldn't get a new team he shortly would get a new manager. But that was the way it would be. This was the last time around for Terry.

Bill had made two notable additions to his squad. He bought Joe Orengo, an infielder and product of the St. Louis farm system, from the Cardinals, and hired Charles Leo (Gabby) Hartnett, who had been fired as manager of the Cubs at the end of the 1940 race. Hartnett, one of the best catchers anybody could remember, ostensibly was engaged to coach the pitchers.

As had become the ordinary with the Giants, there were a number of recognizably grave hazards facing the manager. Gravest of these was the condition of Bill Jurges who, as a result of the blow on the head suffered in June of the year before, had had a troublesome winter and wasn't quite sure how the rigors of training would affect him.

"Take it easy," Terry told him. "Do just as much work as you feel like. When we get around to playing the games, you tell me when you want to play."

Orengo and Whitehead were not among the early arrivals. Both were holding out. More in jest than in earnest, since a natural assumption is that holdouts do not hold out much beyond the reporting date, somebody asked Terry at a press conference, "Who's going to play third base? Ott?"

Terry wasn't jesting when he said, "No. Ott can't play third base."

One of them said, "I'll agree with you he is no third baseman. But he's played hundreds of games there and I just wondered."

"No," Bill said. "He's going to stay in the outfield where he belongs. Orengo or Chiozza will play third. Whitehead will play second."

The Giants went to Havana to play three games with the Dodgers, who were based there, on a Friday, Saturday, and Sunday. The Giants lost the first two games, but Jurges was the best player on their side. Sunday morning, as he arose, he suffered a dizzy spell and fell off the bed on which he was sitting. That the Giants lost the third game went almost unnoticed in the anxiety over his sudden relapse. He was flown to the Mayo Brothers Clinic at Rochester, Minnesota, for a check up.

A few days later there was another press conference with the manager.

"I am going to try Danning in the outfield," Bill said.

"Why?"

"He's not the catching type," Bill said.

Danning had caught more than six hundred games for the Giants.

Nobody said anything.

"What I mean by that," Bill said, "is that he is not suited temperamentally to catching. I think he has the range for an outfielder. And we'll still have the benefit of his hitting."

"How does Danning feel about it?"

"You know Harry," Bill said. "I guess he was surprised when I told him what I had in mind but he said, 'I'll do anything I can to help our ball club.'"

"Who's going to do the catching?" somebody asked.

"O'Dea and Hartnett," Terry said. "I told Gabby, 'I didn't hire you as a coach. You're a catcher. I'm going to give you Gumbert and Melton to work with. I think you can help both of them.'

"Gabby was delighted. So is O'Dea. It means a great opportunity for him."

At the field that afternoon they asked Danning if he ever had played in the outfield.

"I played a few games when I was with Bridgeport," he said.

"How were you?"

"Lousy."

"But you're willing to give it a try?"

"Sure," Harry said. "Whatever Bill wants."

He was wearing a fielder's glove. It was well broken in. They asked him where he got it.

"It's Travis Jackson's," he said.

Travis was back with the Giants as a coach the year before but poor health now kept him at his home in Waldo, Arkansas.

"I gave my mitt to Willie Shafer," Harry said. "I asked him if he had a glove. He said this was Jackson's glove and he didn't think Jack would mind if I used it."

Orengo and Whitehead reported. Orengo was used at shortstop and Chiozza at second base. Whitehead, working himself into shape, wondered where he would play. So did

Terry. Terry also wondered where he was going to get another shortstop, since there was no telling when Jurges would be back. Rucker, who had improved in the confusion of the closing weeks of the race in 1940—had, indeed, got his batting average up to .296—looked good at Miami. So did Demaree and Ott, although Ott's eyes still bothered him. Morris Arnovich, an outfielder bought from the Reds, spent most of his time on the bench. Among the pitchers there was, again, considerable uncertainty. Gumbert seemed all right. Hubbell was worried about his arm. Schumacher was doggedly pegging away. Melton was so-so. Big Walter Brown was trying to make a regular place for himself after five years of striving, on and off, with this club. So was Irving (Bump) Hadley, released outright by the Yankees at the end of the 1940 season. The only department that appeared solid was the outfield.

As the ball clubs were breaking camp and heading North, the Associated Press polled the managers as to where each thought his club would finish.

"I think we'll be fourth," Terry said.

He was the only one to rate the Giants so high.

A week before the season opened, Bill announced that he had concluded his experiment with Danning as an outfielder and that he had told Harry to go back to catching.

"I suppose," Bill said, "everybody will be saying, 'I told you so.'"

"Precisely," a reporter said. "The only reason we didn't knock it from the start is that we didn't want to discourage Danning."

Right after that, Jurges returned from Mayo, bringing to Terry the assurance of the doctors who examined him

245

that his frightening spell in Havana had been brought on only because he had tried too hard and too soon to get into shape. He simply had to take it easy for a little while longer, that was all. Terry was heartened. So were the other players.

The season opened in Brooklyn and the Giants won the first game, and the two that followed. They beat the Phillies in the Polo Grounds opening. Hubbell, as a matter of custom and sentiment, was to have pitched that game but he was flattened by an attack of influenza. However, young Bob Bowman held them off nicely and Ott won the game as early as the third inning when he blasted a home run into the right field stand with the bases filled. They had won four in a row. Things were looking up. Maybe something could be done with this team after all.

In the middle of May, Terry had a chance to get Dick Bartell back. After a year with the Cubs, he had been sold to Detroit. He had had a good season there in 1940, but this year he hadn't been able to get off. The Tigers got waivers on him and released him outright. Bill called him on the telephone.

"Give me a couple of days to think it over," Bartell said. "I've never been in a spot like this before. I want to get as much as I can for signing—and you're the first club I've heard from."

"I'll give you more than anybody," Terry said.

If he hadn't completely changed his mind about Bartell, at least he reasoned Dick would be a good man to have around as an alternate for Jurges. The following day, Dick called him.

"I'm on my way," he said. "Looks like I got a better chance with you than with anybody else."

It proved to be a sound move on Terry's part. Once more in the National League, where he felt he belonged, Bartell picked up quickly. Before the season was out, he would play in more than 100 games at shortstop or third base and hit .303. Terry would say of him at the end of the season that, next to Ott, he was the most valuable man on the team.

By mid-July, although neither Danning nor Young was hitting, the Giants were in third place behind the Dodgers and the Cardinals, and Terry was in a complacent mood.

"If Danning and Young can help Ott out a little bit," he said, "we might really get some place. I guessed right about some things this spring and wrong about others. It might not be much fun if I guessed right all the time. But it looks as if I was right when I said we'd finish in the first division."

Then, candid as always, he added, "Of course, we've had a little assistance from the Reds and the Pirates."

That was true. Neither of those clubs had struck the form expected of them.

"Young Carpenter hasn't hurt us," Bill said.

Nor had he. Bob Carpenter was a pitcher. The Giants had had him in the minors for three or four years and had brought him up from Knoxville late in 1940, and he had won a couple of games for them. Now he was swinging along with the old reliables, Hubbell and Schumacher.

At that point, all seemed well. But the Giants couldn't hold to the pace and when, as August and September came on, the Reds and the Pirates began to move, the Giants had neither the skill nor the stamina to hold them off. They dropped back to fourth place, to fifth, as the Cincinnati and Pittsburgh clubs jammed past them. Then the season was over.

The Dodgers won the pennant in the National League, the Yankees in the American. New York throbbed as they met in a world series for the first time. The Giants were nobodies, lost in the rush and clatter of the crowds headed for Ebbets Field or the Stadium.

Bill Terry

Hal Schumacher

Mel Ott

36

A Surprise Appointment

⊖ IN the twilight of the season, Horace Stoneham had reached a decision. Terry no longer was the man to manage the Giants. His contract had a year to run. As a result of a conference between them, Horace tore it up, gave Bill a new one for two years at a somewhat lesser figure, and opened the front door office to him. Bill would not be the general manager, however. His assignment was to build a farm system, with the Jersey City club as its base.

So passed from the dugout and the clubhouse one of the greatest of Giants, if not one of the most popular. In nine full seasons as manager, he had won three pennants and one world series—but they had been won in the first five years mainly with the players bequeathed to him by McGraw. The last four years had been gray, for few of Bill's deals had panned out well and, in all truth, most of his luck had been bad. Each spring his hopes had been bright; each fall he had been wearied and disappointed. If he were regretful at giving up the controls, he showed no sign of it. After all, he was moving upstairs.

The new manager? There wasn't any, yet. Horace was listening to suggestions, including Terry's, considering some, hastily rejecting others.

On December 2, the minor league meetings, attended as usual by most of the major league club owners as well, were in progress in Atlanta. In Toots Shor's restaurant in New York, a rendezvous for sports writers and sports celebrities, some writers were at lunch and Toots, one of Stoneham's closest friends, was seated with them. Called to the telephone, he was excited when he returned to the table.

"Ottie is the manager of the Giants!" he said. "Horace just called me from Atlanta to tell me!"

The writers dashed for telephones. Thus was the story broken in New York that Melvin Thomas Ott, at the age of thirty-two, had succeeded to the management of a club with which he had spent half of his crowded life. Another of "McGraw's boys" would sit where he once had sat. It was almost like a royal succession.

Still very youthful in appearance, quiet and modest in demeanor, a great figure on the ball field, and yet, at the same time, the perfect player in the ranks, he had seemed almost the unlikeliest choice as manager. The news of his appointment was well received, but no one seemed to know quite what to make of it, including, it developed, Ott himself.

"Like all other ball players, I suppose, I had thought of becoming a manager some day but I had no idea it would be as soon as this," he said. "When Horace offered me the job, I actually was scared. I must have looked it, for he immediately began to calm my fears. He told me that if I wasn't qualified to manage the ball club, he wouldn't have asked me to, and before he stopped talking, darned if he hadn't convinced me. So I took it."

His selection obviously was Horace's own. Horace had,

it subsequently became known, discussed it with Bondy and Terry but had received no encouragement from them. The natural belief of the press and the public was that it had been dictated by loyalty, for there never was a more loyal club owner than this one and it appeared rather plain that in this instance he was rewarding Ott for his great years as a player with the highest prize he had to bestow.

"Either that," somebody said, "or Horace is playing the old army game: when you want to change managers, give the job to the big hitter. That's what his old man did when he picked Terry to succeed McGraw—or went along with McGraw if Terry was Mac's choice, as they said at the time."

Whatever the reason and whatever his fate might be, Ott now was in command and moving rapidly to fashion the team according to his own ideas. Under Terry in the last three years or so, the Giants had possessed little power and stressed a tenacious defense, getting a run ... two runs ... three runs ... then holding on grimly, trying to last the distance in front. But that system had failed because Terry didn't have the highly skilled players he needed. Besides, it had palled on the fans who, like fans everywhere, wanted hitting and more hitting. Mel visioned a team that would come out slugging and win or lose to the accompaniment of the rattle of singles and the roar of home runs.

Having accompanied Stoneham back to New York—and spending his first winter there, by the way—Ott made the headlines with a swift succession of deals within a week after he had settled himself behind his desk. He bought Johnny Mize, power-packed first baseman from the Cardinals for $50,000, and three players—Johnny McCarthy,

Ken O'Dea, and Bill Lohrman, a young pitcher. He brought Hank Leiber back from Chicago, giving up Bob Bowman and cash in an amount not made public. He bought Bill Werber, no slugger but an aggressive, hard-running third baseman, from Cincinnati, where he had landed after spins with the Yankees, the Red Sox, and the Athletics. He bought Willard Marshall, a young, hard-hitting outfielder, from Atlanta.

Five days after Ott's appointment, the Japs had struck at Pearl Harbor. No one knew, within the next few weeks, whether or not there would be any baseball in 1942, but the air was cleared when President Franklin D. Roosevelt wrote a letter, in answer to one from Clark Griffith, giving, in his words, the "green light" to the sport. And so, in March the Giants assembled again at Miami as the other teams opened the training season in the sun belt from one coast to the other.

There wasn't much any one, Ott included, could tell about the Giants that spring. They had picked up some hitting strength but precious little youth with it. About the only young fellows in the camp, as a matter of fact, were Carpenter, Marshall, and an infielder named Connie Ryan, bought from Atlanta along with Marshall.

Mize, of course, could hit but he had a lame shoulder. Young was there but, with Mize on first base, got very little attention from Ott. Witek could hit but he still hadn't learned to play second base very well. Ryan, a good fielder who might have been used at the bag, couldn't hit at all and, before the season was very old, would be in Jersey City. Bartell or Werber would play third base—but which? Jurges was the only infielder about whom Ott was not concerned, yet Bill was thirty-four years old.

In the outfield there would be Ott and Marshall and Leiber, or "Babe" Barna or "Buster" Maynard, Barna and Maynard having been with the club for a while the year before. Demaree was gone, having been sold to the Braves in one of the last deals Terry made. Danning still was the catcher with Ray Berres, acquired from the Braves, to lend him a hand now and then. The pitching staff consisted mainly of Hubbell, Schumacher, and Melton.

It wasn't much of a team on paper and, truthfully, it wasn't much of a team on the field either. But it would be a surprising team, sometimes, along the way through the summer, and it would finish rather surprisingly, too.

On April 14, Ott had his first opening as manager at the Polo Grounds. The band played, the crowd cheered. Then the Dodgers, taking advantage of Hubbell's amazing wildness in the first inning, climbed all over him and scored four runs. They picked up three more runs as Curt Davis held the Giants at arm's length. But there was some excitement in the seventh when the Giants rallied against Davis with two out, and the crowd roared as Mize hammered a home run into the stand. But Johnny Allen was rushed to Davis' relief and fanned Young, pinch hitter—and there was no more excitement, and no more scoring either. The fans, leaving the park, didn't feel too badly. They liked Mize and they liked Marshall and there was the promise that this would be a livelier team than any they'd had in recent years.

For insurance purposes, Ott bought Mancuso and Lohrman back from the Cardinals as the team went West for the first time and reeled through Pittsburgh, Cincinnati, Chicago, and St. Louis. The pitching was good. Schumacher lost a heart breaker, 1 to 0, in Cincinnati when

Bucky Walters shut the Giants out. Carpenter did well and so did Lohrman, but neither could get much support or much hitting to back them up.

In the crisis, Ott reacted strongly. He was firmer, quicker to make decisions. When he had to clamp down on one of his athletes, he clamped down hard. He pulled the team together, got it running smoothly and, alternately leading and driving it, put it back in the race. He, too, had been in a batting slump in May but that soon was over and he was hammering the ball again. He even was arguing with the umpires.

When some one chided him about that, because he never had had any trouble with the men in blue before, he said, "I'm not getting to be a tough guy. You know me better than that. As a player I kept my mouth shut, even when a decision hurt us, because it wasn't my business to holler. But it is now. I'm the manager. I am not trying to make decisions for the umpires but I am going to keep after them when I think they are not hustling—and are missing plays because they're not where they're supposed to be. I don't like to hear them say, as I know they are, that they are disappointed in me because I used to be a good fellow and all that. But I'm going to fight for our ball club."

Near the end of the season, Mel brought up a kid named Sid Gordon from Jersey City who would become very popular. Sid was from the Brownsville section of Brooklyn and his ambition had been to play with the Dodgers. But they had passed him over after looking at him in a try out at Ebbets Field, and the Giants had picked him up. He played a few games at third base where, in the meantime, Werber, Bartell, and Maynard had shuttled back and forth.

At the end of a drive through September, the Giants

pulled up in third place—a long way back of the Cardinals and Dodgers, who had gone head and head to the wire, but in third place, nevertheless. In his first year as manager, Ott had made a very good showing. He also had been, once more, the most valuable player on the team, playing in 152 games and hitting thirty home runs.

Mize had been the leading hitter with an average of .305, and had made twenty-six home runs. Lohrman won fourteen games and lost only five. Schumacher won twelve, and Hubbell and Melton eleven each. Ace Adams, as relief pitcher, had been called into sixty-one games and had been charged with only four defeats.

37

"Ball Players? What Ball Players?"

⊖ TRAVEL restrictions imposed on the general public in the wartime emergency impelled Judge Landis to rule that no major league club could train in the South in the spring of 1943.

"Where are you going to draw the line between the North and the South, Judge?" somebody wanted to know.

"Well," the Judge said, "let's revive the Mason-Dixon line. That will give the folks an idea of what we have in mind."

A friend of Stoneham's suggested Lakewood, New Jersey, for the Giants.

"Have you ever been to Lakewood?" Horace asked Ott.

"Once," Mel said. "We played an exhibition game there a few years ago. I don't remember why."

"I don't even remember the game," Horace said, "let alone the reason. I've been through there but I don't know much about it. I did hear that the pine trees around there keep the winter winds and the dampness out. Let's run down and take a look at it."

They looked at Lakewood, liked what they saw, and arranged to train there. One of the older inhabitants said to Stoneham, "The Giants trained here a long time ago. Back in Andy Freedman's time."

"Where did they finish?" Horace asked.

"I don't remember," the man said.

"Then I guess they didn't do very well," Horace said. "Wish us luck."

The sun at Lakewood was bright most of the time, the air crisp and dry.

"They tell me fighters have trained here for a long time," Mel said, "and they like it. If they can get in shape, our ball players should."

The one to whom he said it was tempted to ask, "Ball players? What ball players?"

In October of 1942, Babe Young was commissioned in the coast guard. In December, Hal Schumacher was commissioned in the navy. Before the year was out, Willard Marshall enlisted in the marines and Dave Koslo, a most promising young pitcher, seen briefly at the Polo Grounds after schooling in Jersey City, was inducted into the army. In January of 1943, Bob Carpenter was tapped for the army. Johnny Mize and Harry Danning showed up at Lakewood but they merely were going through the motions. Mize went from there to the navy in March, Danning from there to the army on April 6.

Left to Ott were but the remnants of a ball club: Jurges, Bartell, Sid Gordon, Barna and Maynard, Mancuso and Berres; Johnny Rucker, back from a cooling out season in Jersey City; Van Lingle Mungo, who always was going to be a great pitcher with the Dodgers "next year" but never had made it and had been brought back from the minors by the Giants late in 1942; Mickey Witek, Ace

257

Adams, the iron man in the bull pen, and The Meal Ticket, Carl Hubbell.

On the opening day at the Polo Grounds, with only the faithful fans, hardened by time and adversity, in the stands, H. M. Stevens, Inc., did a rousing business—considering the size of the crowd—in score cards. That was a day on which the customers really couldn't tell the players without a score card. It was an occasion that grimly foretold the course of the Giants that year. The season opened on April 21, a week later than usual, and it was April 27 before they were unveiled at home. The day was cold and dark and there were fitful showers from the leaden skies. There were cheers for Ott and for Ernie (Botcho) Lombardi, the catcher, whom Ott had got the day before from Boston in exchange for Connie Ryan and a young catcher by the name of Hugh Poland. Botcho, or "Schnozz," as he also was known, had spent ten years in Cincinnati and one in Boston before Mel corralled him. Even as a youth he couldn't get up speed beyond that of a gallop but he could, as they say in the trade, hit that long ball for you, and Mel was looking for hitters. The Giants beat the Braves that day and Gordon, at third base, made an excellent impression. But it is unlikely any one was encouraged enough to believe anything good could come of that team.

Chiefly remembered from that year is that it was Hubbell's last. It was not until May 13 that he pitched his first game and, although he was the winning pitcher in the box score, he did not last the route. In early June, there was the last flash of his greatness. The Giants were in the West and . . . but this is the way Ott told it back in New York a few days later.

"Hub developed what he called his slider at Lakewood.

It looked to me, when he was throwing it, like he was throwing a curve ball but it broke very quick—away from a left-hand hitter and into a right-hand hitter. But there must have been something a little different about it. He seemed to think so, anyway.

"The cold spring around here held him up. When we got to Chicago, I was going to ask him to pitch but it was cold there too. I said to him, 'Do you want to pitch in St. Louis?'

"He didn't say anything and then I said, 'Look. If it is warm in St. Louis and Cincinnati, how would you like to pitch batting practice and then pitch in Pittsburgh?'

"He said, 'I'd like it better that way.'

"So that's what he did. Before the game in Pittsburgh, he said to Lombardi, 'I haven't tried this pitch in a ball game yet but this is how it breaks, so you can look out for it. I'll throw it off the curve ball sign.'

"He worked great. He hadn't given the Pirates a hit and I think everybody in the ball park, including the Pirates —with reservations—was pulling for him. In the sixth inning I got a hit and Elbie Fletcher, the first baseman, said to me, 'If we can't win this game, I hope that old buzzard pitches a no-hitter.'

"So the next time up, what happens? Fletcher hits a home run and it is the only hit the Pirates get."

In July, the Giants claimed Joe Medwick on waivers. It was a sign of desperation. They had a chance to buy Medwick from the Cardinals before the Dodgers bought him in 1940 but had rejected him and scoffed when the Dodgers took him at an over-all cost, including other players involved, of $125,000. Now they got him for $7,500 in a time when, hard pressed, they were claiming players right and left.

By August Ott was almost completely worn down. He couldn't hit, he couldn't eat and he couldn't sleep. As he declined—and his average that year was a pitiful .234—the Giants collapsed about him, hitting the bottom of the league with a dull and sickening thud.

The hero of the Giants that year was Ace Adams, who relieved in the almost incredible number of seventy games and let but seven of them slip out of his grasp.

38

Terry Departs and Hubbell Moves Up

⊖ IN December, Bill Terry's contract expired. There was no talk of a renewal, nor was he interested in any other ball club. Where once he had visioned a career as a baseball executive, preferably in New York, other fields now were absorbing his attention. He already had been successful in real estate operations in Memphis. Now he was to expand them and to enter the automobile business as well.

Meanwhile, he had done extremely well in the development of the farm system, especially in view of the fact that he had had to contend with wartime uncertainties, a wartime economy, and a constantly dwindling supply of player material. He managed, somehow, to haul in enough players, however doubtful their qualifications as major leaguers, to tide the Giants through a troublous time, and when the war was over there would be players of genuine quality, whom he had found and trained, moving into the Polo Grounds and establishing themselves as major leaguers indeed.

Stoneham immediately appointed Hubbell as Terry's successor.

"Loyalty," every one said. "Horace is rewarding Carl as

he rewarded Ott. What does Hubbell know about running a farm system?"

Nothing, obviously. But he learned rapidly. And if loyalty alone prompted the appointment, which is arguable, then Horace, too, was rewarded. Hubbell, taking up where Terry had left off, built on the ground he had laid and evolved a far-flung but soundly organized system which, as this was written, consisted of thirteen farms, from Minneapolis in the American Association (the Jersey City franchise having been abandoned in 1950) to Pauls Valley in the Sooner League.

Had you been at Lakewood in the spring of 1944, you would have said that the Giants must finish eighth again, if for no other reason than that there was no ninth place in the league. But you, along with the experts, would have been wrong. They were destined to finish fifth.

There were, as you could have discerned at the end of the season, several reasons for this. They had a new second base combination in Georgie Hausmann and Buddy Kerr, both rookies, and practically a new pitcher in Bill Voiselle. Medwick, always a great hitter, still could lug his bat up to the plate, although he had gone so far back he could do little else, and he mauled the wartime pitching with joyous ease. And, over-all, as draft and enlistments drained the other clubs as, from the beginning, they had drained the Giants, the league was weaker than it had been the year before.

The player in the camp that year who would outlast all the others as a Giant was Buddy Kerr, the shortstop. Buddy was a New York boy, born in Astoria, just across the East River from Manhattan and a little to the north of Long Island City, and reared on the upper West Side.

He was one of the early farm hands, having gone out to Fort Smith in the Western Association in 1941, and had made his way back through Jersey City. He and little Hausmann, a kid out of St. Louis, tightened the defense. Hausmann would leave and come back and leave again, but Kerr would stay on, even after Ott had passed.

Voiselle also had come up through the farms that Terry had tilled. He had been seen briefly at the Polo Grounds in 1942 on his arrival from Oklahoma City, but had pitched for Jersey City in 1943. Gabby Hartnett was the Jersey City manager. Terry asked him, at the end of that season, "What's happened to Voiselle? I thought he was going to be a good pitcher."

"Nothing's happened to him," Gabby said. "He was the best pitcher in the league."

"But he lost twenty-one games," Terry said, "and won only ten."

"With that ball club," Gabby said, "it's a wonder he didn't lose them all. He's ready, Bill."

So he was. He won twenty-one games in 1944, lost sixteen, and had an earned run average of 3.02. He was the only Giant pitcher to turn in more than ten complete games. A big right-hander—he had been rejected by the army because he was so deaf it is doubtful that he could have heard even a top sergeant—he had a fast ball, a curve ball, and control. All he needed was ego to make him almost a great pitcher and that he did not have. But he was good in 1944.

Those were the bright spots. For the rest, although the team climbed in the standing, it was a pretty dreary season. Names, some familiar, many of them strange, appeared in the line-up, and disappeared. Phil Weintraub, on one of his numerous returns to the Polo Grounds, shared first base with Napoleon Reyes, a young Cuban. Hausmann and Kerr needed no help but Jurges, Reyes, a boy named Luby, and a fellow named Ott, took pot shots at third base. The regular outfield was made up of Ott, Medwick, and Rucker, but, among others, young men called Filipowicz, Treadway, Sloan, and Mead also had their turns.

Steve Filipowicz was no stranger to New York fans, although they had come to know him in another guise, as a football hero at Fordham. As a ball player, his inclination was to catch and, as a catcher, he had a trial with the Yankees and it was Vernon Gomez who, looking at his brawny body and curly head, said, "What a guy! He's even got muscles in his hair!"

Filipowicz caught a few games for the Giants that year but most of the catching was done by Lombardi, Mancuso, and Berres. The pitchers, aside from Voiselle, were Melton, Feldman, Johnny Allen, by then long past his best days, which were spent with the Yankees and the Indians; Andy Hansen, Ewald Pyle, Rube Fischer, Frank Seward, and Louis Polli.

Anyway, they all played baseball, some good, some bad, and, in one way or another, served a purpose.

On October 29, 1944, Leo Bondy died. Little known to the public, he had been an important figure in baseball since 1919, when he entered it with his friend and client, Charles A. Stoneham, as counsel for the club. As already noted, he subsequently succeeded Judge McQuade as treasurer. He had a grim, almost forbidding, countenance and there were not many, even in baseball, who really knew him well. But there was nothing grim about him, at least after office hours. He and Horace had not always seen eye to eye on policies and there had been some difficult times between them but their difficulties had been resolved long before Bondy died. Leo had relinquished his offices in the months of illness leading to his death and was succeeded by Edgar P. Feeley as both counsel and treasurer.

Start with Lakewood again in March, change a few names, a few figures here and there, and the Giant story of 1945 is a repeat of the story of 1944. They made a good run for the first six weeks, with Ott out in front of them, pounding the ball. But when Mel slowed down for a while, they slowed with him, dropping swiftly to fourth place. They bobbed up and down between third and fifth, hung in fourth through August and the first half of September, then settled, slowly but solidly, in the fifth slot, where they remained until it was time for them to pack up and go home.

Ott was the leading hitter with .308, and twenty-one home runs. Lombardi hit .307. Voiselle won fourteen games but lost as many and was not the pitcher he was in 1944—nor would he ever be again. Feldman won a dozen games but lost a baker's dozen. Mungo, although he failed to pitch as many as ten complete games, received credit for fourteen victories. The seemingly indestructible Adams trudged in from the bull pen sixty-five times.

Two rookies, Mike Schemer and Roy Zimmerman, got into the act at first base with Weintraub, Gardella, and Reyes, Georgie Hausmann played every game at second base, being the only man in the squad who didn't miss a day's work. Kerr, with 148 games at shortstop, was the only one who was close to him. Reyes also played third base, understudied by Jurges. Medwick, having played twenty-three games, was sold to Boston. Among the others who helped Ott patrol the outfield were Rucker, Treadway, and Filipowicz.

Two young men joined the club halfway through that year who would not be back for the 1946 season for different reasons. But they would return later and the fans would get to know them well and to like them very much. One was "Sal" Maglie, a pitcher, the other Carroll (Whitey) Lockman, an outfielder. Both were dispatched from Jersey City to see what they could do to help the parent club in distress. Maglie did all right. He won five games and, while losing four, had the low earned run average, especially for a pitcher on a team like that, of 2.36. Lockman did better. Playing thirty-two games in the outfield, he hit .341.

Maglie, who had had a drab minor league record, was twenty-eight years old in 1945 and, but for the war, probably would not have been in baseball at the time. He broke in with Buffalo in the International League in 1938, lasted there for two years, and then dropped down to the Jamestown club of the Pony League in upper New York State. In 1941, he moved up to Elmira in the Eastern League, won twenty games, and was drafted by the Giants and sent to Jersey City in 1942. That season, although he was in fifty games, he managed to win only nine and, with the war on and the minor league situation looking fairly precarious to him, he quit and went home to Niagara Falls, where he had a steady job. But under baseball law he remained the property of the Giants and in 1945, at their urging, he decided to return to Jersey City.

Lockman was only nineteen in 1945. He was from

Lowell, North Carolina, and had had only two and a half years of professional experience, with Springfield, in the Eastern League, and Jersey City, when he reported at the Polo Grounds for the first time. Another season would come and go before he would see the horseshoe stand again, for that fall he was called up by the army.

39

"Nice Guys Finish Last"

☺ THIS was the night of July 5, 1946. The Giants were playing the Dodgers at the Polo Grounds. In the Dodgers' dugout before the game, Red Barber was needling Leo Durocher about the home runs the Giants had hit the day before.

"Home runs!" Leo said. "Some home runs! Line drives and pop flies that would have been caught on a bigger field! That's what they were!"

"Why don't you admit they were real home runs?" Red asked. "Why don't you be a nice guy for a change?"

Leo had been reclining on the bench. Now he leaped to his feet.

"A nice guy!" he yelled. "A nice guy! I been around baseball for a long time and I've known a lot of nice guys."

He walked up and down the dugout, then whirled and pointed toward the Giants' dugout.

"Nice guys!" he said. "Look over there. Do you know a nicer guy than Mel Ott? Or any of the other Giants? Why, they're the nicest guys in the world! And where are they? In last place!"

He walked up and down again, beating himself on the chest.

"Nice guys! I'm not a nice guy—and I'm in first place. Nobody helped me to get there either, except the guys on this ball club and they ain't nice guys! There wasn't anybody in this league helped me to get up there. They saw me coming up and they—"

He stamped on the floor of the dugout.

"That's what they gave me!" he yelled. "Nobody said to me, 'You're in third place now, Leo. We want to see you get up to second.'"

He picked a towel from the bench and held it high and patted it and said, "Nobody said, 'You're in second place now, Leo. We'd like to see you in first place.'"

He threw the towel back on the bench.

"No, sir! Nobody wanted to see me up there. All the nice guys in the league wanted to knock me down, which is the way it should be. But in spite of them, I got up there. I'm in first place now and—"

He waved a hand toward the Giant dugout.

"The nice guys are over there in last place. Well, let them come and get me!"

The Dodgers were at batting practice and Eddie Stanky was at the plate.

"Look at that little ——!" Leo said. "Think he's a nice guy? The hell he is! He'll knock you down to make a play, if he has to. That's the kind of guys I want on my ball club."

He spoke warmly now.

"Look at him," he said. "The little ——. He can't run, he can't hit, he can't throw, he can't do nothing. But what a ball player! I wouldn't give him for any second baseman in the league. Or for any two second basemen."

The bell rang and the Dodgers were streaming into the

dugout. A reporter who had been sitting on the bench got up.

"All right, boys," he said. "Make room for some nice guys."

"Not in this dugout," Leo said.

He waved toward the Giants' dugout again.

"The nice guys are all over there," he said. "In last place."

It was more than an expression of Leo's philosophy. It was a sound forecast. The nice guys finished last.

Now that you know how it ended, this is how it began, this year that was to be a bleak one in the life of Melvin Thomas Ott.

It began brightly, hopefully. The war was over. Playing longer than he had intended to because of the man-power shortage in baseball during the war, Mel had been desperately tired at times and he would say, "When the last shot is fired, I'm going to sit down."

The war had ended in 1945 and he was going to sit down and plan the immediate future of his team. The men were coming back. The boys could be dismissed. The crowds would pick up again. There would be money to spend for players with power—the power that had become Mel's fetish and that, because he placed so much reliance on it, would, in the long run, be his undoing.

On January 5, he called the newspapermen to his office. When they had gathered about him, he cleared his throat and said, trying to be very impressive, "We have bought Walker Cooper from the Cardinals for $175,000."

There was a moment of silence. It was broken when one of them asked, "Why?"

Mel visibly was disturbed.

"Because I think he can help our ball club," he said.

"How?" his inquisitor asked.

"Well," Mel said, "because he is a long-ball hitter and, besides, I am hoping that he will do as much for our pitchers as Bill Dickey has done for the Yankees' pitchers."

Walker Cooper had been with the Cardinals since 1940, and had been their regular catcher since 1941. He and his brother, Morton, had been a battery when the Cardinals won the pennant in 1942 and 1943. For one year, 1942, he had shown great promise but he hadn't paid off on it since. If, as a catcher, he ever had helped a pitcher, including his brother, there had been no visible evidence of it, nor verbal either, if you could believe what the Cardinal pitchers said.

"He's still in the navy," Mel said.

He had been inducted into the navy after the 1945 season had opened.

"We're hoping," Mel said, "he will be discharged soon."

Cooper wasn't discharged in time to report for spring training at Miami, nor was Marshall, although both would join up soon. But Mize, Gordon, Young, Koslo, Carpenter, and Schumacher were there.

One of the old regulars was missing. Bill Jurges had been released soon after the 1945 season and been signed by the Braves. But there were new faces in the camp: Bill Rigney, an infielder, bought from the Oakland club of the Pacific Coast League; Bobby Blattner, bought from St. Louis in 1942 but drafted by the army before he could report to the Giants, and now just back from service; Goodie Rosen, veteran outfielder claimed from the

Dodgers; Monte Kennedy, a pitcher. Kennedy's first year in professional baseball was 1942, when he was with Richmond in the Piedmont League, and he had been in only three games but the Giants had wanted him. Like Blattner, he had gone into the armed forces that year. Now he was up for his big chance.

The spring of 1946 was the spring of the raids on the American baseball structure by the flamboyant Jorge Pasquel, who carried a pearl-handled revolver, apparently had millions of pesos to spend or give away, and was throwing a dragnet over all the ball players he could reach, with the purpose of transforming the maverick Mexican League into a major circuit. He, or his emissaries, fell upon the Giants at Miami and carried off Maglie, Hausmann, and Gardella who, dissatisfied with the terms offered by Stoneham, looked upon this twentieth-century conquistador as a liberator and turned a deaf ear to Horace's reminder that all is not gold that glitters.

Mel was not greatly disturbed over the actual departure of the three, not realizing, for one thing, what a pitcher he had lost in Maglie. But the episode left some of the other players in a state of unrest—two of them, Feldman and Adams, would go south of the border shortly—and, what with one thing and another, including a blow on the head from a pitched ball in batting practice, the stay in Miami was not a particularly happy one for him.

The team, when it finally was put together, had some very obvious defects, yet an observer could write of it, on opening day:

Ott has molded an attack nearer to his liking than any the Giants have had since pre-war days. Being a great hitter himself and having learned his baseball from McGraw, he puts emphasis on the attack whenever he has any one around him who can hit the ball. This year he has the hitters. There are rough spots in his line-up, defensively, but where, for a time, he was the only Giant you could count on to slug the ball, he now has with him Cooper, Marshall, Mize, Lombardi, Young and Gordon. There will be days when that crew will more than offset the shaky pitching and spotty fielding that loom as menaces. Win or lose, the Giants will be a more attractive club this year than they have been in a very long time.

If no one expected the young men to win the pennant—and no one did—no one expected them to do as badly as they did. A week after the season began they were in fifth place. They never rose beyond it all season, spent most of their time in sixth, went to seventh the first week in September, and worked their way by easy stages to the basement before the month was out. Of this fearsome collection of hitters, the only one to top .300 was Mize who, with a mark of .337, was second to Stan Musial of the Cardinals, batting champion of the league. Ott, who had hoped to remain seated, found it necessary to take part in thirty-one games, mostly as a pinch hitter, and came off with one home run and the fantastically dismal average of .074. None of the first-string pitchers won as many games as he lost. The leader, in point of earned runs allowed, was Monte Kennedy, who had pitched in three professional games before he joined the Giants. His average was 3.42. Practically unmarked was the arrival late in the season, of Bobby Thomson. Bobby had come a long way to play ball on the Polo Grounds, for although he was reared on Staten Island, a part of the city of New York, he was born in Glasgow. He was not quite twenty-three years old when Giant fans first saw him playing third base. The Giants had had him in Rocky Mount in the Bi-State League in 1942, and had promoted him to Bristol in the Appalachian League for 1943, but he'd gone off to the army. Assigned, instead, to Jersey City on his return, he had played third base or the outfield in 151 games and hit .280 when Ott called him up. He hit .315, and made two home runs in eighteen times at bat, and his days in the minor leagues short as they had been, were over.

The commotion promised for 1946 materialized in 1947, which was a strange, exciting, and meaningless year. It was the first year the Giants went to Phoenix, Arizona, to train; the first year for "Lucky" Jack Lohrke, for Clint (Paul Bunyan) Hartung, for Larry Jansen; and the first full year for Sheldon Jones. It was the year of the big wind, raised by the Giants' bats, that reached its height in May and June and blew itself out in August. But when all the hullabaloo died away, the team was in fourth place.

True enough, the first division had been regained, which was something, considering that, the year before, the terminus was the basement. But so high had been the hopes of the fans through the first half of the season that the final outcome was a let-down. It had been ten years since a pennant was won. The fans were growing impatient with Ott. So, it seemed, was Stoneham. There were rumors that Mel wouldn't be around for another opening day. He would, but whether or not he knew it, he was on the spot.

274

40

The Crash of Bats in 1947

☺ BUT in the spring of 1947 almost anything seemed possible. The pennant? Well, perhaps not that. But a good run for it from April to September. Everybody was in fine shape. Kerr was being called one of the best shortstops in either league. Rigney was a lively, hustle-and-holler guy and could hit a ball surprisingly hard for one of such slender build. Lohrke—they called him Lucky because as a ball player on the Coast he had been taken off a bus that crashed and burned, and as a soldier a plane from which he had been bumped roared to earth in flames less than an hour later—got a firm grip early on the third base job, thus releasing Thomson and the strong-armed Gordon for duty in the outfield. Marshall, who had proved himself the year before, was certain to do well with a season of big league play behind him. Jansen and Jones, it was believed would supply at least some of the kind of pitching that had been lacking for so long.

But mostly the camp talk was about Clint Hartung. He was six feet, four inches tall, and a raw-boned, 200-pound superman out of Hondo, Texas. He had been returned to the Giant farm team in Minneapolis in 1943, after a season with Eau Claire in the Northern League, where he pitched or played first base and hit .351. But the army wanted him and he went that way. Released from service in the winter of 1945, he was notified that the Giants had ordered him up for trial in the spring of 1946. He sent back word that shocked Stoneham and Garry Schumacher, former sports writer, now promotion director of the Giants, who already had begun to build him up in the New York papers. He had re-enlisted in the army for one year.

"Why?" Horace demanded. "Why? Doesn't he know the war is over? Is he out of his mind? Would he rather be in the army than play for the Giants?"

No, he wasn't out of his mind. He hadn't been told what his status was as a player. He didn't know whether he was going to stay with Minneapolis or be sent back to Eau Claire. And there was something about bonuses and allotments somewhere in his figuring, and his family could use the money.

"Money!" Horace screamed. "If he's as good as we've been told he is, we'll pay him more money than he ever saw!"

But it was too late. He already was in the army. All the Giants could do was to wait another year for him.

Now he was at Phoenix. Ott asked him if he wanted to pitch or play in the outfield—it was explained to him the Giants already had a first baseman. He said he'd rather play in the outfield. So that's where he started. The distance he got with his hits, the range of his throwing arm, soon won headlines for him. His size and over-all strength and the tall stories told of his exploits as a player in the Paul Bunyan country of Wisconsin made the tag a natural.

There was one other they talked about in Phoenix, and

with greater justification. He was Larry Joseph Jansen, twenty-seven-year-old right-hander from Verboort, Oregon, and, as already was suspected, the best pitcher the Giants had had since the passing of Hubbell and Schumacher. With San Francisco the year before, he had won thirty games, lost only six, and had an earned run average of 1.57.

When the season started, the bats began to crash. Ott had the hitters he'd wanted all along. They would hit more home runs in one season than any other major league club, including the Yankees, ever had hit—221. Mize wound up with fifty-one, Cooper with thirty-five, Marshall with thirty-six, Thomson with twenty-nine, Rigney with seventeen, Gordon with thirteen, Lohrke with eleven . . .

They brought the crowds in and they made the crowds howl. They were in first place through the last week in May and the first week in June. Jansen, a control pitcher, also delighted the crowds and wound up with twenty-one triumphs and only five losses. Thomson, Marshall, and Gordon formed a strong outfield. Lockman suffered a broken ankle in an April exhibition game with Cleveland and was out of action all season save for two appearances as a pinch hitter. Rigney was, literally, almost all over the infield, playing 137 games at second base, third base, or shortstop. Marshall played in every game. Mize missed but one.

Yet, with all that, due to a slow start in spite of the banging of the wood against the ball, they had a hard time reaching the .500 mark and as hard a time keeping far above it. Their percentage at the wire was .526.

The main reason, the big drawback? The pitching. Jansen won twenty-one games and Koslo won fifteen. The only other pitcher—and Hartung was tried as a pitcher too—worth his salt was a kid named Ken Trinkle who, as a trouble shooter, was in sixty-two games. Voiselle didn't last out the season. Ott, in a fury because Bill threw so many home run balls, fined him $500 for throwing one one day—although, as somebody pointed out at the time, the other Giant pitchers were throwing them every day for nothing—and that was the beginning of the end for Bill. Mel traded him to the Braves for Morton Cooper, thus reuniting the Cooper brothers as a battery. But this was 1947, not 1942, and Mort was no improvement on Voiselle. He just did make it to the end of the season.

With all this going on, people were asking how many pitchers the Giants could have bought for the $175,000 they had paid for a catcher.

The complacency that set in that winter in the front office was incomprehensible. Although the thundering attack in 1947 had failed to move the club past fourth place because it was not supported by pitching, not a single off-season deal was made for a major league pitcher. Maybe no deals could have been made. Good pitchers were scarce around the league, the club was short of trading material, and prices were high for any one wishing to do business on a cash basis. But as spring loomed again, the town suddenly was flooded with little white buttons for the fans to wear—little white buttons bearing in blue lettering the simple legend: "Giants in '48."

The Giants to do what in '48? Win the pennant? Apparently that was the idea. With that pitching staff, which consisted in the main of Jansen, Koslo, Kennedy, Jones, Ray Poat, a kid who had come up late the year before, Trinkle, and Hartung, who, having failed as an outfielder,

278

now was being geared for the box? A sports writer in Shor's one night said to a young woman wearing one of the buttons, "You may take that home, my dear, and put it in your jewel case with your Willkie button."

Trained at Phoenix again and shaken down in a series of exhibition games with the Indians, as usual, the Giants opened with Mize, Rigney, Kerr, and Gordon in the infield; Lockman in left, Thomson in center, and Marshall in right; with Cooper back of the bat, aided by Wes Westrum, brought up from Minneapolis late in 1947. The power was there still but there wasn't much speed in the infield, while the outfield, which received rave notices at Phoenix, had its lapses on defense, for Lockman, who played deep, couldn't come in on a ball, and Thomson, who played shallow, couldn't go back for one.

But, as a crew, they were exciting, as they had been the year before. They were bound to be, with that hitting and that pitching. They almost always had to come from behind in a ball game. Sometimes they won and sometimes they didn't. Even when they didn't, they nearly always put on a thrilling show. The greatest of these was in a late May night game with the Cardinals, when they came slugging up from the rear to batter Howie Pollet and Red Munger for eight runs in the eighth inning, and Jansen, coming in to pitch the ninth, sealed the victory by fanning Erv Dusak, Stan Musial, and "Nippy" Jones.

Jerry Mitchell of the *Post*, thinking back to the time when Dizzy Dean used to pitch like that in a clutch, said, "I wonder if Jansen has a brother named Daffy?"

But it was mostly tumult and shouting and the Giants were rocking up and down between fourth and fifth places.

Horace was looking dubiously at Ott and one day when, in a pinch, Mel ordered Cooper to bunt, Horace almost fell out of the clubhouse window. Rumors were recurrent that the great little man from Gretna, Louisiana, by way of Right Field, N. Y. was on his way out.

Johnny Mize smashing one of his 51 home runs in 1947

International News Photo

Whitey Lockman, during 1951 spring training, practicing his new position at first base.

Wide World Photos

Eddie Stanky putting the ball on Carl Furillo of the Brooklyn Dodgers to complete a triple play started by Captain Alvin Dark, running behind Stanky.

41

The News Nobody Believed

⊖ IT was the morning of July 16. Telephones rang in the offices of the newspapers and the news associations, in the homes of reporters and columnists. There was the voice of Garry Schumacher: "We are making a very important announcement at noon in our office. Please be here."

One to whom Garry talked said, "Thanks, Garry. I'll be there."

And to himself he said, "Mel Ott has been fired."

Arriving at the building in which the Giants are housed on the corner of Forty-second Street and Sixth Avenue, he met Pat Robinson of the International News Service, who was dashing out of an elevator on the way to a telephone booth in the lobby.

"Has Ott been fired?" he asked.

"Yes," Pat said, "and Durocher is the manager."

"Fun is fun," he said. "Who's the manager?"

"Durocher," Pat said.

Durocher manager of the Giants? It was unbelievable. The first one he met on the Giants' floor was Max Kase, sports editor of the *Journal-American*.

"Certainly it's true," Max said. "Don't you read your own paper?"

"Generally, yes. But I haven't seen it yet."

Max held out a copy of the paper. There it was, spread all over the front page. Bill Corum's exclusive story of the release of Ott and the signing of Durocher. It was the biggest sports beat since Tom Meany's story of the resignation of John McGraw. Durocher, a close friend of Corum's, had called him the night before, saying he had something important to talk to him about, wanting to ask his advice. Wanting, really, assurance that he had acted wisely. The Giant management had been offered to him and he had accepted it. Did Bill think he had acted wisely? Bill did. And had a story.

What Leo didn't know was that when Horace Stoneham finally had made up his mind to change managers, he first thought of Burt Shotton, Leo's stand-in in Brooklyn through 1947, when he was under a year's suspension by Commissioner Albert B. (Happy) Chandler. Since Shotton was bound to Branch Rickey, in a personal sense if not actually under contract to him, as a sort of consultant and super scout, Horace arranged a meeting with Rickey in the office of Ford Frick, President of the National League, to ask his permission to talk to Burt.

Rickey, having heard Horace's request, began to talk. Since Branch, when it pleases him to apply it, has a gift for talking around a given point for minutes on end without actually getting to it, it was some time before Horace realized Branch was offering him, not Shotton but Durocher. Once that was made clear, Horace moved in and an agreement was reached, subject, of course, to Durocher's approval. This Leo gave at a meeting in his apartment that night.

But now the Giants' office was boiling with excitement, the newspapermen milling about, the telephones jangling, everybody talking at once. Then there was a lull. Garry Schumacher looked at his wrist watch.

"I guess we'd better be starting," he said.

The Giants had gone to Pittsburgh. Horace and Garry were flying Leo out, to take him into the clubhouse at Forbes Field and introduce him to the players as their new manager. There was the bustle of departure. Ott was talking to two newspapermen.

"So long," he said to Leo. "Good luck—and say good-by to the fellows for me."

"Thanks, Mel," Leo said. "Sure. Sure."

"Good-by . . . Good-by . . . Good-by . . ."

They went out to the elevator.

"Well?" somebody said.

The group began to break up. Going to the elevator. Going to their offices. Going to lunch.

"You'll be around for a while, won't you, Mel?" one of them asked.

"Yes," he said. "I don't know for how long. You know, I'm going to be Hub's assistant in the farm system. I suppose I'll do a lot of traveling. But I'll be here for a little while, I expect."

"Well, see you at Shor's."

"Fine," Mel said. "I'll be seeing you."

As they left, he still was standing in the corridor.

"Wouldn't you think," one of them said, going down in the elevator, "they would have taken Mel to Pittsburgh with them so that he could—well, you know, sort of turn the club over to Leo and say good-by to the players?"

"Yes," another said. "Horace usually is such a very thoughtful fellow. I guess he was a little excited."

The news of the change of managers hit the Giant fans with a terrific impact. Ott, whatever his shortcomings as a manager, still was a hero to them. Perhaps a change was necessary. But Durocher! Of all persons, Durocher the manager of the Giants! The man they had learned to hate as manager of the Dodgers? The more fervent among them vowed they never would go to see the Giants play again.

On hearing them, a cynic said, "Not until Durocher gives them a winning team."

Ott, who never had played in the minor leagues, shortly was on the road, Hubbell's assistant and field agent in the rapidly expanding farm system. Durocher, only the fourth manager the Giants had had over a span of forty-six years, was installed at the Polo Grounds. Leo had told Stoneham, on accepting the appointment, "You know, Horace, this is not my kind of ball club."

Nor was it. Ott, who had fashioned it, couldn't win with it. Nor could Durocher, nor, for that matter, any one else. There would be a lot of changes made, but not right now. Leo would have to go through the balance of the season with the outfit he had and make the best of it. The best was fifth place. Mize hit forty home runs, Gordon hit thirty, Lockman eighteen, Cooper sixteen, and Marshall fourteen. But Jansen, with a record of eighteen victories and twelve defeats and an earned run average of 3.61, was the only pitcher to complete ten games or more. Jones—they now were calling him "Available Jones," after Al Capp's comic strip character—was in fifty-five games;

Trinkle in fifty-three. Leo even brought in "Ol' Bobo" Newsom, that restless roamer of the baseball trails, to help out for a while.

Hubbell sent in a couple of young men for inspection. Sal Yvars, a catcher from Jersey City, and Don Mueller, an outfielder from Jacksonville. They weren't quite ready but it wouldn't be long before they would be. Yvars went to Minneapolis and Mueller to Jersey City.

That fall Durocher released Travis Jackson and Hank Gowdy, who had served Ott as coaches. They weren't the kind of coaches he wanted for the kind of team he had in mind.

42

Leo's in Trouble—and Out

⊖ BRANCH Rickey had broken the color line in baseball by signing Jackie Robinson for the Montreal club, a
Brooklyn farm, in 1946, and introducing him as a member of the Dodgers in 1947. Since the heavens hadn't
fallen upon his head, nor the earth erupted, at least in the
vicinity of Ebbets Field, in consequence of his defiance
of the taboo, other clubs were encouraged to explore the
possibilities of the vast pool of Negro ball players, hoping
thus to tap a new source of material and, equally important, a new source of revenue.

In January of 1949, the Giants, with their home base in
Harlem, followed the trend. They bought Henry (Hank)
Thompson from the Kansas City Monarchs and Monte
Irvin from the Newark Eagles and assigned both to Jersey
City. Thompson, who had been tried and rejected by the
St. Louis Browns in 1947, had demonstrated that he could
play the infield or the outfield. Irvin was an outfielder. In
June, the Giants would buy Ray Noble (pronounced
Noblay) a native Cuban, who was catching for the New
York Cubans. He also went to Jersey City.

At the time, that is, in January, the purchase of Thompson and Irvin was merely an item in the news. Interesting,

to be sure, but they had not yet appeared in Giant uniforms and, more interesting as of then, was the formation of Durocher's new coaching staff. Soon after he became manager, he called in Herman Franks, who had been a catcher with the Dodgers in the early forties and meantime had managed St. Paul and been a coach with the Athletics. Then Herman's name did not mean anything at the Polo Grounds, but now Leo, wise as all get out, brought in two men whose names meant much, Fred Fitzsimmons and Frank Frisch.

A small unpleasantness was caused by the signing of Fitzsimmons. It was no fault of Durocher's but since he technically did violate one of baseball's oldest rules and since he was Commissioner Chandler's favorite whipping boy, he was caught up in it. Fitzsimmons, who had left the Dodgers to go to Boston as a coach under Billy Southworth in 1948, still was a Giant at heart, and when Leo, as manager of the Giants, visited Boston late in the season, Fitz said to him, "You wouldn't be needing a coach next year, would you, Leo?"

And Leo, already having made up his mind to dismiss Jackson and Gowdy, and liking Fitz and being aware of his value as a sop to the hostile old line Giant fans, said, "I certainly would! Talk to me about it later. But you're in, brother."

When all this came out, as it did, they were both in—in the bad graces of the commissioner. The incident having been duly reported by the Boston club—and only Fitzsimmons, in all innocence, could have revealed what happened—Chandler had them on the carpet. Their offense? Fitzsimmons was under contract with the Braves when he asked Leo for a job. Leo, aware of Fitz's status, not only had encouraged him but virtually had hired him. In so doing, he had, in the phraseology of baseball, tampered with him. Chandler did not set aside the agreement entered into by Fitzsimmons and the New York club in the winter of 1948-49. But he did suspend Fitz for thirty days of the training season and give Leo a sound going over.

The signing of Frisch, who had broadcast the Giants' games since his release as manager of the Pirates after the 1947 season, also had its repercussions. Frank had grown to greatness as a player with the Giants. In 1932 there were many who thought that he, not Terry, should have succeeded McGraw, although by that time he was with the Cardinals. Still looking upon him, and rightly, as a great figure in baseball, there were as many who, in 1948, thought that he, not Durocher the interloper, should have succeeded Ott. Durocher, accepting the challenge, hired Frisch, knowing that Frank could help him and certain that, in no way, would Frank try to hurt him.

Although once, when they were playing side by side in St. Louis, Durocher and Frisch had not been too friendly and Durocher had indicated his belief that Frisch had dictated his transfer to the Dodgers because he feared that he, Leo, was a potential rival as manager, they had maintained a great professional respect, one for the other. And out of his brief time as a Giant coach—he would leave New York in June to become manager of the Cubs—Frisch was to say, much later, "I never worked for a greater guy than Leo."

But that was in the winter and now they were at Phoenix and this wasn't Leo's kind of team, as he had said, but he was trying to put it together as well as he could. Mize was at first base. Little Georgie Hausmann, whose

Leo Durocher, with Horace Stoneham, left, and Eddie Brannick, signing the two-year contract in 1949 that made him manager of the 1951 pennant winners.

Larry Jansen and Sal Maglie, whose 23 wins apiece made the 1951 pennant possible.

The first all-Negro outfield in Major League history, Willie Mays, Monte Irvin, and Hank Thompson with Manager Durocher.

sentence of five years in exile for having jumped to the Mexican League had been reduced, along with the sentences of the other rebels, was at second. Kerr was at shortstop and Gordon at third. Thomson, Marshall, and Lockman were in the outfield. Cooper was the first-string catcher but his number was up. The pitchers? Jansen, Koslo, Jones, Hartung, Andy Hansen, Kirby Higbe, Hank Behrman, and Poat.

It was not a happy season for Durocher and, considering Chandler's attitude toward him, there were a few anxious hours in which it seemed perilously close to being his last. As every one was aware, he virtually was on probation as a result of his transgressions while manager of the Dodgers and now, on April 28, he was accused of slugging a fan at the Polo Grounds.

The background of the alleged assault was a game in which the Dodgers beat the Giants, 15 to 2, and during which Durocher took a frightful verbal raking from the crowd, made up in large part of Brooklyn rooters. Most offensive, according to the New York players, was a man who later identified himself as Fred Boysen, a Puerto Rican. Boysen, they said, appeared late in the game in a box close to their dugout and from that short range poured a relentless fire of abuse at Durocher. When the game was over and the crowd swarmed at the heels of the players bound for the clubhouse in center field, Boysen, who had run up close to Durocher, was struck so violently by somebody that he sprawled on the ground.

He said that he was running after Robinson, wanting to shake his hand and that Durocher, on seeing him, had flattened him with a left hook. This Durocher denied vigorously.

"Do you think I'm crazy?" he demanded. "That's all I'd have to do to get thrown out of baseball, hit somebody. I heard the bum yelling at me from the box but I never so much as looked at him. I didn't even know he was on the ground in center field until I got in the clubhouse and somebody told me there was a fight on the field and a guy was knocked down."

With Boysen at the game was his lawyer, Ben J. Chasin. They went to a magistrate's court and got a summons for Durocher and, in Cincinnati, Chandler sprang into action. Since the incident took place in a National League park and involved a National League manager, it seemed to lie within the jurisdiction of Ford Frick, then the National League president, but since it was Durocher who was in the middle, Chandler figuratively brushed past Frick and said, "I'll handle this."

That was when it appeared that Durocher had reached the point of no return, especially as the commissioner obviously was girding himself for a major engagement. But the affair ended as suddenly as it had begun. Chandler, questioning Frisch and Fitzsimmons, among others who were on the scene, could get no corroboration from them of the charge laid by Boysen, nor could Boysen produce any witnesses in his behalf when the magistrate heard the case.

So Leo's professional life was saved and, to make sure there would be no recurrence of the incident, Stoneham ordered that, in the future, no spectator be allowed on the field until all the players had entered the clubhouse.

That was almost the only excitement generated at the Polo Grounds all season, but Leo wasn't marking time.

He was making moves that, he hoped, would result in the making of a team he could call his own.

In June he traded Cooper to Cincinnati for Ray Mueller, also a catcher. In the same month, he brought up Thompson and Irvin, sent Gordon to the outfield and tried Thompson at third base. Not satisfied with Kerr at shortstop, he encouraged Lohrke to make a place for himself at that position, but that didn't work too well. He tried Irvin in the outfield but Monte didn't hit and Leo decided to send him back to Jersey City the following year.

On August 22, he asked for waivers on Mize. The Yankees were battling for the pennant in the American League. Casey Stengel called Frank Frisch in Chicago.

"I could use some more hitting," Casey said. "Can Mize help me?"

"Yes," Frisch said. "He can't play every day any more but he still can belt that ball. I think he can help you a lot."

Stengel claimed the one whom the players called "The Big Cat."

Of the pitchers, Koslo had the best season. He won only eleven games and lost fourteen, but he led the league with an earned run average of 2.50. Jones and Jansen each won fifteen games. The others were nowhere. Thomson led in batting with an average of .309, and hit twenty-seven home runs. Marshall and Lockman were the only other .300 hitters, but Gordon, hitting .284, made twenty-six home runs.

The attendance was poor as the Giants meandered through the season and closed it in fifth place. The more stubborn fans were sticking to a vow they had made not to go to the Polo Grounds as long as Durocher was the manager. The others who stayed away, or were content to take the games on radio or television, simply couldn't see any difference in the team under Durocher. To them it was just as futile as it had been under Ott and not nearly as exciting. With the Yankees and Dodgers winning again, the plight of the Giants was desperate.

43

"The Brat" Becomes a Giant

ⓔ ON December 14, Leo made a decisive move—a move he had been contemplating for months as he had watched his ball club sag. He outraged most of the fans and strengthened the Giants by trading Kerr, Marshall, Gordon, and a young pitcher named Sam Webb, to the Braves for Eddie Stanky and Alvin Dark.

As it had taken courage for Leo to assume the position that Mel Ott had held, so it took courage for him to bring Stanky, alias "The Brat," into the Polo Grounds. In the minds of so many Giant fans, Stanky was linked with Durocher from his days in Brooklyn. That Stanky had said Leo had "stabbed him in the back" during his salary dispute with Branch Rickey in the winter of 1947-48, and so helped to force his sale by the Dodgers to the Braves, made no difference. Nor had Eddie's two-year stay in Boston purged him. He was one with Durocher. If not, why had he said, when he learned he had been traded to the Giants, that he would be glad to play for Durocher again? For Dark, they had no feeling whatever. But first it had been Durocher and now it was Stanky.

And what had Durocher given for this hammered down monster and Dark? Three of the most popular players on the ball club, whether Leo liked them or not. Gordon, Marshall, and Kerr. Nobody talked about Sam Webb. Nobody seemed to realize he had been with the Giants.

As the storm of criticism swirled about his head, Leo had only this to say: "We haven't had a good second base combination for a year or more. Until we can get better pitching, that is what we need. Two fellows out there who can make double plays. The one player I didn't want to give up was Gordon. But unless I did, I couldn't have made the deal."

There was one more important addition to the club that winter. Sal Maglie, the hard-eyed, blue-jawed "Sal the Barber," who had been pardoned for jumping the Mexican border, returned with no questions asked.

Leo was beginning to get his kind of ball club.

At Phoenix in the spring of 1950 there were new faces, new hopes, and the kind of days that caused Garry Schumacher to say, "I wonder what the Spaniards thought when they came up through here? They must have come for gold, all this way through the desert. But when they got here and saw this sky and the light, like the sun shining through the stained glass windows of a cathedral..."

A light was shining in Leo's eyes that spring. He had Stanky and Dark and Tookie Gilbert and Hank Thompson for his infield; Lockman, Thomson, and Don Mueller for his outfield; Wes Westrum, the best receiver the Giants had had in years, to do his catching; and Maglie, for whom he was hoping great things, to go with Jansen and Jones on the pitching staff. A balanced team, he thought. Not as much power as the Giants had had in 1947, but a much better defense and, he thought, much better pitching.

Mize had faded and gone, and in his place was Tookie

Gilbert, whose square name was Harold, and in whom baseball was bred in the bone, for his father was Larry Gilbert, who had been with the miracle making Braves in 1914 and, in the years since then, a successful minor league manager. (There were sports writers from Memphis and New Orleans and Atlanta and Nashville at the Kentucky Derby in May of this spring of 1950, who said Tookie had been called up too soon, for they had seen him with Nashville in 1949. And they were right. But he looked good in Phoenix and he would play 111 games with the Giants that year before Leo made up his mind to send him out to learn a little more.)

Stanky was at second base and Dark at shortstop, of course. Dark, as far as New York fans had been concerned up to the time Leo had made that outrageous deal with the Braves, was simply another young man in a Boston uniform who occasionally visited the Polo Grounds. Most of the New York sports writers had regarded him as casually. Those who were at Phoenix and looking at him closely for the first time, thought he was a surprisingly slight-looking young man for his height, five feet eleven and a half, and his weight, 185. They would have guessed, had they been asked to do so, that he was no taller than five feet ten and no heavier than 160. But he was a ball player, they knew. He'd had only one year in the minors. That was in 1947, with Milwaukee, after he'd spent a full season with the Braves in '46. He was back in Boston in 1948 and, helping to win the pennant for the Braves, he had been voted the rookie of the year.

Thompson had shown a catlike quickness at third base the year before. He could hit, too. He hit .280, and made nine home runs in 1949. There was life, there was zing in this club. It would move, Leo was sure.

Unforgettable was the opening day at the Polo Grounds. April 18, and the Braves playing the Giants and only a fairish crowd in the stands. A crowd that didn't like Leo and didn't like Stanky and hooted them. And poor Alvin Dark was hooted, too, not because he'd ever done anything to make the Giant fans dislike him but simply because he was seen in the company of Durocher and Stanky.

It was a long, slow, hard climb for the Giants, up through that spring, and the second division. But they were moving and things were happening that portended a brighter future. Maglie was winning. Stanky and Dark were clicking. In June another Negro ball player was bought. He didn't get any headlines in the papers then. Nobody, save the Negro league fans, ever had heard of him. He was bought from the Birmingham Black Barons. He was an outfielder. His name was Willie Mays. He was sent to Trenton.

In July Jim Hearn, a pitcher, was bought from the Cardinals. He was twenty-six years old and had been with the Cardinals or one of their farm clubs since 1942, with time out for the war. As a rookie he had shown early foot, as they say on the race track, but he had been used seldom and shown little. Eddie Dyer, the Cardinal manager, had lost confidence in Jim, if, indeed, he'd ever had any. Leo was willing to take a chance on him, to give him a fresh start and let him go, not saying too much to him, picking spots for him, giving him plenty of elbow room.

Monte Irvin was brought back from Jersey City. He hadn't hit in New York the year before but Leo knew he could hit. He'd hit everywhere else he'd been. In eighteen games in Jersey City that spring he had hit .510. Give him time on the Polo Grounds, Leo figured, and he'd hit there, too. Leo didn't know quite where to play him so he played him here and there. At first base when Gilbert wavered, at third base when Thompson needed a rest, and in the outfield.

The Giants moved up. They were sixth in June, fifth in July and August, fourth going into September, and third when the bell rang. The only attendance records they set at home were in the low numbers. But they were getting on. When the figures were totted up all over the league, they had three of the first four pitchers in the earned run averages— Hearn, the league leader, with 2.49; Maglie with 2.71, and Jansen with 3.01. Maglie pitched twelve complete games and won all of them. Hearn pitched eleven and won all of them. Stanky was in 152 games, and Irvin in 110, and each had hit an even .300.

Happy days, if not precisely here again, seemed not too far off.

In the press room at Philadelphia the night of the first game of the world series between the Yankees and the Phillies, Barney Kremenko of the *Journal-American* broke a story. Mel Ott had been released by the Giants. So the last of "McGraw's boys," bar Eddie Brannick in the front office, passed from the New York scene which he had entered as a stripling twenty-four years before.

44

Never a Year Like This

⊖ THE Giants, as you know, had their beginning in 1883. They have had many exciting, almost incredible years. But never had they known a year such as they were to know in 1951.

It began in St. Petersburg, Florida. Del Webb who, with Dan Topping, owns the Yankees, was born and raised in Phoenix and wanted to show his 1950 world champions to the home folks, so he arranged a sort of lend lease deal with Stoneham under which, for this year, the clubs would swap training bases. And so it was that the Giants worked on Huggins Field, named for the little man who was Durocher's first major league manager, when Hug was the boss of the Yankees and Leo was a fresh busher out of Springfield, Massachusetts, come to the Yanks by way of Hartford, Atlanta, and St. Paul.

Maybe just training his ball club there did something for Leo. He was a tough, brash kid when Huggins had him, afraid of nobody, respectful of nobody, but Huggins. A kid, as Branch Rickey once described him, in a leather wind breaker, out of a pool room in Springfield, when you backed him up against a wall. But Huggins was thoughtful and patient with him and tried to show him the right way, the nice way, to go. Now, in the spring of 1951, he had his ball club training on Huggins Field. Maybe . . .

But, whatever Leo's thoughts, he had a pretty good ball club with him. There were some rough spots to be smoothed away. Who, for instance, was going to play first base? Who was going to play third? But the core of the team was solid. Westrum to catch. Maglie, Hearn, Jansen, and Jones to pitch. Stanky to play second base, Dark to play shortstop, and Thomson, who had got over the notion that he could play as close to the infield as Tris Speaker did in the dear, dead days of the dear, dead ball, to play center field between Mueller and Lockman or Irvin. Lockman? With Irvin to play left field and nobody to play first base, why not Lockman at first?

So began the education of Whitey Lockman as a first baseman. It was dreadful to see. After a short time, Leo shut his eyes, too, and began to think of Irvin as a first baseman. Did you ever see a first baseman who had a horror of thrown balls? That was Irvin. Still, somebody had to play first base.

Meantime, there were pleasanter things for Leo to think about. The pitching looked better. There was a laughing Negro boy named Artie Wilson, an infielder whom Leo liked and who also was useful as an interpreter for Ray Noble, since Artie had learned to speak Spanish in Cuba but Ray hadn't learned to speak English in Jersey City. The laughing boy didn't last too long, once the season got under way, but at least he had taught Noble to understand Durocher and to order a steak in English.

The opening of the season was bright and gay as Jansen shut the Braves out and the Giants won, 4 to 0. Shortly after, there was the deluge. The Giants lost eleven games in a row. A writer who had picked them to finish third, having awarded the pennant to the Dodgers and second place to the Phillies, solemnly set forth that they would be lucky to finish fourth.

Then, on April 30, with Maglie starting and Jones finishing, they ended their losing streak by beating the Dodgers at Ebbet's Field—and were off and running. It was a long run but they made it.

On May 21, Leo took compassion on Irvin and restored him to left field. This meant that Lockman had to play first base. So he did, not very well, to be truthful, but at least he showed up there every day. After a while, Whitey got used to it. Pop flies didn't bother him so much.

On May 24, Willie Mays was called up from Minneapolis, where he had been farmed, ostensibly for the season. Calling Willie up wasn't as easy as it sounds. Willie, who had played in thirty-five games, was hitting .477, and was the darling of the Minneapolis fans. A personable kid, nineteen years old, he could hit, run, and throw and had that flair which great ball players have. Stoneham would have liked to have kept him in Minneapolis but the struggling Giants needed him. The howl that went up in Minneapolis when Willie's transfer to New York was announced was terrifying. Horace didn't dare go there to answer it in person. He knew a safer way. He explained his reasons for taking Willie away in quarter-page advertisements in the Minneapolis newspapers.

Willie didn't hit when he first joined the Giants. He made one hit in his first twenty-one times at bat. Some of these times at bat were against the Dodgers, with Roy Campanella catching. The first time Willie met Roy,

"Preacher" Roe was pitching. Between pitches, Roy said, "What do you think of him, Willie?"

"He's a mighty good pitcher, Mr. Campanella," Willie said.

"You're lucky today," Roy said. "Wait till you get Don Newcombe tomorrow. He hates colored rookies. He'll blow you down!"

But Willie got straightened out. He began to hit and his fielding was remarkable. One day, playing center field and running for a line drive to right center, he ran from under his cap—but he caught his cap with his right hand and the ball with his left. There was another day, this time with the Giants playing the Dodgers, and another line drive to right center. There was one out and the Dodgers had Dick Cox, a fast man, on third base. Willie caught the ball while running full tilt toward the right field wall, made a complete spin, and threw Cox out at the plate.

In the clubhouse after the game, Durocher said, "What was so remarkable about that? He does it every day! Every day!"

Of course Willie didn't do it every day, but there was this early afternoon in the clubhouse when a reporter said to Leo, "Is it true what you say about Mays?"

"Anything I say about Mays is true," Leo said. "But if you will pardon my formality, sir, just what is it you have in mind?"

"I heard you said you wouldn't trade Willie for any other player in baseball."

"You heard right," Leo said. "I wouldn't trade Willie for DiMaggio, Williams, Musial, or anybody else you can name. They're great ball players. Sure. I'm not knocking them. But Willie Mays is nineteen years old and ..."

Leo didn't have a chance to turn down any offers for Willie. Whoever else might have wanted him, there was a draft board in Westfield, Alabama, that had first call on him. But the drafting of Mays was away off in the future, as the Giants struggled to get out of the bucket.

On May 27, they rose beyond the .500 mark for the first time as Maglie shut the Phillies out with two hits. Jansen and Hearn were swinging along with Sal the Barber. George Spencer, equipped with the best of all weapons for a relief pitcher, a sinking fast ball, was doing a fine mopping up job. The Giants hadn't had pitching like that for years. But Leo wasn't satisfied. As the season advanced, he bought Al Corwin down from the club's farm in Ottawa and Corwin reeled off four victories in a row.

In July, Thomson moved in from center field to third base. The same month, Mueller ran up a hitting streak of nineteen games, and Westrum and Dave Williams, young infielder, hit home runs with the bases filled in the same game with the Cardinals. On August 11, the young men were in second place—but thirteen and a half games back of the Dodgers. Then, on the following day, it started. Corwin and Jansen beat the Phillies in a double-header, launching a sixteen-game victory parade. By the time that was over, the Giants were only six games behind and the Dodgers had taken fright.

The crowd was slow to catch on, not thinking the Giants had a chance to win, thinking they merely were putting on a show after the main bout was over, that they were winning now because they were under no pressure. But they kept plugging or banging or pecking away, winning far off, winning the close ones. Losing, but slamming right back, cutting down the Dodgers' lead and, on Sunday,

September 30, the last day of the season, beating the Braves, 3 to 2, in Boston and locking themselves into a tie with the Dodgers.

It hadn't seemed possible but there it was. In a six-week drive, they had closed a gap of thirteen and a half games separating them from a club that was supposed to be so much the best in the league it couldn't lose. The Yankees had won in the American League again but the world series would have to wait for a decision in the play off, two games out of a possible three.

45

With One Swipe of His Bat

⊖ NOW the crowd was on. Now the town stood still. The first game was played at Ebbets Field on October 1, and the Giants won, 3 to 1, as Hearn outpointed Ralph Branca. All the runs were scored on homers. Andy Pafko put the Dodgers in front with a drive into the left field seats in the second inning, but Thomson won the game with a slam in the fourth with Irvin on base, and, in the eighth, Irvin clinched the victory.

The second game, played at the Polo Grounds, was a rout, young Clem Labine shutting the Giants out with six hits and the Dodgers walloping Jones and Corwin for thirteen, including homers by Robinson, Pafko, Gil Hodges, and Rube Walker, who was catching in place of Campanella, injured the day before.

So great was the superiority of the Dodgers that day that it seemed to foreshadow the ultimate defeat of the Giants on the morrow. Even the Giants fans felt that way but they had no complaint to make. After all, their guys had tied the Dodgers, even won one play-off game. Maybe it was too much to ask them to take the whole thing. Then the impossible happened—happened so dramatically that

Durocher hugging Bobby Thomson after his homer won the 1951
pennant playoffs from Brooklyn.

Monte Irvin stealing home in the 1951 World Series. Yogi Berra is the Yankee catcher, Bobby Thomson (23) the batter.

there are no words to describe it other than in the barest terms.

The third game was, up to the last half of the ninth inning, exactly as every one had expected it to be. Big Don Newcombe had outpitched Maglie and the Dodgers had had command all the way. The score was 4 to 1 as Dark led off. He singled past Hodges into right field. Mueller also singled to right and Dark raced to third. Irvin fouled to Hodges. Lockman doubled to left, scoring Dark and sending Mueller to third. Mueller twisted his left ankle sliding into the bag and was carried from the field on a litter. Hartung was put on to run for him. Charlie Dressen took Newcombe out and waved Branca in from the bull pen. Thomson was the hitter. Branca laid a fast ball across the plate and Thomson took it for a strike. Branca threw another fast ball and Thomson hit it into the lower deck of the left field stand, scoring Hartung and Lockman ahead of him.

With that one swipe of his bat, Bobby had settled everything. The Giants had won the pennant for the first time in fourteen years. He was a hero and Durocher a genius. Branca's heart was broken and Dressen was a dolt. Manhattan rocked on its foundations. Brooklyn was as the dismal swamp. Hoary-headed baseball writers swore they'd never seen anything like it. Durocher and Stanky wrestled on the third base line. The other players pounded Thomson, but he was numbed by the excitement and felt nothing, nor could he speak. For an hour after the game thousands of fans stood on the field in front of the clubhouse, yelling for Thomson. Every once in a while he made an appearance in the doorway. In the Dodgers' clubhouse, Branca lay, stunned, across a short flight of steps leading to the lockers.

"It was the most famous home run ever made." Garry Schumacher said. "He hit it in 3,000,000 living rooms, to say nothing of the bars and grills."

In the tumult the Yankees were forgotten. Of course, they would have to be reckoned with, beginning on the morrow. But on that wild afternoon, the world series didn't matter. That which Willard Mullin, sports cartoonist of the *World-Telegram and Sun* called "The Little Miracle of Coogan's Bluff" had, for a day, robbed it of its significance.

But the tumult passed—and there stood the Yankees. They were favored to win the series, yet the Giants obviously had something more than an outside chance. They were red hot and dead game and they had good pitching. Maglie and Jansen each had won twenty-three games. Hearn had won seventeen.

The series opened at the Stadium on October 4. Durocher picked Koslo to start and Stengel countered with Allie Reynolds. Koslo and Irvin were the whole show. Koslo scattered the seven hits he yielded, while Irvin got a triple and three singles and stole home. The Giants won, 5 to 1.

Ed Lopat pitched so well for the Yanks in the second game that he nullified an almost equally fine performance by Jansen, the Yanks winning, 3 to 1. Irvin got a double and three singles.

"Monte doesn't know he's in the world series," Red Smith of the *Herald-Tribune* wrote. "He thinks this is the Darktown Strutters' Ball."

Now the teams switched to the Polo Grounds and the

Giants again took the lead, knocking Vic Raschi out in the fifth inning when Lockman climaxed a sharp attack with a home run in the right field stand. Hearn, although unsteady, managed to keep going until the eighth inning, when he hit Rizzuto, was tagged for a single by Mc-Dougald, and, after he had retired DiMaggio and Berra, walked Brown and Collins, forcing in Rizzuto. That was the Yanks' first run and the Giants had six, but Durocher derricked big Jim and put Jones in to finish. Woodling hit a homer off "Available" in the ninth but it didn't matter and the final count was 6 to 2.

The next day it rained and it was as if the rain cooled the Giants off, for they were not the same again. Reynolds took a decision over Maglie in the fourth game, the Yanks winning, 6-2, and tieing up the series. In this game poor Willie Mays, who had made only one hit, slapped into three double plays.

The fifth game and the last at the Polo Grounds was marked by a startling collapse of the Giants' pitching. Jansen, who started, was flattened in the third inning, when the Yanks made five runs and, as it developed, won the game. The blow that felled him was a home run by McDougald with the bases filled. After him came Kennedy, Corwin, and Konikowski. Lopat gave the Giants five hits. The score? 13 to 1.

It was taken for granted that, when the athletes switched back to the Stadium for the sixth game the Yankees would win it and wind up the show. They did, but the Giants, who took nothing for granted, fought them right down to the last out and came very near to winning. Sain, who had relieved Raschi in the seventh, was pitching when the Giants went to bat in the ninth trailing, 4 to 1, and quickly loaded the bases on singles by Stanky, Dark, and Lockman with none out. Irvin and Thomson, the two most dangerous right-handed hitters in the batting order, were coming up, but Stengel gambled with a left-hander, Bob Kuzava, because of his control.

"Get it over. Make 'em hit it in the air. We'll get 'em out," Casey told Kuzava.

Irvin drove a long fly to Woodling in left field and Stanky scored, Dark hustling down to third. Irvin also hit deep to Woodling and Dark scored. Durocher brought Sal Yvars, the catcher, in from the bull pen to hit for Hank Thompson and Yvars smashed the ball low and on a line—but straight at Bauer in right field and Bauer, judging it perfectly and sinking with it, was almost on his knees when he caught it.

So ended a fine and thrilling season for the Giants, a season in which Durocher had, in spirit at least, his kind of team. Leading it, he had gained stature as a manager and even the most obdurate of his critics found it difficult to fault him.

Horace Stoneham, for whom it had been a long haul between flags—and, at times, a very unpleasant one—accepted victory graciously, as he always had accepted defeat.

"It would have been nice if we could have won the world series, too," he said. "But I'm satisfied. Nobody reasonably could ask for anything more after the way the guys came up to win the pennant."

That was the way almost everybody seemed to feel.

Index

Leverett T. Smith Jr. of the Society for American Baseball Research prepared this index, which is simply a list of all people whose names occur in the book. In all cases, the names—including nicknames—have been reproduced as Graham has used them in the book. When Graham has not included a first name, one has been provided in brackets, with the Macmillan Company's *Baseball Encyclopedia: Complete and Definitive Record of Major League Baseball* as the source. In a single instance (Billy Cox), Graham was revised with the placement of the player's correct name in brackets.

310

312

315

317